Number One
Pacific Island

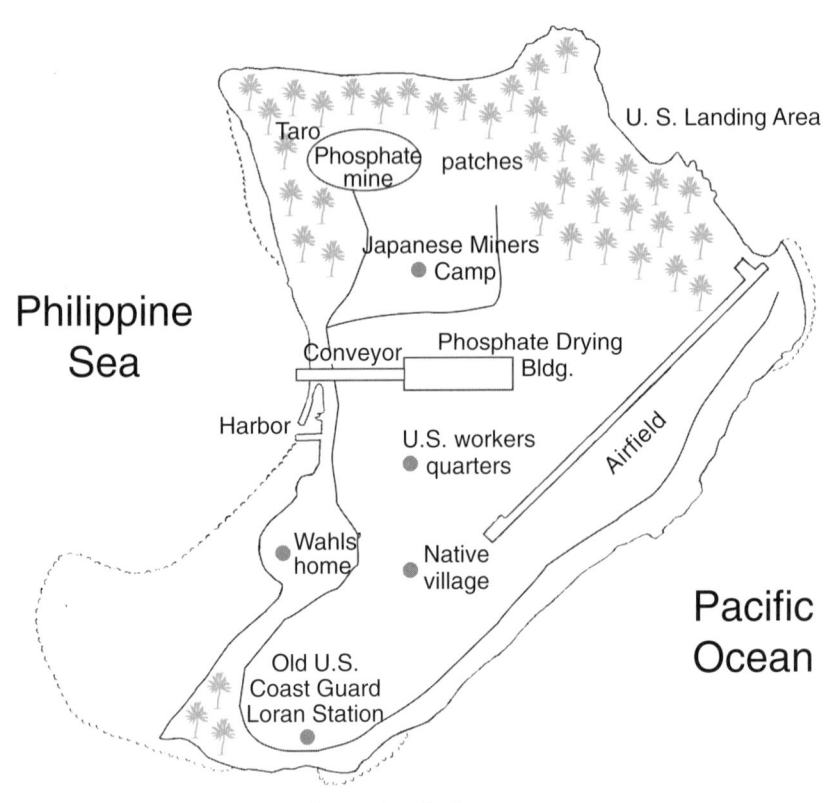

Island of Angaur

- Philippine Sea (west)
- Pacific Ocean (east)
- U. S. Landing Area
- Taro patches
- Phosphate mine
- Japanese Miners Camp
- Conveyor
- Phosphate Drying Bldg.
- Harbor
- U.S. workers quarters
- Airfield
- Wahls home
- Native village
- Old U.S. Coast Guard Loran Station

Number One Pacific Island

Cecilia Hendricks Wahl

Woodcrest Publishing
BLOOMINGTON INDIANA

Copyright © 2000 by Bloomington Hospital Foundation
All rights reserved
ISBN 1-878318-50-0
Library of Congress Control Number: 00-132164

A limited edition was printed in December 1999
for friends of Cecilia and Henry Wahl.

Design by J. Vint; composition by Bruce Carpenter
(All queries to: P.O. Box 1149, Bloomington, IN 47402)
Printed in the United States of America

CONTENTS

List of Photographs vi
Foreword vii
Acknowledgments ix

ONE	Deep in the Heart of Palau	3
TWO	Tour of Inspection	14
THREE	Somebody Tell Me	26
FOUR	At Home on Angaur	41
FIVE	The Boat	55
SIX	Trouble, Trouble, Boil and Bubble	69
SEVEN	Henderson Heyday	88
EIGHT	The Phosphate Problem	110
NINE	Just Us Natives	123
TEN	Rough Sailing	148
ELEVEN	Tell Me a Sea Story	155
TWELVE	In Topical Climes . . .	178
THIRTEEN	Mariana	191
FOURTEEN	Dog Days	204
FIFTEEN	Angaur, Here's to You.	222
SIXTEEN	Going to Town	239
SEVENTEEN	Safari	254
EIGHTEEN	"Back Home Again"	265
	Epilogue	268

LIST OF PHOTOGRAPHS

Tulop	9
Henry at ease in the "library"	29
Angaur's blowhole	47
The Wahls at home	50
Our pride and joy, overhauled and repainted, . . .	61
Admirals Andrus and Pownal, Mr Causey and Henry	93
Phosphate rolls up the conveyor and . . .	93
pours into a ship's hold.	93
Away they go! Nobody left but "us natives."	109
"Nan Dog King, this is Nan Dog George."	129
Moses, net fishing	130
A fine specimen of a sailfish	133
Rosco, Buck Harlan, Cecilia, Lt. Richards	159
A native outrigger canoe	179
Johannes and Tumiko are married.	181
Palau money	183
Chief Uherbalau with his three grandchildren	185
Mariana, our housegirl	192
A rare sight was the dance done by the older women.	199
Tulop and Joseph call the names.	201
Takahashi and his granddaughter	202
The crowd that appeared every time the three blonde . . .	219
81st Division Cemetery, Angaur	231
Chief Aibeduul and the Airii chief	236
Little Sisiniya, who was named for Cecilia	257

The photographs are from the Wahl collection.

FOREWORD

Following World War II the former Japanese mandate in Micronesia was turned over to the United States by the United Nations. The U.S. Navy was delegated the administering authority.

Micronesia covers an ocean area larger in square miles than the United States. In this vast area of over three million square miles, approximately sixty thousand Micronesians are scattered among several hundred islands and islets. All of these people must be furnished health and education; their handicraft and copra must be picked up, and trade goods left in exchange. Typhoons, heavy seas, tropical downpours, and many small problems keep business from becoming routine.

Here is a story of fifteen months spent in the Palau Islands, the westernmost group in the Trust Territory of the Pacific. Henry and I were there in the days when Naval Military Government was just getting underway in its guardianship and rehabilitation of the natives of the former Japanese-mandated islands.

Those of us close to the problems of the mandated islands, who saw the complete devastation of the areas, feel that the Navy in the first couple of years made as much rehabilitation for the people and the islands as was made in any other wartorn area of the world. This certainly speaks well for the men who asked for the work and the training they received at the School of Naval Administration at Stanford University. The Naval administrators, all volunteers, trained for America's first colonial experience, may not have had previous experience in that field, but they were long on conscientious desire to do what is right for the islanders. They came to the islands at the low ebb of demobilization, when personnel and material were short, and Americans, weary of Pacific war, had happily

FOREWORD

turned their thoughts elsewhere. These administrators found a seven-day-week job waiting for them, with long hours and meager facilities. Their reports should effectively dispel all the dreams of those who think that life in the Pacific Islands is one long idyll of hammocks, tall drinks, and small boys with fans.

We were in the Palaus too long to be experts, and not long enough to know the whole, real background of the people. Too many two-hour experts had come to the islands with preconceived notions about the native peoples, and had gone home to preach the gospel about the customs and needs of Micronesia. About all we could actually be sure of, after we knew the people a little while, was that they appreciated America's efforts in trying to do a job for them. We did not become members of their "secret" lodges, nor were we taken into the native tribes and made chiefs or high potentates. But we had many friends among the people whom we shall never forget, even if we do not pass that way again.

We hope for the same high ideals and the same zeal, with no thought of personal gain, in the administrators who come in the future to live near the people of the Pacific and help to improve their lot.

In most instances I changed the names of the Americans herein, and many of the characters are composite. The natives, however, carry their own names, and are reported as faithfully as I could observe them.

Bloomington   CECILIA WAHL
1948

ACKNOWLEDGMENTS

In 1947 Cecilia Hendricks Wahl joined her husband, Henry, in a memorable experience on Angaur Island, southernmost of the Palau Islands, approximately 800 miles southwest of Guam. This was her first experience in a tropical environment.

Her life on far-away Angaur, now over fifty years ago, Cecilia preserved in a manuscript. Following her death in 1998, I decided to memorialize Cecilia by publishing this manusript. We hope our friends and relatives will enjoy reading about an important period in our lives. We spent seven years in the U.S. Navy Administered Trust Territory of the Pacific Islands. The Department of the Interior assumed the administration afterwards.

I would like to thank our niece, Nancy Hendricks Cahill, who keyboarded the manuscript on computer; Bruce Carpenter, who put the material in book type; and John Vint, consultant, editor, and friend. The book represents the dedication and labor of three talented, generous, and loving persons, and honoring Cecilia in this way has given me much pleasure.

Bloomington   HENRY WAHL
January 2000

Number One Pacific Island

CHAPTER ONE

Deep in the Heart of Palau

"Thirty minutes to Peleliu, Ma'am."

The coveralled sailor on the Navy Air Transport plane was bending over the narrow canvas rack on which I had been trying to rest for the past couple hours. Thirty minutes! I suppose that solicitous attendant thought I had been asleep while the plane droned on and on through the blackness of night over the Pacific. He couldn't know how many butterflies were looping the loop in my middle. Seventeen days out of San Francisco by boat and plane, and now I was nearly there.

Stiffly I swung down from that torturous canvas shelf and picked my way over sleeping figures sprawled on the floor of the plane to the heaped up luggage. The boy helped me find the shopping bag which contained the dress and good shoes I had saved for this moment. As I stepped to the small, curtained restroom at the rear of the plane, sailors bound for Samar and Manila, and China, were stirring and disentangling themselves from their pretzel sleeping positions on the floor. In uncomfortable "bucket" seats along the sides of the plane, other Navy wives, some with tousle-headed children asleep across their laps, were aroused, sensing by the stir of activity that we were soon to land.

Inside the curtained privacy of the restroom I braced myself against the cold aluminum wall of the plane and tried to slip out of my slacks. Just then the plane dipped and jostled, losing altitude for the landing.... Never wear a girdle under slacks again, I warned myself as I regained my balance. It had been a nuisance every minute of the four hours of flight from Guam. But the arrival costume had been thought out carefully, and no amount of discomfort would have changed my mind. . . . Must look my best for the arrival . . . wear something dark, but smart and unmussed as if the trip had been nothing at all . . . must impress Henry with a smooth, bright look at dawn . . . green gabardine dress he likes . . . brown pumps.

The dignified Navy captain who had talked in low tones all during the trip with another officer and had made notes in a small black book looked surprised at the sudden change in costume when I emerged from the curtained space to walk down the aisleway to my seat.

Down, down the plane dropped. My ears plugged up and I swallowed to make them pop. . . . Outside was only inky blackness. Then as we turned in for the landing, and the plane dipped its wing, tiny lights winked up from below. Bigger and bigger they grew as the plane leveled off, and before I realized it we were down. There was a bump and the sudden screech of tires squealing onto the runway. . . . The plane trundled toward a row of lights.

What's the last minute before arrival feeling? Stomach tight. Muscles tense. A foolish grin plastered across the face. Furtively I looked around to find out if everyone saw how silly I looked. The plane rolled to a stop. The motors roared, coughed, and then were quiet. The cargo doors were banged open and the moist, black velvet tropical morning rolled into the chilly plane interior. A ladder rattled against the plane's side and a Navy officer clambered up.

"Good morning," he said. "Is there a Mrs. Wahl aboard?"

"Me, I'm Mrs. Wahl," I blurted.

"Hey, Wahl, She's here," he sang out the doorway.

Another head appeared over the bottom edge of the door, one wreathed in a big grin and stubbled with day-old whiskers. It was Henry, in wrinkled green shirt and shorts, and scuffed G.I. shoes. This was our dramatic reunion, seven thousand miles away from Indiana! I got a quick peck under the nose and a hurried squeeze; but the big grin more than made up for it. There had been no word from Guam that I would be on that plane. But Henry, knowing I was due, had come over from Anguar, our island, the day before just in hopes I would be on the next plane.

It was an exciting bustle, the unloading of baggage, and the good-byes to momentary traveling acquaintances, the introductions to new people on the ground. As we climbed into a waiting jeep I thought to myself . . . this reunion is just like all the others during the war. It's just as if he had been out of town overnight and now is back in the old routine. All the lonesomeness, the unshared thoughts, the uneasiness melt away like hoar frost before the sun. Being here is the most natural thing in the world. . . . There remains no time we were apart, only a lot of catching up to do. Being on a far off Pacific island now seemed perfectly natural.

The sudden tropical dawn was coming up like stage lights smoothly brightening. A line of lumpy, dull green hills loomed up ahead of us, the only high spot on the island. The white coral airstrip and the road alongside appeared gray in the half-light. The dawn gave a softening touch to the war-battered island where splintered tree trunks rose gauntly above the tangled green of the new underbrush. Broken concrete block-houses took form, squatting alongside the airstrip; a young coconut sprouted from the roof of one. Rusted tanks and trucks and smashed airplanes lay in a heap beside the building.

"Breakfast isn't until 7:30. Want to take a look around? I'll show you our island across the channel." Henry drove the jeep away from the group around the plane and headed toward the abrupt, ugly ridge which dominates Peleliu.

"That's Bloody Nose Ridge. Some of the war's worst fighting went on there," he pointed out. "There're still Japs holed up in caves up there. Some Marines were fired on while they were on patrol just a couple weeks ago. You won't catch me wandering around those rocks!"

We moved along the coral road where underbrush fought to crawl across the open space. Three little native boys stopped as we passed, peered at the strange woman in the jeep and called, "Gooood mahning," giggled and skittered on down the road.

"They're cute!"

"Wait till you see the kids around our house," Henry replied. "They play ping pong on the front terrace and swim in the water in front of the place all hours of the day and night. Now look! There's Angaur."

Lying flat across a stretch of choppy, gray ocean was a small piece of land, pale green in the long rays of the sun. There was Angaur, where Henry was the only Navy Military Government officer, and where, for nine months I would be the only white woman except for occasional visits by other Navy wives.

"It's certainly flat! You're sure that's south, Heinie? It ought to be north."

"No, dearie. You'll get your directions in a little while. Now we live on the far end of the island from this view. Angaur's about seven miles from here. And you're finally here to see it. We've waited for this a long time, haven't we. Hello, my dear."

Breakfast in the screened-in quonset mess hall was a babble of introductions. Too many quick impressions, none of them clear, flashed through my sleepless, excitement-dulled brain. Too strong coffee . . . condensed milk . . . dining room an open room overlooking the water . . . nice of the Peleliu skipper and his wife to have met us at the plane before dawn . . . so that's Harry. "Yes, Henry has written so much about you, Harry,.." Wonder how he likes having his wife, baby, and mother-in-law arrive all at once. "No thanks, no scrambled eggs." Not really hungry you know! That tableful of fellows must be enjoying a good stare at us!

"Hey, Heinie, want to fly over with us this morning?" A gay, curly headed chap leaned over our table and grinned his greeting. "We're going to get some hours in the air this A.M. and might as well land on your strip."

"How about it, dearie? Do you want to go home in a Navy bomber? These guys are the Air and Sea Rescue Squadron pilots, and this is Lt. McDougall. You don't have to be crazy to be a flier, but it helps, and these guys qualify! How about it? You'd get a ride in a PB4Y2."

"A bomber! Sure, I'm game. It sounds wonderful."

"Thanks, Jack. We'll pick up Cec's gear and meet you on the strip right away," Henry said. "Boy, that's a relief. I hated having you wait till noon for the trip on the construction company's rolling tug."

The airstrip at 8:30 was a bright glare of white coral. Brighter yet in the morning sun was the clumsy, pot-bellied plane. The luggage was swallowed into the rear compartment, and we squatted down and waddled under the belly of the bomber to the opened bomb bay doors. Strange hands reached down to grab mine, and I was hauled up a long leap into the elbow-bumping narrowness of a passageway through the forward section of the plane. Surrounded by the bare structure of the warplane, I was confounded by a dizzy array of wiring, parts, and gadgets. My respect for flyers and aeronautical engineers suddenly grew much healthier.

The young pilots were already in their comfortable, over-stuffed seats, verbally banging each other over the head.

"Well, Red, do you think you can fly this thing this morning?" yelled the pilot over the roar of the motor.

"Fly her? Hell, all you can do with this tub is follow her wherever she decides to go. If I had an experienced co-pilot I might feel as if we were going to get off the ground once in awhile. Do you supposed those bomb bay doors will hang on one more time?"

"Yeah, if the damn piece of wire the mechanic stuck on holds. Well, Mr. Woods, shall we go to work?"

"Right, Mr. McDougall."

McDougall let us stand right behind the pilot's seats so we would have a panoramic view. The old plane ambled to the end of the strip like a pregnant dachshund. Then, suddenly, the air strip whisked from under us, blurring as it went. Peleliu fell into order beneath us, and from a narrow vista of land and trees we suddenly came into a wide blue world, dotted by white clouds above and whitecaps below. To our left drifted the entirety of a tiny squall . . . a perfect circle of rain showers slanting to the ocean like a spotlight through a smoke-filled hall. Another light squall obscured Angaur, and we swung around to the west to avoid it.

Then, as we turned again, there was our island, a small green-shaped comma, fringed in the white lace of the surf, the dark blue water beyond. Henry put his mouth close to my ear and shouted.

"Look down at the southern end, the tip of the island. There's a V-shaped reef pointing west from that sandy beach. Middle of that beach is our quonset. Can't see it too well because of trees. But you know this spot now." It sped by too fast for me as we circled and started gliding down toward the water.

"Watch now! This is how the pilots will get the construction company men out to the strip to meet us. If they wanted us they'd come over our house."

The plane leveled off about a hundred feet above the water and roared across the buildings of the camp.

"I felt as if I could touch them," I gasped.

"Wait till you see them buzz us! You'll really think they're low. By the time we land now they'll all be there," Henry shouted.

"Who's 'They'?" I shouted back.

"Civilian construction men, fire truck, native policemen, probably half the village. You're quite an oddity here, you know. I don't think they've ever seen a redhead. In fact, the villagers have seen only a couple of white women before."

"Oh golly! Do I look all right? Will they understand me? What do I say? Oh, Henry, I look so tired!"

"No, joe, you're fine. Just be yourself. You are almost home."

Standing on tiptoe, I gripped the backs of the seats and peered down as we swung around and lined up over the Angaur strip. We seemed to be floating down slowly; it must be the airstrip bounding up to meet us! We touched at the end of the landing field and sped past a group of jeeps and trucks. Taxiing back the length of the strip seemed to take an hour after the skimming trip down. At last we were stopped, the engines cut, and all of us were still shouting a little in the sudden silence.

DEEP IN THE HEART OF PALAU

We skimmed down through the bomb bay doors and out from under the plane.

"Ah! Meestahr Wahl! You back!" A slim, brown figure in neatly pressed Navy green shirt and shorts, and white tennis shoes stood grinning beside the plane.

"Yes, Tulop. A good ride this morning. Tulop, this is my wife."

A strong, brown hand shot out to grasp mine firmly. "Ah! Meesus Wahl. Goood mahning." Tulop, the native chief of police and Henry's right hand man, bustled to the plane to take our luggage and throw it into the waiting jeep. A hesitant line of natives approached us. Henry made the introductions.

"There is Merep... John Telei... Gullivert... Charlie Eduardo... Takime... Balau." As each was introduced he stepped up with a wide grin and shook my hand, and then ducked back embarrassedly. How many weeks would it take for me to connect these strange names with the shining, friendly faces? I didn't know until months later that two whole truckloads of natives were parked at the edge of the airfield ogling me.

Tulop

"Hey, Wahl, you old goat, you finally got her," a distinctly American voice boomed out. "Now maybe we'll have some peace around this joint!" A jolly, solid man bounced down from the seat of a huge red fire engine.

"Your husband, Mrs. Wahl, is a heel! He beat me at two measly games of cribbage last week, and he now maintains that he's the champion. How'd you ever happen to get caught by this old codger?"

This was Jack Pleasants, the island fire chief, and security chief for the Henderson Construction Company, which was bossing the removal of phosphate from the island. It was a small deposit but one of the richest in the world. Sensing my tenseness and exhaustion after the long trip, he kept up a stream of lighthearted banter that soon had me grinning at ease. Then there were more introductions as others of the island's temporary inhabitants arrived. Sexton, the personnel man; Harlan, the project manager; Buck, assistant manager; Anderson, Antone, Sheffield. finally we were off in Henry's jeep to our house by the sea, which he had written so much about while I was waiting for my travel orders.

Chickens fluttered out of the roadway as we headed through the first native village I had ever seen. It was a modern version of a Pacific island community, though; gray quonsets lined the road in a palm shaded area. Native women, swathed in loose dresses, looked up from their work and waved. Youngsters, with dogs at their heels, came tearing around corners to stare. Again the sun-white coral was so bright it blinded. The low brush, grown and tangled since the devastation of the war, bordered the roads. A vine-like sunflower twined over a couple old rusty tanks. The drive from the airstrip took only a few minutes, and we drew up in a driveway which ended at a shed large enough to hold four jeeps. The sea was beyond.

"There, madam, to the right is your happy home," Henry beamed.

The long, low gray quonset lay some thirty feet from the beach. It was almost hidden by what Henry called Australian pines. He helped me out of the jeep and led me across a concrete porch to the door in the middle of the south end of the building. Three rooms lined up the length of the hut . . . we could bowl the length of this house, I thought irrelevantly.

Henry bustled in like a real estate agent.

"Now here's the kitchen. Seems funny to enter a house by the kitchen all the time, but you'll get used to it. You like?"

"I like. But what's this tremendous console?"

"That, dear, is the stove. I just got it. Scrounged it. It's a field range. Army. See, you pull open the top and here is a big kettle. It's made for feeding stew to a couple hundred men; but I think we can make it work for two."

"It looks a little overwhelming," I said dubiously. "How does it work?"

"Well, I've had it going only once, and I'm not too sure. I do know it sounds like a plane on the takeoff. But, come, see the rest of the house."

Our home was airy, almost to the point of being open on all sides, I felt at first glance. The whole ocean side of the living room was screened along the curve of the quonset ribs, and protected by a canvas awning. The two bedrooms opened onto the covered terrace on the beach side. They, too, were screened on the western side. It was like a summer camp cottage, plain but comfortable.

"Here it is! This is my pride and joy! Kindly note the size of this masterpiece, my dear. Feel those springs."

The masterpiece could not be missed when we entered the main bedroom. A bed almost seven feet square, it completely filled one corner of the huge room. The natives had made it to specification, Henry declared, and had used two sets of springs set lengthwise, and six narrow mattress pads, three each way, to make the finest bed in the Pacific. It sat beside the screened side of the room which opened onto the beautiful, roofed, cement terrace. What a place to sleep with the sea breezes blowing in and the sound of the surf to lull us. I looked longingly at the bed because the excitement of arrival was beginning to wear off and exhaustion was setting in.

Henry was explaining that the building once was the Officer's Club for the 484th Army Bombardment Group. "They left this thing," he pointed to a combination love seat-radio-shelf-speaker-outlet-table-bookshelf, which we promptly dubbed "The Throne." Its mattress cushions were covered in screaming bright blue cretonne with violent red roses. The room also sported a packing box desk and several cabinets, all painted gray.

"I waited till you came to have the boys build us a closet and hotlocker. We'll fix that up in a day or two; then there'll be a place to put your clothes."

We investigated the rest of the building, which included a fine bath with two showers and a toilet with a window opening directly

· 11 ·

into the bedroom. There was also the extra dormitory room with five beds. We walked along the beach for a few feet. Then we sat on the terrace while Henry got out the gifts the natives had been giving him. Soon I realized I was growing droopier and nearer tears. That long boat trip across the Pacific, two exciting days in Honolulu, three in Guam, the cramped plane ride to Peleliu, the lack of sleep were all getting me down. Henry wisely suggested that I rest for awhile till he got me some lunch.

"What do you want to eat?" he asked, popping into the bedroom just as I began to relax.

"I haven't the vaguest notion, darling. What do you have?"

"Well, there are four warehouses, an abandoned reefer, and the icebox full of food. We ought to be able to find you something in all that. Let me see; there's a slug of C-ration; but I don't think that'll do. I know! first I'll bring you some cold tomato juice. That ought to be good. Then how about some pea soup and some bacon and eggs. I got some fresh ones from the construction company kitchen yesterday. And the natives brought you a stalk of bananas this morning."

I couldn't have though up a menu at that point if my life had depended on it; so I just nodded dumbly and let him go, barely wondering how he was going to cook the stuff. He was back in a few minutes.

"How do you fix this pea soup?"

I sat up wearily and took the five-pound box of dehydrated pea soup. Trying blindly to figure how to reduce a recipe for one hundred to two, I finally said, "Oh, mix a couple tablespoonsful of this in a couple cups of boiling water. Do you have the stove going?"

"No, I gave up on the field range. There's gasoline all over the floor, so I decided something was wrong with the darn thing. I have a Number 10 can filled with sand and gasoline out on the back porch."

"Some stove," I muttered to myself as I lay down again and closed my burning eyes.

"Here's your tomato juice." He was back almost before my eyelids were closed. I had to admit it was delicious even if it did stick a little going down.

"Could you come show me how much bacon we'll eat, dear? I have the can almost open."

I plodded out to the disarray that was the kitchen. Standing on the counter was a 14 pound tin of bacon and a huge butcher knife with which Henry had started to slash open the can.

"How wonderful to have bacon. But how'll we get away with that much?"

"The best we can, I guess. Most of these canned things are big cans. Either Number 10 tins, or bigger stuff like this." He sawed away with the knife and finally had the lid off.

"Help me pull this slab out now."

"But it isn't sli-i-i-iced!" I wailed. The sight of the slick, huge slabs of salty bacon did it. The tears cascaded.

"My god, honey, what did you expect? You're a pioneer now and lucky to have this stuff." But he set down the can and pulled my head over on his shoulder while I sobbed.

"I'm sorry, dear, but I'm just so tired, and everything is so new, and I don't think I could eat much of anything, anyway."

He led me back to the bed, and in a little while brought the soup, which insisted on separating continually into a tasteless past and water, some excellent bread with canned butter, and a couple bananas. I gulped it down between sobs, tried to smile my thanks, and then curled up to fall into a dead sleep.

I must have slept three hours, waking now and then to hear the surf lapping on the beach, being conscious of the warm, fragrant breeze wafting in through the screen.

From far off down the beach came the voices of small boys singing loudly, "da-da-da-da, da-da-da-da, DEEP IN THE HEART OF TAXSIS."

I chuckled sleepily. Home in the Pacific!

CHAPTER TWO

Tour of Inspection

The sound of a discreet cough, followed by the cascade of water from the back porch faucet to the concrete, wafted in over the open-topped partitions of the quonset.

"Henry, someone's at the back door!" I nudged the sleeping form beside me in alarm, for it was only seven o'clock.

"Huh? You wake up too easily," he muttered into the mattress. It's just someone walking through the yard."

"Honey! Get up. I'm sure there's someone there. Roll it!"

He staggered out of the comfortable, big bed, reached for his shorts, toed into his slippers, and shuffled out to the back door.

It was a bright, warm morning. Through the shady terrace just beyond the screen the ocean shimmered. So this is Angaur; curious possibilities sauntered through my mind . . . a completely new experience, nothing in the past on which to base this. Will I be disappointed, or scared, or lonesome so far from home? Henry said we'd be twentieth-century pioneers in a sense, and we were excited with the prospect. Ah, Two in the Tropics . . . will the tropics take its toll of the Wahls . . . will the natives like the Wahls . . . will the Wahls like the natives . . . tune in tomorrow! I giggled at this silly trend of soap-operaish thought, and turned my attention to the voices in the living room/office.

"We go to Peleliu today. Meestahr Wahl find parts for village truck. Construction company boat goes eight o'clock." This was a soft, throaty male voice.

"O.K., Balau. I'll make pass for you. Who all goes?"

"Charlie, Takime, me. No more."

The typewriter spattered a few words, then the sheet of paper was ripped out, and Henry apparently gave it to the native, for I heard him say, "O.K., Balau. See you later."

TOUR OF INSPECTION

The screen door was closed quietly, and Henry came back into the bedroom explaining, "The Henderson tug goes to Peleliu every morning, and the natives have to have passes to ride it. So we'll be starting most of our days typing passes for some of the villagers. Come on, get some clothes on so we can have breakfast and look over our domain. You'll have a lot of new impressions today."

While I was in the kitchen opening a can of grapefruit juice a strikingly handsome native knocked at the door. He'd padded soundlessly across the yard and the concrete porch, and his rap was a startling sound. He was a lithe, slender young man with a head any artist would dream of painting against a backdrop of ferns and magenta bougainvillea. Café au lait skin, tremendous deep set brown eyes, a faraway meditative look about them, an almost feminine mouth, and black, shiny hair that waved away from his forehead.

"How do you do. I am Mrs. Wahl. Will you come in." I tried to speak slowly and clearly. But he stood where he was.

"Mr. Wahl?" he asked softly.

"Just a moment. I'll call him. Henry! Someone is here."

As soon as Henry appeared from his desk the visitor stepped in the door. I wondered at his hesitation, but marked it up to shyness. However, my first introduction to native customs came later when Henry explained that no native man goes into a house where there is a woman alone, even his sister. Unless the father or husband is in sight he waits.

"Good morning, Gullivert. Lesson time? Gullivert, this is my wife. Gullivert is our village school teacher, dear. Every morning he brings an English lesson that he has prepared for the children and for himself to learn more English. We'll go out to the terrace, Gullivert."

Henry had not been any great shakes at English in college, but this was another of his duties as a military government officer. They ranged from organizing village baseball games to sitting on the local court, and enforcing military law.

The English lesson done, we set off on my first official tour of the island. We drove in the jeep to the village, over the white coral road with thick vegetation growing close to the edge. It was an unusual village made up of abandoned Army quonset huts which had been a hospital area tucked neatly in rows in the shade of coconut and ironwood trees. The natives had moved in, when at the end of the war they returned from Babelthaup, the big island at the north end of the Palaus, where they had fled for refuge when the bombings threatened Angaur and when the last rough fight against the Japanese had been waged along the ridge on Angaur.

We caught glimpses in the open doorways of glistening floors, neat interiors with little or no furniture. There were barefoot women clad only in white chemises, or bare from the waist up. On the doorsteps gnarled old men and women sat comfortably with grandchildren in their laps. Everyone waved in friendly fashion. For my money, Gullivert remained the handsomest native I'd seen; but all the Angaur people were attractive . . . not at all the fuzzy-wuzzys in the pictures Henry had sent from the Solomons during the war. This was a brown race of people, well built, with straight hair. Henry explained that their language and general characteristics pointed to a Malayan background.

Three little barefoot boys wearing shorts handed down from the Army and gathered by twine around their beanpole waists, stood aside and giggled and waved as we passed them.

"Why it wasn't a dream!" I gasped.

"What do you mean?"

"I thought that I'd dreamed that just when it was beginning to be light this morning there were three little boys standing right outside our screen on the terrace staring at me. I thought it was so ridiculous it had to be a dream. But those are the boys I saw! Why those little rascals!"

Henry howled. "Yes, they were undoubtedly there. I tell you, these natives will know more about us and how we live than we know about ourselves. Don't ever worry if they seem to be around. They're naturally, not nastily, curious. And remember you're quite a rarity in these parts. Only one other white woman has been on this island for any time, and that was a decade ago. There have been visitors since, and a Coast Guard officer's wife was here for several weeks. And furthermore, you have red hair."

"This is going to be like living in a fish bowl! They won't miss a thing with us in that house that's half screen!" I wasn't quite used to the idea yet.

Angaur was a montage of white and green and blue that first day. White coral shimmering from the heat waves rising above it; light green underbrush and young jungle encroaching on the white roadways; cobalt blue sky afloat with fat white clouds. The coral and phosphate dust grayed and whitened the greens of the jungle. Ragged skeletons of banyan trees, battered by the wartime bombardment, towered above the new growth. A distinctive odor soon identified itself with the island: a moist, verdant, musty smell from the jungle and a milky smell from the coral on the open beach, freshened and stirred by the salty trade winds from the sea.

We drove along the back roads comfortably settled in the jeep, each with one foot propped upon the sides, the cool breezes blowing above our "kneezes". A jeep is a wonderful, informal institution. Scarcely any springs . . . definitely no knee action . . . canvas covered boards for seats.

"Henry, do you suppose after our informal life out here I'll ever be able to ride in an automobile again like a lady with my feet inside, not propped on the seat or the dashboard?"

"Treat this jeep kindly, Madam," he bantered. "It is the aggregate of many a junk pile. I point out to you that we have a horn, which is quite a distinction among island jeeps! We also have a solid wooden top, handy for hanging on over rough spots. Wait till you go to Koror; you'll wish you had this commuter's strap to hang on over their horrible roads! We're lucky to have sixteen miles of smooth, coral-surfaced roads on Angaur."

I could feel the sun biting into the skin of my right arm and leg which were not shaded by the jeep. I moved over closer to Henry.

"Sudden burst of affection, joe, or just sunburn?" he quipped.

"Sunburn," I answered dryly.

A flock of white herons fluttered awkwardly up from the underbrush by the swamp we were approaching. The sudden sputter of our jeep in the morning quiet had startled them, and they rose with heavy wings flapping. They circled annoyedly behind us till quiet prevailed, and then drifted back to their interrupted sunning. The whole island seemed to be dozing in the increasing heat of the day, and we were the only disturbance in its midst.

"Let's drive the length of the airstrip," said Henry. "I like to go there in the morning to find any new birds that might be around. I can usually find some turnstones or golden plovers, and I don't think you've ever seen any before."

The commotion that greeted us at the strip had driven away all the birds; but it was so hilarious and ridiculous that we didn't think of them again. Toward us roared the huge, red Henderson firetruck . . . driverless! It steered a straight course as if guided by an automaton. The possibilities of imminent disaster struck us suddenly.

"My god, what's happened to Pleasants," screeched Henry. "He couldn't have fallen out and left this thing out of control, could he?"

Then we spied him sitting at the back of the truck, cross-legged atop all the hoses and nozzles, monarch of all he surveyed, and having a huge time for himself.

We collapsed in gales of laughter as the truck rolled by at about forty miles an hour. Pleasants swept off his baseball cap in deep salute as he passed, and then rose and casually climbed along the fender to the steering wheel. He turned the truck around and steered back to where we sat.

"You crazy nut," Heinie shouted over the noise of the engine. "What are you trying to prove? Or are you just island happy?"

Jack jumped down from the driver's seat and came over to the jeep. "Hi, you two. Well, I discovered a couple weeks ago I could set the steering wheel on this bucket of bolts and take a straight course down the 6000 feet of the landing strip. Even if I did veer a little I was on flat ground and couldn't hurt anything. Then I began to have a little fun. Only trouble was that just about the time I got up on the truck, who should come along but Bill Henderson himself . . . the boss down from Guam on an inspection trip. How do you think the supposedly sane police chief looked about then!

"Incidentally, Mrs. Wahl," he grinned at me, "when will I be welcome at that vine covered cottage of yours. I am in need of a beer . . . or worse."

"Give us another half hour," Heinie returned. "We'll be officially at home then. I'm taking Cec on a tour of inspection.

"Well, I'll be down to show you how officially I can down a can of brew." So saying he climbed aboard his red wagon and karoomed off down the strip, siren screaming.

Our tour took us to the rugged north end of the island, where the limestone rock, a honeycomb of knife-sharp ridges, rises thirty feet above the water. Gray little crabs, camouflaged on the rocks, sunned themselves and became visible only when we approached and sent them clattering into hiding. What Henry dubbed baby "octopussys" lay in the puddles left by the receding surf. We sat for a moment looking at Peleliu across the channel, and northward to the rest of the islands, which were softened by haze and mist, and seemed green mirages rising from the sea. It was a comfortable feeling to see the islands stretching away to the north. That meant contact with other Americans, and mail at Koror, the headquarter island. We knew we were going to be perfectly comfortable and happy on Angaur; but the presence of those other islands was soothing . . . just in case.

There were very few flowers blooming on Angaur. Having been brought up on the idea of a gardenia-in-your-hair-daily, and orchids-outside-the-door school for the tropics, I had packed several of my favorite vases to make the house a blooming bower. Henry explained that because of its coral and limestone soil Angaur was a marginal tropical island so far as plants were concerned. A pink and a white ground phlox thrived in the sand; there was a spider lily, which was a fragrant cluster of white blossoms reminding me of the lemon lilies planted along our ditch banks when I was a little girl. There were strings of papaya blossoms in the trees; but they hardly looked as if they would fit in a vase, being small white blossoms that should be strung in a wedding bouquet. There were a few hibiscus bushes, and some dwarf poinsettias which grew along the ground. These wilted before we could get them back to the house. The only other flower was a brilliant red cluster of small-petaled blossoms on a shrub in the jungle. But they were so covered with pesky ants they weren't worth picking.

We waved at everyone we met, for all the natives were shyly friendly, and the construction men a highly informal group. Heinie already had the advantage of knowing almost everyone, so he hailed them as we passed, and it was an easy habit to acquire. We passed several native women walking very straight and easily, carrying tremendous long machetes in their hands and baskets made of coconut palm leaves on their heads. Then we passed a bunch of boys, girls, and dogs.

"They're going to set traps for land crabs," said Henry.

"Land crabs! Are they good to eat?"

"Just you wait. They are ambrosia, the way the Angaurese fix them. These kids are carrying a little lunch for themselves in those baskets, probably some taro and dried fish, and the rest of the baskets are filled with split coconuts. They'll walk the road we just traveled to set the snares under trees . . . a half a coconut tied down. Then the whole young set will spend most of the night waiting by the traps till they hear a crab ticking up to the bait. They'll flash a light on him, which freezes him to the spot, pick him up, and put him in a basket. Simple! Huh?"

The youngsters waved merrily, too.

"This waving business had me thinking I was rock happy a couple months ago," Heinie laughed. "I got in the habit, as soon as I arrived, of waving at all the villagers when I passed them. One morning I was rolling along this road, thinking about something I had to do, and I waved at a couple I passed. A minute later I did a double take and remembered I hadn't recognized the folks I'd waved to. I looked back and discovered it had been a couple of dogs!"

By afternoon Henry's brief vacation was over. A stream of people came through our living room office to air their troubles, to chat pleasantly awhile, and to move on.

Round-faced Carlos coasted into the backyard with his tiny son on the back of his bicycle. Carlos didn't speak English very well, but he explained softly and uncertainly that the village water plant, which he ran, needed more chlorine, and would Mr. Wahl get some at Peleliu. In answer to Henry's question about the current state of the water supply, Carlos said that the pump was okay, well pumping very much water, wooden tanks all okay. He went away smiling, little Carlos hanging on around his waist.

Harlan, the project manager for the construction company, stormed in. "Now, by god, Wahl, those natives of yours have got to quit riding our tug to Peleliu without passes. We can't be responsible for them, and that tug's not seaworthy at all. These damn gooks'll get away with anything they can, and I'm by god not going to have it."

Henry pointed out that the natives, as well as the tug boat operators, knew that no one was to get on the boat without passes. If the Henderson police would only check a little more carefully for passes, and quit winking at the regulations for the return of special favors from the native girls, there wouldn't be any trouble. A beer and fifteen minutes of conversation cooled Mr. Buck Harlan considerably, and we parted affably.

Tulop came in most excited, walking as if he had springs on the balls of his feet. "Meestahr Wahl! You come with me? Obisong say Henderson men take big bulldozer in her garden, garden no good now. She is very angry; she talk about everything! You come look, tell us what to do."

We set out in the jeeps with Tulop and the angry, excited native woman. We found that the construction men had been clearing a storage place for empty oil drums and had dragged a rusted old landing boat directly across Obisong's patch of tapioca and sweet potatoes. The men probably wouldn't recognize tapioca from roses, and didn't understand that the natives scattered their gardens all over the island wherever there was a tillable bit of soil. Poor Obisong was so angry she was beside herself. She spit out a streak of Palauan, slicing off the tops of bushes with furious slashes of her long, sharp machete as she howled. Tulop grinned understandingly, but amusedly, at her vituperation. Then he interpreted to her that Meestahr Wahl would speak to the Henderson manager about paying her for the damage. Would she take some canned food to last till she could get another garden going? She agreed with some relief, but still muttered a string of invectives to the native woman with her.

Back at the house, Henry made out a written report of what he had found, talked to Tulop about a proper settlement in the matter, and prepared a note to the project manager. This matter taken care of, Tulop brought out a note from the Henderson doctor.

"Meestahr Wahl! Amanya sick . . . here." He pointed to his lower abdomen. "Henderson doctor say she better go to Koror hospital, have Navy doctor fix."

Henry looked at the note. "My gosh, what next! Amanya's got gonorrhea. O.K., Tulop, I'll fix her pass. You think she can go to Peleliu on the tug tomorrow, and catch a native boat from there?"

Just as Tulop was preparing to leave, the Angaur Chief, two other older men, and a woman came in for a conference. Tulop stayed to interpret. Uherbalau, the Chief, was a slender old gentleman of some seventy years. His thin, lined face with its sharp cheekbones and high ridged nose was distinguished by a trim mustache, and once piercing brown eyes now watery with old age and blurred by cataracts. He limped stiff-legged into the room and settled down in a straight chair with his bad leg stretched out in front of him. Twenty years ago a Japanese doctor had removed the knee cap in mending a broken leg.

TOUR OF INSPECTION

Henry greeted the Chief and the two village elders, or *rubak*, with the Palauan afternoon greeting, "*Ungil odo osong.*" They laughed, delightedly, as they always did when Henry attempted to struggle with their language, but they replied with the same greeting.

Uherbalau said through Tulop that he was very happy to have Mrs. Wahl come live on Angaur Island. He nodded his head as Tulop translated. Although the Chief spoke little English, he appeared able to understand it well, and he vocalized his understanding by a constant, "hnnh, hnnh, mhnnh" at the end of each sentence of translation. The visitors kept watching me closely, and I began to feel uneasy under their eyes. Tulop sensed this and explained that they were saying Meesus Wahl has very pretty hair, ah, number one good, not like Palau hair, very fine, this color not like Palau hair.

Compliments over, Henry took advantage of their presence to talk business with the *rubaks*. He explained that it was time to clean up the American cemetery on the island. Would the women of the village do it for him the next time they cleaned their village cemetery?

The Chief wanted to know how much money the women would be paid for this work. (The natives has soon learned the American way of getting paid for services rendered.)

"M.G. has no money to pay the women for this job, Uherbalau. In America things like churches and cemeteries are things of the heart and mean much to the people; so everyone helps take care of them without being paid. Uherbalau, these men in American cemetery come to this island and drive away Japanese so all Palau people be free like Americans. Uherbalau, you think money can buy this thing? This belongs in man's heart. How can you put money on this thing?" He spoke quietly, emphasizing the sentiment with his hands.

The Chief nodded vigorously, as Tulop translated and conferred with the two *rubak*. Then he turned back and said, "What Mr. Wahl say is good. In two days all women in the village spend three days and fix up American cemetery."

"Ah, thank you very much, Uherbalau. Tulop, tell the Chief that although I cannot pay the women I will give them American food so they can eat and be happy. Tell Uherbalau I will give each woman who works nine cans of C-rations for three days' work."

The elders smiled and nodded their heads. Henry decided it was the right time to present the village with the gifts I had brought from the States . . . two brass candlesticks and two pairs of candles for the little Catholic church. There was a chorus of surprised "oh!"s and "ah!"s, when the gifts were brought out and set on the table. "Number one fine," they exclaimed. Before they had had only wooden ones. One of the *rubak* disappeared and came back in a few minutes with a half dozen natives ranging from six to sixty years. One, a handsome, quiet woman, was Elena, the village virgin in charge of the rosary services at the church. Henry said she could do the entire church rites for any festival or service from memory.

Elena glided into the white *rubak's* house, respect and dignity in every movement. She looked curiously, but coolly at the white woman. Then her gaze caught the pair of candlesticks on the table. Every motion stopped. Her eyes widened perceptibly and became wide chocolate pools. Tulop explained to her they were for the church. She moved forward through the circle of men to the table and reached out a hand timorously to touch a candlestick. "Ah," she whispered, "this is for my church?"

She lifted one candlestick slowly and stroked its satiny finish. "We have nothing like this before," she said to us. "You give something to church Palau people can never have any other way."

Uherbalau broke the spell by indicating that she should take the candlesticks to the church. She started to pick up a piece of paper from the table to wrap them in, but Tulop jumped forward.

"Ah! Too strong! Too hard! This!" He thrust to her the cotton and tissue paper in which the candlesticks had been packed. After almost ceremoniously wrapping the gifts she tucked one under each arm, smiled beatifically to all, and fairly floated out of the room.

And to think, I chastised myself, you begrudged the space those bulky packages took in your suitcase! Uherbalau's thanks brought me back to the room. "Chief say," Tulop translated, "if you give him one hundred dollar he could not like more. This present very, very fine."

The meeting broke up then with firm handshakes all around. The delegation departed; but Tulop paused at the back door, and with a wide show of white teeth, grinned, "Ah, Meestahr Wahl! You got Number One good mind!" He disappeared.

CHAPTER THREE

Somebody Tell Me

Tulop was the epitome of all the Palauans we came to know. We saw more of him than of any other native, for he was Chief of Police on Angaur, and more than that to us. He was interpreter of language and of the people, general Man Friday, sounding board, and confidant. Furthermore, it was clear that he interpreted us to the people of the island. It was Tulop we saw first in the morning when he came with the list of people who wanted to ride the tugboat to Peleliu; he was usually the last person we saw in the evening when he came from his last round of the island to report quietly, "Everything is okay, Meestahr Wahl."

Tulop could be any other Palauan in color and size . . . the average five and a half feet, smooth brown skin, sleek black hair. But he was distinguished by keen eyes that missed nothing, the wide mouth of a happy person, the most beautiful pair of legs we ever saw on a man . . . smooth and slender, but like molded steel. And lastly the deep, confidential voice of a perfect detective. He would come upon us with his springy, catlike walk without a sound, and announce diplomatically in the tone of a practiced detective, "Meestahr Wahl! Somebody tell me . . . " We knew, without questioning, that his informants had given him the exact information about the subject at hand, but that we would never know the source.

Tulop was in his mid-thirties, a substantial family man, and a young rubak. His eleven-year-old daughter and three-year-old son, whom he adored, were being brought up in strict Palauan customs, and were quiet, well-behaved children. We often wondered why they did not come to the Sunday open houses we held for the island children. Tulop never told us; but we suspected that he disapproved of the boisterous manners some of the youngsters had picked up from the Americans and that he felt his children should continue in their careful training.

He commented to Henry one day on his happy marriage. "Meestahr Wahl, I am married to my wife fourteen years now. I think I make present to her father and mother."

"Is this something everyone does, Tulop?" Henry queried.

"Oh, no. But sometimes man who has very good wife like to . . . Ah! I can no speak English so good to make you know. I can no say good what I mean." He hesitated. "But my wife very good to her mother, father. She give me two very fine children, she makes very good house and fine clothes. I make show she very good wife."

"I think that is a very fine thing to do, Tulop. You mean that sometimes a man who is happy in his marriage likes to show this to the man and woman who trained his wife?"

"Yes, that is so. This is good way to say so."

"What kind of present will you give your father-in-law, Tulop?"

"I am very lucky man. I am policeman for Japanese when they live here. Now I work for Americans. I have some money. So I make present two hundred fifty dollar to my wife's parents."

Tulop combined his police training under the Japanese with a natural intelligence and a spy system of his own. Given a misdemeanor or a crime to solve he could give us a list of suspects and the most logical offender in a matter of minutes. This he could do because he had all his people, as well as the Americans on the island, mentally catalogued. We never knew who his informants were; but we did know that whenever he wanted information about someone, he sent small boys to play in the neighborhood. They apparently gathered a great deal of pertinent information innocently.

As long as the construction company and the Japanese workers were on Angaur there were many problems of petty theft, drunken and disorderly conduct, surreptitious gifts of liquor to the natives (which was strictly forbidden by law), and woman trouble. It was a common failing among the Americans to blame the natives immediately for anything that was missing in the construction camp.

Tulop knew his people to be honest, with a few incorrigible exceptions; and he bore the accusations quietly while he made his private investigations.

The construction company store was robbed one night of nine hundred packs of cigarettes. First thing the next morning, Jack Pleasants summoned Tulop to the construction camp police quarters and told him to find the native who had committed the robbery.

Tulop softly protested that a native was not the guilty one.

"Now, Tulop, the stuff's nowhere in our camp! Who else could have taken them!" Pleasants blazed back. "Now dammit, I want you to search the village, every house. We'll find that man."

The search was fruitless, as we were sure it would be. The next morning Tulop brought to Henry his own solution.

"Meestahr Wahl! You know Henderson store. Somebody cut screen in small window, back side of quonset hut, open window, climb in."

He gestured with his fingers as he talked. "Meestahr Wahl! This man climb into window. But very funny, Meestahr Wahl! Not enough foot prints. I think this man . . . veeery long legs. I think he tall man."

"Meestahr Wahl! I see many things in store . . . many times. You know, Meestahr Wahl, one truck driver very tall man, very slender! I think he open the window, climb in with long legs, throw cigarettes out window. Somebody pick up and carry away, and then this man go out the door! What you think, Meestahr Wahl?"

Henry could only tell Mr. Pleasants, who said it was the most ridiculous damn thing he ever heard of. But, strangely enough, after several days of apparent quiet over the matter, the truck driver suddenly left to return to the States. We learned that an investigation by the Henderson police found the driver had been engaging in several kinds of undercover activity.

There was a sequel to the story. A few days later one of the Japanese ships left, loaded with phosphate. It pulled out at dusk, and just after dark Tulop came in with a slip of paper.

Henry at ease
in the "library"

"Meestahr Wahl! The name this man go to Japan with cigarettes. Somebody tell me."

The Japanese sailor was apprehended in Tokyo with the cigarettes as he left the ship. Tulop had been right from the beginning.

Tulop had mastered the English language in three years, and though he claimed he could not speak it "so well," he understood it excellently. Palauan has only about a two thousand–word vocabulary, which makes translation into English difficult. The customary procedure was to go from Palauan through Japanese to English, a slow process with frequently amusing outcomes. Tulop's court files at the native police station, for instance, were labeled, "Records of Criminal Psychology of Angaur Island."

The first time we left Angaur for Koror, the headquarter island, we were forced to stay away much longer than we anticipated. Henry sent a note back to Tulop just before Easter, making arrangements that any native who wished might come for the Easter church services at Koror, where the missionary churches were located. Tulop typed his answer on an old communications typewriter that fairly creaked the capital letters onto the paper.

NUMBER ONE PACIFIC ISLAND

Dear Mr. Wahl:
Many thanks for your kind letter which was delivered to me at 3 PM 3rd April.

Every Catholic on Angaur is appreciating your kindness very much. All of these people are anxious to go to Koror. However, on account of the boats narrow space and the present rough weather by which the boat may roll and pitch we decided to send 8 men and 10 women only this time. We shall be very much obliged if you kindly to them favor there.

Feel easy about Angaur, as everything is all right during your absence. As soon as you finish your job there, please return to Angaur safely with Miss Wahl.

Mr. Buck and Mr. Pleasants come to patrol your quarters every night. I have never failed to inspect your ice chamber and to feed your dog. You wife will be satisfied if you tell her so.

Please give my best regards to Mr. Suwachi and Mr. Abina [M.G. officers, Schwarts and Avila].
                Sincerely yours,   TULOP

After several weeks at Koror we had an opportunity to go home on a native boat, and grabbed the chance. It was a most joyful homecoming, for we had been away much longer than we expected, and without adequate changes of clothing. And we had missed peaceful Angaur more than we could describe. The sunset was darkened by a very black rain storm, and night fell suddenly, as we rounded the northwest pont of Angaur. There along the west side twinkled the lights of our home harbor, and the village. The rain began peppering down barely five minutes before we were tied up safely at the dock, and we jumped ashore and hurried to Pleasants' office to borrow a jeep to get home, thinking that the natives had not seen our boat coming in. Jack loaded us and our gear in his jeep and started down the wet, dark road to the village. Half way we met

Tulop on his way in the police jeep to meet the visiting native boat. Jack hailed him.

"Hey, Tulop. Got somebody here for you."

Tulop peered through the dark. Suddenly he recognized us and almost stood up in the jeep so surprised was he. "OHH!" he exclaimed. "Meestahr Wahl! You home. You come on this boat? We did not know. Ah! I am very glad you are home!"

The boys dashed ahead of us to unlock the quonset, and to settle our packages. They made a trip to the construction company mess hall to get us some leftover supper. Jack stayed for a beer and a short visit, and later Tulop came for a long, lazy talk with Henry about affairs during our absence.

We came to expect two things on each return from a Koror trip: some pleasant surprise for us at the house or in the village, and trouble. One time Tulop had the prisoners from his jail clean our whole yard and the beach front. Another time he had a Japanese phosphate worker paint and erect a magnificent mural of a south seas scene above the native police station. Palms hung over the sunny beach, and large black letters proclaimed,

INSULAR CONSTABULARY
PALAU
ANGAUR ISLAND

The warehouses might be cleaned for a surprise, or the hut scrubbed, or a mess of fresh fish cleaned and placed in our refrigerator. All these things made each homecoming exciting and friendly.

But we also approached our home shores with some apprehension because trouble had a habit of happening most often when we were away. Henry would hand Tulop the suitcase and ask, "Everything okay, Tulop?"

And Tulop would answer, "Hello, Meestahr Wahl. Everything okay. . . . Oh! Meestahr Wahl, while you gone we have much trouble . . ." and on into the story.

Usually one of the natives had gotten beered up and on his false courage decided to settle forcibly all of his outstanding gripes; a couple times the village store had been robbed; the most serious was the accidental death of one of the natives when a Japanese laborer backed into his road grader with a tractor. This nearly resulted in a native-Japanese riot, and we came home from Koror through treacherous waters to straighten things out. One of the more serious incidents, although it ended humorously, was the fracas in which Tulop was nearly shot by an irate, well-tanked villager.

Tulop had, by a process of resignation and reassignment, become the only policeman left of an original force of three. The job was really too much for him, for it meant patrolling and vigilance at all hours of the day and night, with little time left for his private life. And, as is natural in our own country, the person vested with the maintenance of law and order is sometimes the target of unkind words from the populace. While we were away one weekend, Taro, one of the young village bucks, had had access to the liquor supply of an American worker. He took on a considerable load, and then raced a jeep through the village, scattering chickens and scaring children. He was sobered suddenly when he rounded a corner too fast and turned the jeep over. Tulop hurried to the scene, arrested Taro, threatened him with dire punishment, and with the Chief's permission forbade him to drive again, and fined him $10. Taro was utterly penitent, apologetic to everyone in sight, and took his punishment like a man.

But his cousin, Eang, got hold of the remaining liquor, and, strengthened by its warming effects, suddenly remembered a time a year or so before when Tulop had hauled another of his relatives into court. Tulop, he decided fuzzily, was no good, a menace, and he, Eang, son of a *rubak*, was just the man to avenge the family honor.

Now, Eang not only had broken a law by getting drunk; he was unlawfully in possession of a gun he had gotten on Peleliu. He staggered into the village to Tulop's door and began to shout insults.

"Tulop, I come to kill you. You make much trouble for my family. You no good bastard. Hey, Tulop...come out!"

Wham...wham...wham! He let go with the .45. Fortunately his aim was bad and he missed Tulop. However, Tulop's house, his radio, his wife's sewing machine, and their clothes closet suddenly sported many air holes.

The harsh pistol report brought the villagers pouring out of their houses. The women, terrified, grabbed their children and ran for the safety of the nearby underbrush. Several of the bolder men moved cautiously toward Eang trying to reason with him. Joseph, the storekeeper, spoke quietly.

"Eang. Stop this wildness. Put your gun away. Tulop has done you no harm. Why do you do these mad things? Come give me your gun."

Eang fired blindly again, the bullet spurting up the dirt at Joseph's feet; and the village elder retired quickly to attempt some more remote means of subduing the wild man. Eang staggered off at a tangent along the main village street, which was now deathly quiet on this late, dark night. He had not gone far before his sudden bravado began to pale and he began muttering and sobbing to himself about his family's persecution. This was the sign for Tulop to pounce on him and lead him away to jail.

When Tulop met us at the dock the next afternoon his eyes were wide and dark. He was furious and frightened that he and his family had been in such danger, and he was eager to pour the whole story out to Henry.

"Meestahr Wahl, I can no more be policeman. This man frighten my wife, my little boy. This I cannot have. I try very hard to make Angaur number one island, but I can no do, just me. Taro, he is not angry with me; he knows he does wrong. But Eang...ah...he is bad man; he cause me much trouble."

Henry called a court session immediately that evening, and Eang was brought before the village panel. Chief Uherbalau brought his imperial wrath down upon the boy's head and sent him to the higher court at Koror for trial, which meant that a far greater sentence could be passed on him than in the small local court of justice. Tulop was calmed and reassured, and Henry promised him that we would try again at Koror to have more policemen assigned to Angaur.

Eang cooled his insolence in the village jail for several days until the boat could take him to Koror. Henry and Tulop made a raid on the village and uncovered several more guns which had been brought over from Peleliu. Possession of a gun seemed a fine thing to an Angaurese, as it does to an American, and they disregarded the law against such ownership by smuggling in weapons from the nearest island, where arms and ammunition could still be found in the jungles. We spent the morning after the raid packing the guns Henry had confiscated and the surplus arsenal which had recently been turned over to him by the Henderson Company. We cleaned the guns and listed the serial numbers preparatory to sending them to headquarters at Koror.

One of the submachine guns from the construction company police department was jammed. Henry tried unsuccessfully to remove the clip of bullets; so he decided to take the gun out to the beach and shoot off the clip instead. We looked carefully around to be sure no one was in the line of fire. Then Henry aimed the gun into the sand and pulled the trigger.

A rain of sound split the morning air. The force of the rapid blam-blam-blam-blam drove Henry back several feet, and we went back into the house laughing about the horrible noise and the power of the gun. Not two minutes later Tulop came rushing into the house without knocking, his eyes white, his brown face blanched.

"Meestahr Wahl!" he gasped, "You shoot?"

"Why yes, Tulop. What's the matter? This gun was stuck, so I took it to the beach and fired it."

"Oooooh!" He sighed with relief and collapsed panting in a chair. Everyone in the village think somebody come to shoot them again. Women and children already hiding in bushes!" He laughed shakily, "Everybody hear too much guns this week."

Henry was most embarrassed, for it hadn't occurred to us that the people would think anything of the shooting. So he went with Tulop to allay the villagers' fears.

Not a week later the south end of the island was rocked one sunny morning by a loud explosion which sent the shy women and children hiding again and brought Tulop out to find the source of the blast. He and Henry searched everywhere for a culprit, thinking it might be small boys with some explosive snitched from the construction company. Not a sign could be found of gun, shells, or dynamite. Finally Tulop hit upon the source.

"Meestahr Wahl! I think I know. I think somebody make agi. . . . I think you maybe call this in America 'home brew'. . . use banana peel, anything he can find, put in big five-gallon gasoline can. I think this man very much sorry because he should not make agi, so he cannot tell us when this can go . . . bang!"

Henry howled delightedly. "Okay, Tulop, I think you are right. You see if you can find this man, so we can talk to him. Now we must tell the women not to be frightened any more. Everything is okay in this village."

As the only man on the native police force, Tulop was nearly run ragged, for the construction company was still on Angaur, and constant patrol of the village and the garden area was needed. The beer problem was always present; whenever a ration of beer came in, the phosphate workers went on a rampage, and there were bound to be reverberations in the village. And during Henderson's last days a good bit of their dining room and kitchenware disappeared, plus personal belongings. The usual accusations that the natives had taken the items flew thick and fast, and it wasn't until Tulop insisted on making his own knockdown of the Japanese laborer's camp that the loot was discovered. The construction company police always arrived noisily at the front gate of the Jap camp and proceeded to search methodically through the row of huts. Tulop ranged a force of native helpers along the outside of the wire fence around the camp, and went in himself to make the search. As soon as the word spread that the camp was being searched the Japs ran to the back fence with their loot and dumped it . . . right into the hands of the waiting natives. Some items had gone into the village as gifts and some by being picked up. It was reasonable to the native that if the very generous American gave him many things when he was getting ready to leave Angaur, then these other items left lying around were surely his for the taking.

The strain of the days and nights of constant surveillance finally became too much for Tulop, and one Saturday afternoon he was nowhere to be found. Both he and the police jeep had dropped out of sight, and though we knew the small island well, we had learned there was simply no way of finding a native unless he wanted to be found. Henry had searched fruitlessly off and on for several hours and finally had given up. He busied himself at his Saturday job of spraying the exterior screens and eaves of the house thoroughly with D.D.T. late in the afternoon we started for a short ride through the village. We had gone barely a block's length when we spied the police jeep parked by one of the homes.

"By gosh, there's that rascal, Tulop," Henry muttered as he stopped. "Tulop! Hey, Tulop! Where have you been. I hunt all day for you!"

Tulop bounced up from the ground where he squatted talking with a couple of men and walked slowly and uncertainly toward us. "Hi, Meestahr Wahl!" He waved widely at Henry. "Hi, Meesus!" He clapped me on the shoulder, an unprecedented gesture. Henry was too surprised to speak, and sat looking squarely at his police chief. Tulop stood limply by the jeep for a minute, his hands stretched up to the canvas top, then abruptly giggled, and scratched his nose.

Tulop, our paragon of law and order, was drunk as a lord! Someone had a fresh batch of agi, and had found a willing imbiber in Tulop. And, like all the other natives, with a little liquor under his belt, Tulop was an entirely different individual. Usually quiet, completely polite, and utterly respectful of the authorities, a drunk native could become surly, full of braggadocio, threatening, and really dangerous, for he didn't know a thing he was doing.

Before I realized he was drunk my spine began to crawl with the sensation that something was not quite right with his demeanor. I couldn't look at those wide, blotchy eyes, at the usually broad grin turned down into a menacing line. He and Henry stared intently eye to eye for several acutely uncomfortable moments. Then the silence was broken when a jeep load of village girls went by, driven by a construction official, generally the object of Tulop's respect.

"You see that Meestahr Harris?" Tulop snarled. "He no—in good! All the time he sleep in village, want to make push with Angaur girls. But he too old, girls laugh. This man I no like. Someday I make stone on his house."

"Tulop, you say this man sleeps in the village. Before you tell me he does not. Many times I ask you. He has native girl friend, I know; but you say he does not stay in the village. Why do you say this?" Henry was trying to keep calm.

"Oh yes, he come to village every night. Someday I take my knife and go . . . keeeek. . . ." Tulop demonstrated violent motion with an imaginary knife across his abdomen.

"Tulop, I think there is something wrong with you today. Where did you find agi?"

"Agi? I find no agi. Nothing wrong with me. I am Number One policeman. I know everything goes on on my island. But policeman got much trouble." He fell morosely silent again, staring wildly at Henry. Henry was having trouble deciding whether to be furious or to be amused at Tulop's outburst.

"Tulop, I think you find agi. You do not talk so plain now. This does not sound like other Tulop I know. When you feel okay again you come see me at my house."

Henry muttered as we drove on, "Well, I'll be. . . I never thought I'd see that. You know why he got drunk, don't you?"

"Oh, I guess because he just got tired of being on the go morning, noon, and night, and because he couldn't resist the temptation."

"Well, that reason, and more. He did it methodically and with forethought because he wants to be fired. Remember, Merep definitely expected to be seen driving that Henderson man and the native girls around the village in the middle of the night because he wanted to be released from the police force. He had another job he wanted to do; but this is essentially the same principle Tulop talked to me about during the week, being the only man left on the force. He really is overworked; but no more native police are forthcoming, even though I've asked several times. So poor Tulop is the victim of overwork. I ought to fire him for this, but he's indispensable. You know, we just couldn't get along without him, and we should be thankful he's on our side most of the time."

"He certainly was a changed person," I said. I've heard the men say several times that a native is just like an Indian when he gets drunk. Tulop lost all his reserve, all of his sophistication, and was almost primitive again. I really felt he was capable of murder when he was talking about Harris."

"Yes, he was! That's why I worry so, and probably lose so many friends with the construction men over this law against giving liquor to the natives, who simply don't know what they're doing when they're drunk."

"But Henry, would they all drink if they had the chance?"

"Yes, I think so. That's why there must be rules against it. These natives have few outlets for their emotions, and if liquor is sometimes available it becomes a disproportionately large influence in their lives. Their society is communistic in a sense, and to be sure that the little liquor they might get isn't given to everyone, a native would drink it all up at once. That's when the trouble begins. But the society is also a very rigid one, and there are few deviations allowed from the norm. So a man who gets drunk and misbehaves may have seriously transgressed. Now, Tulop, like the others I've seen, will be dreadfully sorry when he sobers up, because he may find he has broken some tabu."

Tulop didn't show up that night or the next morning. But he

apparently sobered up rapidly after we had encountered him, for an emissary in the form of Jack Pleasants came to see us Sunday morning.

"Say, that Tulop is one worried man!" he said as we stirred our coffee.

"Well, he'd better be!" Henry grunted. "Because he's going to get one hell of an eating-out when he comes in. I'm sure he knows it, and that's why he's delaying."

"He came up to headquarters to see me last night, and was practically sobbing. 'Meestahr Pleasants,' he said. 'You go see Meestahr Wahl and tell him I am very sorry? I not do this thing again. I think he is very angry with me.'"

"Migod, Tulop," I said. "You know there's a law against getting drunk. How'd you happen to do it?"

"But Meestahr Pleasants, you police chief too," he said. "Sometimes y-o-u get drunk and do things not so good!"

"Bygod, he had me there! Remember the time I got a load on and took the fire truck out through the village raising all hell in the middle of the night? I'm no paragon of virtue, but that got me!"

Tulop was indeed penitent, the most sorry individual we had seen in months. He and Henry talked the problem over when Tulop finally slipped in late in the afternoon. Henry said he understood how hard it was to handle the big job of police work alone and that he would try again to get reinforcements. He read the resignation Tulop had carefully typed, and said that he would like Tulop to reconsider, at least for the months we would be on the island.

Tulop agreed. "Okay, Meestahr Wahl, I stay police chief as long as you are here. But when you go I want no more to stay on Angaur. You make this very good place, everybody happy . . . good laws for everybody. But when you go I take my family to Peleliu, where my wife's father and mother live."

Henry was pleased with such flattery, but salted it down a bit, remembering that the natives are quite clever in the Japanese sense of giving false impressions.

Our love for Tulop was certainly not lessened by the incident, for we knew the motives behind it, and knew Tulop's inherent intelligence, plus our dependence on him.

"You know," Henry said after it was all over, "even though I'm the M.G. officer and he is the native police chief, I sometimes feel that it is he, not I, who is running Angaur. He's certainly keen compared to any American; and we've commented before on his understanding of English and his interest in world affairs. I've kept a close check on him, and I've never caught him in a lie, though I've tried, just to be sure. I think one of the many things I've learned here is that Tulop reflects as a mirror the moral and ethical code of his superior officer. If the man is a libertine, Tulop makes every effort to keep him supplied with attractive native girls. If the man is grasping for money, Tulop makes the necessary arrangements to see that he accumulates money. If his superior has moral and spiritual ideas, Tulop then treats his constituents in the same manner. I don't think personal beliefs or disbeliefs enter into it with Tulop; whatever the authority is, that is what Tulop himself is."

"And can't you see how that appears in a bigger scale in the general relations between the Americans and the natives? We must maintain a high level of behavior because we're looked up to. If we can't give the Palauans something of a constructive nature, we've no reason to be here."

CHAPTER FOUR

At Home on Angaur

The practical side of Henry's education for Naval Administration work came bit by bit in his contacts with the Angaurese. It was slow going at first, one cautious step after another in learning the natives' ways, and showing them assurance that the Americans were not on the islands for the purpose of exploitation. This theoretical training at Stanford University, where Henry had been a member of the first School of Naval Administration, was known as SONA.

After the end of the war, when he was almost due to be released from active duty, Henry had learned that application could be made to SONA for an approximate two-year assignment in military government in the former Japanese mandated islands in the Pacific. This was what we were looking for! Jokingly, we had always said that since we had no rich uncles to send us traveling around the globe, we would have to work our way. Working in Pacific islands, some of which Henry had seen and loved during the war, would be a wonderful beginning to our travels. Only two weeks before we were to start home to Indiana from San Francisco where he had been stationed, the letter came from the Bureau of Personnel, and he was accepted as a member of SONA I.

And so began our plans for a tour of duty overseas together. The class work was excellent, bringing to the members a group of experts in anthropology, history, geography, geology, and international law. We digested the day's lectures with our evening meal when Henry described the day's activities; and we researched and theorized together over the weekly reports he handed in.

It was a happy time of preparation, and of assuring our friends that we were not completely daft. "The wandering Wahls" we were dubbed by some of our correspondents. One of Henry's best friends at home wrote him letter after pleasing letter saying, "for heaven's sake get these ideas of trailing about the world out of your mind. Come home and go in business with me while we can still make some money."

The months I spent at home with the family waiting for my travel orders were filled with explanations of where and why we were going. Miss Eastburn, a shy, unmarried business lady voiced the general feeling about this jaunt.

"My dear Cecilia, you must tell me just where you are going."

Here we go again, I thought, trying to give my oft-repeated speech as accurately as possible. "To Angaur, the southernmost of the Palau Islands, Miss Eastburn. The Palaus are about 800 miles south and west of Guam. They are the westernmost of all the central Pacific islands, and are about 500 miles east of the Philippines. And they're about seven degrees north of the equator."

"Oh my goodness, my dear, isn't that an awfully long way from home? I should be quite afraid to be so far away."

"Well, seven thousand miles isn't the distance it used to be, you know. Henry says it's the most delightful spot he's ever seen; and I can hardly wait to get under way."

"How long will you be gone?" she asked fearfully.

"Henry's tour of duty is scheduled to be eighteen months. We think it really should be longer, for in that time we feel we'll just get to know the natives and the language and that he'll begin to do his job efficiently."

"Well," hesitated Miss Eastburn with an uncertain laugh, "at least your experience will be . . . will . . . will be (at last she found the word!) *interesting!*" And, feeling that she had said just the right thing to these crazy people who were off to the wild ends of the world, she trotted off to her familiar world of a one-room apartment, women's clubs, and dieting.

"At least it will be interesting." That seemed to epitomize our projected year in the tropics to all our friends at home. More than one of them thought we were plain crazy. Anybody who would leave these good old United States of their own free will, and go to the stinking, steaming tropics where there was nothing but tarantulas, coral snakes, mosquitos big enough to wear pants, and dumb, black natives!

Bill and Connie wrote, "If you people are so unlucky as to be on one of those islands which Heinie and I had to inhabit, your evening clothes will have to be long enough to hide the hobnail boots which will be necessary to tramp the coral. I can just picture you now . . . Cec in her long, flowing gown and Heinie in his whites, doing pirouettes in the moonlight on the veranda of your quonset hut, dancing cheek to cheek . . . so the mosquitos can bite only one side at a time. The tempo changes, and amid the strains of the jitterbug tune comes the ghostly sound which resembles a skeleton clacking in the breeze. Cec feels a tug at her dress as if someone wants to cut in for a dance. She turns and looks into the limpid, romantic eyes of a land crab as he waves and scrapes and taps his claws to a devil's tattoo on the floor. It proves the last straw for poor Cecilia. She gets a fiery gleam in her eye, imagines herself an auburn KiKi Bird and takes off like a rocket in small circles among the palm tree tops, screaming, 'Ki-ki-rist it's hot down here.' The responsibility for the collapse of his loving wife bears too heavily upon him and Heinie slowly turns into a large gray-green iguana and ambles into the brush scratching his scales and muttering to himself all the while, 'Why did I ever stay in the Navy.' If you think I'm kidding you, Cec, just you wait!"

So we waited for Angaur. And we found it all we had hoped for, and more. The newness to us of every detail on the island was delightful. Henry's duties were demanding, but they left us time for daily explorations to the old phosphate mining areas, now brackish lakes, where we sat hushed for half an hour at a time watching for birds. His favorite hobby showed us a string of new birds for our books . . . purple gallinules, golden plovers, sharply marked black and white turnstones, two pairs of ducks who seemed far afield in that area, and the ever present brilliant blue, noisy kingfisher. The first black honeyeater with his brilliant red throat and breast was exciting, as were the graceful white-tailed tropic birds.

Most of the island was now covered with a tangle of young vines and trees, and studded with scarred white skeletons of old trees, a sign that the 1944 bombardment from U.S. ships has been heavy before and during the landings in the Palaus. The American landing on Angaur was made in late September, 1944, a few days ahead of the Peleliu landing; and operations here supported that bloody fight seven miles across the channel.

When the American softening blows began on Angaur, the Japanese gave the natives a choice of moving north to the larger island of Babelthaup, or remaining on their home island and taking their chances. About half of the village moved to Babelthaup, but even they were the victims of the bombings and the malnutrition that went along with the beaten-up land. There had been three small villages on Angaur in the north, central, and southern sections of the island. But the fighting, and the placement of the American installations all over the island had forced the returning natives into one crowded area at the southern end where the Army had their hospital wings, barracks, and theatre. It was in this area, along the sandy beach, that our house was placed. The construction company had taken over the Army quonsets in the center part of the island, and the battered Japanese phosphate works near the boat basin on the central west side.

The north part was now deserted except for the American military cemetery and the majority of the natives' gardens. We visited the cemetery often to walk among the rows of crosses, reading the names of the Army, Navy, and Marine boys there. No lovelier resting place could they have found than this clean, sunny spot of coral sand. The natives had landscaped the grounds with palms, hibiscus, colorful croton bushes, and border shrubs. A pair of plumeria bushes bloomed fragrantly at the gates on either side of the iron plaques, donated by the division general, which proclaimed this to be the 81st Division Cemetery. The native women spent several days each month cleaning the grounds and trimming the shrubs. A little chapel of smooth, gray stones gathered from the landing beaches stood on the grounds.

The east side of Angaur seemed the most desolate. The flat beach is rocky and unprotected by a fringing reef, and the sea pounds in heavily leaving broken pieces of coral and heavy round rocks worn smooth from the force of the waters. We saw few natives along the road that skirted the island here, for the area was too barren for gardening. There was an old coral gravel pit full of the waste of war: twisted steel beams, oil barrels, maimed machinery, all rusted to a reddish copper hue. And always there was the tangled underbrush spreading away from the road.

Hidden in this brush was a trail just wide enough for a jeep to bump down to a narrow cove where the skeleton of a C-47 lay nosed ever so gently against the rocks. Here was a story for speculation, and a rare sight to show any visitor. Our best guess was that the plane didn't quite make it home, but had slipped in low to the water at the island's edge, and floated in on the shallow tide for a beautifully executed crash landing.

Stretching more than two-thirds the length of Angaur on the flat east side was the seven thousand foot airstrip. From its eye-burning coral expanse were flown the first B-24 strikes against the Philippines. Deserted now, though still usable, the strip showed few signs of the great activity it had known. There were a group of stripped huts where the operations area had been, hard-stands still resisting the insistent weeds, a parachute rigging loft, and the bomber graveyard at the north end of the island. A half dozen B-24s rested tiredly on their bellies where they had been pushed out of the way for fresher planes. Gay Disney-like mascots, boastful titles, and beauteous, bumptious maidens adorned the noses of the retired raiders. Rows of bombs were stenciled against their sides, and Rising Suns and ships were enumerated. After the planes had been pushed off the field they were still visited by mechanics who dismantled all the usable parts. Even now flyers from Peleliu slipped over to hunt spare parts for their aging patrol bombers.

"Scrounging is the word," explained Henry. "It'll be one of your most used figures of speech here, for that's the way we get half of our material. It means to find usable items in deserted camps, to bum things from ships that anchor in, or to pick them up off junk heaps . . . from the boondocks, that is!"

Natives, too, had looked over the deserted bombers and found seats and pieces of metal they could use in their homes. And the kids salvaged aluminum tubing, straightened the pieces, and used them for blowguns with which they hunted wild chickens and little fat, green lizards.

Our tours of inspection were never complete until we had covered the road above the sharp rocks at the northwest corner of the island to see how rough the sea was this day, to look at Peleliu (as if it might float away between our daily rides), and to see our Blow Hole.

Here was the best spot on Angaur to see the ever-changing ocean . . . cobalt blue, under brilliant, clear skies, gunmetal when the rain clouds hovered, blue-green near the shore where fingers of rock made the water shallow. Some mornings the sea was violently choppy, as if a giant churn were being operated beneath the surface. Then the little tug boat on her way to Peleliu for Henderson Company errands, or the picket boat returning from a special trip hopped about, and completely disappeared between the waves.

If there had been a storm at sea near the Philippines, we knew the sea would be going by in long, slow, boat-rocking rolls, as slick-surfaced as if it had been oiled. When the big storms came at the change of seasons the spray beat far across the road, which was more than thirty feet above the water. And around the northwest point the waves always broke fanlike and angrily.

"Our" blowhole was a particularly satisfying replica of Old Faithful. The waves, through many seasons, had worn a subterranean cavern in the limestone rocks. Each breaker which rolled in forced water up through the cavity into a spurting geyser.

Angaur's blowhole

"Now wait a minute," Henry always warned when we had climbed to the old gun mount platform, "As soon as that good wave hits the ridge she'll blow. Hear that?"

"Vrrroooom!" The water had blown high and the spray wide. On stormy days when the waves were heavy the blowhole would spout a plume of water as high as sixty feet. The average thirty feet came just to our eye level. On dead calm days there was only a little spray, and a faint "Whoosh" as the waves patted into the cavern.

Our daily rides over various parts of the sixteen miles of fine crushed coral roads on Angaur were usually after the morning or afternoon radio checks with Koror. Combined with the hunt for new birds, and color shots for the camera, was the search for ripe papayas. There is no lovelier tree in the tropics than the slender papaya, and no more delectable fruit than its bland, cantaloupe-like fruit. Bouquets of leaves top the straight grayish trunk, large, veined leaves like several oak leaves fastened together in a fan-shaped leaf. The fruit hangs in a cluster all around the trunk, perhaps two dozen dark ovals, the lower ones tipped and spotted with orange. Young trees five and six feet high send showers of white hyacinth-like blossoms down threads of stem from the midst of the leaves. The most desirable fruit grows on such tall trees it is difficult to find sticks long enough to push it loose.

Each of us watched our side of the road for signs of the ripening fruit.

"Hey, whoa!" I yelled. "Back up. I think I saw one. . . . Yes, look up in that second tree from here. Oh, it's a luscious ripe one."

Henry hopped out and found a dead limb just long enough to reach the tempting orange papaya flecked with green . . . just the right shade of ripeness. He reached to his full length pushing and prying at the short, tough stem.

"Oh damn! Too late" Henry howled. "Those robbers beat us to it again. You stinking bats and birds, you!"

Neatly concealed from the perfect front of the fruit was a gaping hole from which the small black seeds were falling. Some bird had dined sumptuously ahead of us. Muttering uncomplimentary phrases about the darn old bats we resigned ourselves to canned fruit again and climbed back in the jeep.

A check on the progress of the conveyer belt usually wound up our daily ride. It was being rebuilt on the site of the old Japanese belt in order that dried phosphate could be loaded directly into the cargo ships again. Angaur's phosphate had been mined by the Japanese during the years between the first and second world wars and used in their homeland for superphosphate fertilizer. Their plant on Angaur had been a complete one, with approximately three thousand Japanese, Okinawans, and natives living on the island. Pictures showed that a handsome white tropical camp had sprung up and that the Angaurese had been busy, well dressed citizens. But the whole island was a shambles now: phosphate drying plant, storage building, and conveyer belt in utter ruin, natives clothed in castoff Army and Navy clothing and engaged in a struggle to recover some semblance of their former living standard.

It was the job of the Henderson Company, on Angaur under Navy contract, to rebuild the conveyer belt, and to mine the phosphate at the same time. Until such time as the mechanically operated belt would be ready, the phosphate was dredged out of the swamp area, stockpiled for partial drying, and loaded onto Japan-bound ships in cargo nets from shore to barge to ship.

The long conveyer belt would be finished in June, and the ships would be able to tie up directly underneath, only twenty feet from the shoreline, but in nearly three hundred feet of water, so abruptly did the shelf of the island fall away. When the belt was far enough along that I could edge out on it without too many fearful shudders, we liked to climb to its top, some fifty feet above the island. There was a fine spot for photography of both Angaur and the surrounding water. There we could look down into the deepening blue of the water and see the limestone ledge clearly, see long, slender fish swimming in the shallower water, and an occasional sting ray undulating by.

By the time we got back to the house there would be several natives sitting under the trees in the back yard, waiting to talk with Henry. Between the village and the construction camp, and maintenance jobs for the vehicles and our house there was enough business to keep him on the go most of the day. The village generator, which gave us light from seven to eleven in the evening, was old and rickety, and needed constant checking and overhauling. The water plant must be kept in fuel and chlorine. The jeeps and trucks must be taken to the native garage or the Henderson mechanics for checking. Our water heater and refrigerator were salvaged items, and most temperamental. Neither could be counted on for efficient operation two days running. The tanks had to be filed, and the wicks cleaned regularly. And if we went to Koror for several days someone had to keep an eye on the refrigerator, or else we had to unload it completely and take the contents to the Henderson reefers.

The Wahls at home

The refrigerator wick had a maddening way of filling with carbon and going out. That meant taking it apart, cleaning the whole works with a toothbrush, and carefully reassembling it and lighting it. Moments of suspense lengthened while Henry adjusted the wick for a blue flame, which meant the freezing process would begin again. Invariably the flame would burn a bright, cheery yellow, and the ice cap on the unit would melt slowly away. That was a sign for Henry to stamp out of the house to bring Clyde Baylor down from the construction camp. Clyde was a master mechanic who claimed he knew nothing about kerosene refrigeration, but he was the only one who could keep the reefer going.

"Next time I will do that myself," Henry would mutter. "No blasted ice box is going to get the best of me!" Next time he struggled for three days, disassembling, cleaning, and replacing the unit. Every time the yellow flame sprang up. The kitchen floor was sooty, and the contents of the ice box had long since gone to the camp reefers. But Henry persisted. His temper mounted at each try.

"Dear, why don't you get Clyde?"

"No, damn it, I am going to fix this thing if I die in the attempt. Watch it this time. Now work, you bastard!"

In the end Clyde came down. He looked at the parts lying in a row in front of the refrigerator, sat down crosslegged in front of them, and shook his head. He reassembled them gently, put the wick in place, and touched a match to it . . . Blue flame! One try, that's all it took.

"There you are, Mr. Wahl. I don't know why you couldn't get it. Did you say you had a short snort for me?"

Henry nearly bit the corner off the table in frustration.

Even after we began to write glowing letters home about the joys of Angaur, and the happy days we were having, the questions rolled in with our mail. "What ever do you DO all day long? "Isn't it frightfully lonesome, dear?" "We hope you're not a *bit homesick*, but how do you manage all alone?"

The answers were easy. There would not have been time to be lonesome even if we had been so inclined, and the days went by so busily that we never had time to do many of the things we wanted to do. Two radio schedules a day, natives in and out from early morning till the lights went out at night, supervision of maintenance for the village and ourselves, police court sessions, port director's work whenever Navy or phosphate ships came in, monthly reports to write, three-day trips to Koror, and a steady stream of interesting visitors. This was how the days went by, leaving us time now and then for a little reading, swimming, and exploring the island, and for our collection of records.

We were usually getting breakfast when our most exciting visitors "dropped in." Henry would be in the living room with his glass of Toddy, that canned chocolate milk drink which was in great demand in the islands, and I at the refrigerator pouring a second glass of fruit juice. A faint, low rumble would drift through the screens from the beach, and we would both suspend motion for an instant to listen.

"Airplane! Airplane!" Heinie yelled as he raced through the bedroom to the terrace. I banged the juice can and the glass down on the counter and ran through the house, leaving the plywood floor shaking. Henry was pointing directly west.

"It's the PB4Y2. Look, here they come to buzz us!"

The pot-bellied plane leveled off a bare fifty feet above the water and seemed to be racing directly at us. Standing in the opening at the edge of the terrace we waved madly, feeling as if we could have touched the black flash of her underside as she roared overhead.

"Megawd, look at those tree tops blow! I swear they nipped them this time. Come on Cec, they'll be down before we get there!"

We picked up our hats and colored glasses as we hurried back through the house. Henry gulped down the last of his Toddy on the way to the jeep.

Talk about going down to the station to watch the daily train go through your village! The airstrip took that place in our lives. We didn't have a plane in every day. But the familiar low-throated roar would send us dashing to identify the plane and then to the strip to see what surprise was in store. Most often it was the Air and Sea Rescue boys from Peleliu to bring a passenger to Angaur on business for the construction company, or to scrounge from the graveyard of planes. Occasionally the captain from Peleliu dropped down in his SNJ for a short conference. There were several official inspection parties from Guam in the admiral's plane. These were expected, and were preceded by much polishing and pressing, which was seldom noticed in the hours the parties stayed.

Regardless of whose house was buzzed, the Wahls, Tulop, the Henderson manager, their fire truck manned by Pleasants, and anyone else free at the moment would drop everything, jump in his jeep and dash madly for the strip.

Round the corners we roared, hanging on to our caps, the wind and dust whipping into the jeeps. The plane whistled over our heads and disappeared behind the green growth at the end of the strip.

At the main cross road to the strip we met the red fire truck and two jeeps. Heinie gestured gallantly to Pleasants to get the heck on with his red wagon, and Jack answered with an earsplitting wail of the siren as he swept by. We joined the procession and arrived at the edge of the strip in time to see a black rear fin racing detachedly along behind the row of brush, the only part of the plane visible until she swung into the clearing.

Henry joined the rest of the men to see what the business was this time. The pilots waved to me in the jeep when they swung down out of the plane. All the men stood or squatted in the shade of the wing, talking leisurely, and juggling handfuls of gravel which they scooped up as they talked. Shortly the group broke up. The crew piled into Henderson jeeps and took off up the road toward the bomber graveyard. Henry brought several men over to the jeep.

"Dearie, let's take the boys to the house for a brew while the crew does some scrounging. You know McDougall and Woods. These are a couple officers from Peleliu, just along for the ride. My wife, gentlemen."

They piled in the jeep, and we drove back to our beach. Two of the men slipped into swimming trunks and spend most of their visit in the cool morning high tide. The rest of us sat comfortably on the terrace with our cold drinks and chatted pleasantly and aimlessly for a half hour.

When we returned to the strip the crew was already warming up the plane. Our guests stepped lively and could soon be seen adjusting their headphones and waving from the cockpit. The bomb bay doors rumbled shut and the plane swung around to the south end of the strip near us. As she turned, the backwash of the propellers sent a hail of sharp coral pebbles in our faces. We all yelled, and turned our backs till the bomber was out of the way.

After each of the four motors was carefully revved, the plane started a slow, easy roll forward, suddenly gaining speed, and then thundered past us with an earth-shaking vibration. The pilots were intent on their most important moment of work and ignored our "thumbs up" salute. Pleasants gunned the motor of the fire engine and moved out onto the strip to watch the plane rise . . . just in case.

Quiet settled down again, and we moved back into the jeeps to get out of the burning rays of the sun and back to the morning's work.

CHAPTER FIVE

The Boat

I didn't dare move my mouth to call Henry. Saliva was already gathering under my tongue, a cold sweat covered me from head to foot, and my scalp began to crawl. The Henderson tug boat rolled like a bucking bronco gone berserk. If I let go with either hand I would roll off the hard seat. The cabin was filled with a bunch of grinning, ungrateful men, just waiting to see a woman get deathly sick. Mac, the operator, took one look at me and guffawed, "Hey, Mrs. Wahl, I'm gonna get that forfeit case of beer this time! You're gonna get si-i-ick!"

I am not going to get sick, I am not going to get sick, I am not . . . oooh these awful diesel fumes. Why the one seat has to be right over the engine room in this horrible boat! Isn't there some other way to get to Peleliu . . . going to get sick!

With a great show of effort I looked up at Henry, standing beside Mac at the wheel. Some sound must have come from my tight lips, for he stepped across the feet of the men sitting around, pulled my rigid weight up from the seat and maneuvered me across the small cabin to the open door.

The salt spray and the fresh air helped a little, but this time I most definitely was going to be sick. Henry put an arm around my waist to steady me while I bent over, and said soothingly, "Take one deep breath . . . now another. We'll be in quiet waters in just a minute. See, you can see the end of the heavy waves right ahead. Now another deep breath."

Looking at the pitching waves was the last thing I could have done. I closed my eyes and breathed as deeply as I dared.

"In a minute now . . . in a minute . . . you'll make it." Henry spoke calmly.

At last a healthy, if unsocial burp rolled out, and I could take a relaxed breath again. The tug steadied and moved into shallower water as we neared the entrance of the Peleliu boat basin.

"Dawgonnit, Mrs. W." Mac grinned, "I thought sure I had you that time. 'That's a bird's nest on the ground,' I said to myself. But, by gosh, you fooled me. I'm sure disappointed."

"You're a heartless Texan, Mac," I answered weakly. "I came within a tonsil of being seasick that time. But if I didn't do it this trip, I don't think I ever will. I'm sorry to leave you so thirsty; but we will offer you several beers if you come to the house when we get home this afternoon. That is, if I live!"

As soon as we had tied up and jumped to the solid ground of Peleliu, Henry said, "Come with me a minute before we go in to the post office. I want to show you something I'd like to fix up for the natives and us."

He led the way along the refuse-strewn docks to a narrow slip between log pilings where a dirty, scaley boat lay tilted on her side, stern ground into the sand. She looked little different than the other wrecks that cluttered the dirty water of the boat basin which lay to the southeast of Bloody Nose Ridge.

"What on earth is that?" I frowned.

"That's the picket boat I hope to get, all forty-five feet of her. It would be wonderful for the Angaur people to have a boat they could use. And when Henderson leaves we're going to need a way to get to Koror for mail and supplies. What do you think of her?"

My head still ached from the ordeal of crossing the channel from Angaur, and nothing looked very cheerful at the moment. "Well, if it will ride smoother than that tug, I'm for it. But I don't see how anything could ever be done with it. How in the world could a boat get in the shape that thing is in?"

"Oh, when the war was over out here, and the big campaign to 'get our boys home' was on, somebody tied this boat tightly at high tide, put on his hat, and went back to the States. With the changing of the tides she was left to batter herself to ruin." He helped me up onto the sloping deck and starting talking, almost to himself.

THE BOAT

"The leather bunk seats aren't hurt. That cabin deck is shot . . . have to re-cover that. Starboard deck's pretty well battered. What really worries me is that aft end. I'm sure both rudders have gone through the hull, and the drive shafts will be bent like corkscrews." He turned to me.

"Remember, Cec, I asked the skipper at Koror a couple months ago if we could get the boat for the natives at Angaur while it was still afloat. 'No money for such a questionable project,' he said. So I was turned down. But I know darn well the natives could fix this boat. I think it's worth another try with the skipper to see if we can't get it."

Henry was right; we did need a boat badly at Angaur. All we had for our use and for the natives was a small, open craft that right now lay beached with a broken drive shaft. It was too small for the open sea, too.

A week after we had looked at the picket boat at Peleliu we had a hurry-up message on the morning radio schedule. Peleliu was to have an admiral's inspection and the wreckage in the boat basin must be cleared out before I-Day. If we still wanted that boat we'd have to get it out of the channel in forty-eight hours or it would be towed into the open sea and sunk.

Elated, Henry hurried to find Tulop. He gave hurried instructions to round up Chief Uherbalau, Tomas, Joe Mrar, Charlie Eduardo, Singinari . . . "anybody who wants a boat."

The men gathered in the office-living room and listened as Henry explained the problem. Earnestly he leaned forward. "You have all seen this boat at Peleliu. You know it is in very bad shape; but I think we can fix it. You know we need a boat very much. We can bring supplies from USCC stores at Koror by this boat. Maybe somebody get very sick and we must go to the hospital at Koror."

There was a long pause between each sentence while Tulop interpreted. The afternoon light in our quonset shone on serious faces.

"Some things are not so good about this boat," Henry pointed out. "Koror tells me we can have no Navy money to fix the boat. That means Angaur people must do all work for no pay. I do not know what will happen to the boat when I leave. Maybe somebody at Koror will need it. Maybe Navy will take it back. But if you fix it, as long as I am here we will operate it for Angaur people. And I will do all I can to make this your boat. Uherbalau, you and your people must decide if you want to do the work."

Henry sat back. The natives talked a moment among themselves. Then they turned to Henry, a grin in every face. Nodding their heads affirmatively they chorused, "*O oi, O oi.*"

Caught up in the excitement of the Angaur people for the task ahead, I had no idea then what the boat meant to them and to Henry, and no conception of the marvelous job of reclamation I was to witness in the next few weeks. What a lesson it was in the mechanical genius of a so-called primitive people.

When the tug left for Peleliu the next morning five natives were aboard with a two-inch pump and several tool kits. Arriving, they clambered all around the wounded craft, looked her over, and consulted seriously on what was to be done. As soon as the tide had fallen below the holes in the stern they went rapidly to work. Deftly they removed the bent rudders and twisted screws. Then they patched the bottom and rear with pieces of rubber tires for a seal, reinforced with plywood. The pump was started, and six hours later, when the tide came back in, it had lifted three thousand gallons of water out of the hull and floated her above the holes in the stern.

The little pump put-putted all night long while the natives slept on the deck and the nearby dock. By morning she was completely afloat and nearly dry inside. At noon, the tug took her in tow and headed across the channel. The men watched her apprehensively all the way home, fearful that the patches would not hold and that she would sink again, this time for sure.

When we saw the returning tug with her tow we jumped up from lunch and hurried down to the harbor to watch the arrival. It could have been a spanking new craft coming into the harbor, excitement was so high. As the boats came within halloing distance the repair crew sang out gaily, and the natives on shore shouted

THE BOAT

back at them. The Japanese laborers ran up and down the dock area chattering like magpies, and even a group of construction men off duty for dinner gathered above the basin to watch the scene.

Henry's grin was the widest of all. He turned to Tulop and yelled, "Hey, Tulop! You think you can make this boat strong?"

Tulop swung his forefinger up and down for emphasis. "Meestahr Wahl, I think this boat be Number One Boat in all Palau Islands. My people can fix strong." He was fairly bursting with pride and excitement.

The young men of the village ran along the dock as the boats pulled in, vying for the honor of catching the lines to tie them up. Grinning broadly, Singinari gave a mighty heave of the first line from the deck of the picket boat. Matthias caught it and gave it a turn around the post. Our boat was home.

Chief Uherbalau had been sitting on the bank above the dock. Now he moved quickly down the hill to survey the boat. Several of the *rubak* joined him. They nodded together. "Ah, *mal ungil a bos*!" Uherbalau puffed dignifiedly on a cigarette; but there was a give-away twinkle in his watery old eyes.

A jeep came scooting into the crowd, and Buck Harlan, the Henderson manager, stepped out.

"All right now, you guys, let's get this floatin' wreck outa the water before she sinks and holds up my phosphate loading. Hey!" He beckoned to the crane operators, "Get those 80's movin' down here. Get your cable reeved and we'll drop this thing up on the bank."

Two huge cranes rumbled to the pier's edge, and rolled into position facing each other, their long arms swinging out over the water. The oversize "dogs" plummeted down and were hooked to cables fore and aft on the boat.

Buck presided like an orchestra conductor, waving his arms, his hands, his fingers. In response, the operators manipulated the boat up out of the water and laid her gently in the cradle waiting on the beach.

· 59 ·

NUMBER ONE PACIFIC ISLAND

She was a disheartening picture, for the damage was worse than at first appeared. Mud and sand everywhere, on the leather cushioned bunks in the after cabin, through the sink and pantry, stopping up the little toilet and lavatory. When the rotten timbers had been torn away and the mud scraped off the hull, it was found that the fantail was broken out, and most of the hull in the after quarter. The deck on the starboard side was shattered where the boat had rocked against the piling of the docks at Peleliu. And where she had grated to and fro with the tide on the coral sand the forward keel was worn so thin it would have to be replaced.

That was May 22. The skilled natives were still working for the Henderson Company and could spend little or no time on the boat. So for the next month the only work that went on was a little paint scraping and removing ruined parts. On June 18 the phosphate contract was finished and all the Americans left. The natives were now free to work on the boat.

Next morning, as soon as it was light, twenty men started in earnest, and for the next fifteen days there was scarcely an hour when work wasn't progressing. They made it a festival. Sitting around the working site, there were always a half dozen extra natives chattering away with directions and suggestions. The skilled men replaced the keel and the whole rear end of the hull, and repaired the deck line. They worked partially with American tools, to which they had access in the shops left by the construction company. But the larger part of the woodwork they hacked out with rough hoe-like adzes, a relic of earlier days in the Palaus. We never ceased to marvel at the smoothly turned wood that took shape.

To me was accorded the honor of choosing the color the boat was to be painted. We could select only from the cans of paint left over by the armed forces. There were black, gray, white, and zinc chromate. We knew the natives like bright colors, and felt that the yellow chromate would be easy to spot in the water in case of trouble. So our color scheme became yellow for all the top work, and gray for the hull.

· 60 ·

THE BOAT

Our pride and joy, overhauled and repainted, goes into the water.

The job of painting the boat was a picture straight out of Tom Sawyer, but in reverse! The straw bosses moved up closer on their logs till they were holding the cans of paint. Then they chattered advice to the painters till they wheedled their way up to the brush. Every man and child on the island took his turn in slapping a few inches of paint on their boat. It was a gay, happy time for the Angaurese, for they were people of the sea, and to build a boat was one of their greatest joys.

Joe Mrar and Oligriil had rebuilt a Gray Marine engine, and the American Army major on Angaur, now in charge of the phosphate mining which the Japanese had taken over, gave them another. The boys used the machine shop to turn propellor shafts, to temper new rudders, and to fit the propellers.

Here was a group of South Sea islanders, "gooks" some of the Americans persisted in calling them, who had made contact with American machinery only a couple years before. They could already match many of the trained American mechanics. We constantly marveled at their skill, and found each day more reasons to consider them among the most intelligent people we'd ever seen. Aniichi, a handsome man of twenty-five, could handle every piece of equipment on the island from a gasoline engine to the tremendous Northwest 80 cranes and the dredges. Joe Mrar was an expert with Gray Marine engines. Charlie Eduardo kept up all the village's trucks and jeeps. The fact that they had been assembled piece by piece from junk heaps and broken down chassis didn't deter him. Balau ran our village electric light dinky, a generator with no spare parts, which would have failed months before without his daily ministrations. And Joseph, the storekeeper, who would likely become chief some day, kept double entry books, and read the Japanese version of the Honolulu newspapers.

The boat began to take shape as the work went on from early morning till dark. Then one afternoon a flash of reflected light stabbed on to the terrace where I was reading. The boat was in the water! She fairly skimmed along outside the reef, making a tour around the island. The sun had glinted against one of the cabin windows to catch my eye.

The trial run was made on July 2, only thirteen days after concentrated work had been begun. And they had said at Koror the boat couldn't be fixed in a year!

The first official trip was set for July 3, when we were to go to Koror to take the Angaur baseball team for a game on the Fourth. For the last fifty-four hours before we were due to start five men worked continuously to finish the job. Singinari brought his phonograph to the beach and the boys played it day and night while they worked. Whenever we stopped by, the men were carefully listening to the throbbing engines, shouting directions above the noise.

This was truly a labor of love. Everyone on the island had an interest in common, and any village frictions were forgotten for the time being while we all watched the boat emerge a smooth-running, gray and yellow beauty.

THE BOAT

The Fourth of July celebration at Koror was to be a great occasion. The admiral was coming from Guam, with a party of gold braid, for an inspection trip. We too were gathered up in the excitement of preparation, Henry wondering which uniform would be worn for the Fourth, and I gave special care to ironing my best yellow cotton dress that would match the boat. The village lights stayed on till almost 1 a.m. the night before the trip, for there was much preparation of food, and many strategy meetings over the starting lineups for the ball game.

On the morning of the third we began to think everyone in the village was going, for the crowd at the pier grew larger and larger as departure hour neared. The boat was covered with packages of food, baseball gear, and gay villagers.

Finally the engines had been tuned to the satisfaction of Joe Mrar and Charlie Eduardo. The visitors began to jump ashore. We took our places in the front cabin on the wide leather bunk-bench, and Henry handed me the log.

"This, and the radio checks every half hour, will be your duty for the boat," he said. "Make a note of departure time, arrival time, number of passengers, and any special cargo. Then keep a log of the running time on both engines."

3 July 1947

0930 Departed Angaur, first trip to Koror.
    Aboard: Wahls, 43 natives, mail, baseball equipment.
    Total running time: Port engine   0 hours
                               Starboard engine 0 hours

Just as the lines were ready to be removed, Henry called, "Hey, Singinari, you forgot the flag!"

"Ohh no, I got it, Mr. Wahl. Right here!" He jerked open the table drawer and brought out the carefully folded American flag, which he passed to Henry. From hand to hand it went to the rear of the boat, to the steel-pipe staff. Henry stood at attention while the flag was being tied to the pole; everyone grinned. When it was secure Henry came back to the forward cabin.

"Ready Captain?" he briskly asked Singinari, who was our pet. He was a gay bantam rooster of a native, whose wardrobe of fancy Army, Navy, and Japanese military caps distinguished him as Master of the Boat.

Singi grinned from ear to ear, adjusting his yachting cap, which was spanking clean for the occasion, saluted snappily, and answered, "Yesss, Sir!"

"Then give her the works. Let's go!"

Singinari tried each throttle, and then gently put the boat in motion, and we moved away from the dock. A babble of Palauan, Japanese, and American goodbyes and last minute instructions came out to us from the pier. We might have been starting for the States, not just Koror.

It was a wonderfully uneventful trip. We had no sooner cleared the harbor than the ever-present fishing began. The two mechanics disturbed the jammed crowd on the deck every hour or less to move the deck sections and check on the precious engines. Everyone above the age of eighteen took a short turn at the wheel. When lunch time came we passed the oranges we had brought along, and were given in return smoked fish, bananas, and tapioca. Nobody aboard but us natives!

 1340 Arrived Koror. Trip time 4 hours, 10 minutes.
      Total running time: Port engine   4 hours 10 minutes
                               Starboard engine 4 hours 10 minutes

That businesslike entry on the first page of our log could never show the elation that surged through all of us from the minute we sighted the dock at Koror till we jumped triumphantly ashore amid an admiring crowd of natives and a surprised group of Navy personnel. We were secretly pleased that the arrival of the skipper from Peleliu just ahead of us had brought to the dock a good many of the Koror officers, for it meant more of a crowd saw our arrival and could admire the beautiful boat.

Ensign Ned Elliott voiced their amazement. He was Officer of the Day that busy day, and he roared down in his jeep just as we slipped in to the dock.

"Migod, Wahl, you really made it! When you radioed up this morning that you were coming, we said you'd never make it. When you came around the bend from Ngarakebesang, all we could see through our glasses was a mass of people . . . no boat! We thought the damn thing had sunk and you were walking in!"

From the appearance of some of the people at the dock, however, the reaction was not entirely one of joy and appreciation. The coldly appraising glint in their eyes as they surveyed the craft gave us a chill of apprehension. To have was one thing; to hold another.

Our five man crew went over the engines and the steering gear, and checked all the compartments to be sure they were watertight. They swabbed the decks with salt water and a broom, and proudly held open house to show their Koror friends the "Number One Boat of the Palaus."

Our belongings were loaded into Ned's jeep and we bounced up the bumpy road to the American housing area on the hill to begin the Fourth of July celebration.

Quick to pick up the American customs, the Palauans were celebrating the Fourth as we would in the United States. It was a gala day from beginning to end. And the high spot of the day was the baseball game between Angaur and Koror.

The Palauans are excellent baseball players, having learned from the Japanese. Our Angaur team had been beaten only once, by an American team, and were a proud and cocky bunch. At a weekend series at Angaur the month before our team has swept the field, beating Peleliu, Koror, and Babelthaup teams. So they had come to this holiday game with great expectations. Henry had boasted of them loudly and long, and his fellow officers at Koror were ready to lay large bets against our team. Heinie had been in his element during all these weeks of preparation for the ball game, for he used his college and semi-pro baseball experience in helping coach his boys.

NUMBER ONE PACIFIC ISLAND

At the beginning of the game, both teams lined up facing each other at home plate, doffed their caps and bowed formally like the Japanese who had taught them the game. Then they took to the field amid shouts from the fans. The equipment was odds and ends willed the natives by the Navy and Army. A few of the players had real baseball shoes, the majority wore canvas sneakers, and a number played barefooted, digging their toes into the dust for a starting grip. For nine innings their babble of Palauan was mixed with loud, clear "batterup, "sliide," and "yer out;" for long before they began to speak English, the Palauans were fluent in the baseball slang terms they had acquired from the Japanese.

The umpire and the yell leaders were worth any price of admission. Ngirathmetuul, the umpire, was a dapper, slender school teacher from Peleliu. He wore Marine khaki pants and shirt, tailored as tight as ever a dude Marine wore them, and a white linen umpire's jacket after the Japanese fashion. His hair was plastered smoothly back with glistening pomade. And he wore dark glasses. Such windmill gyrations, and bellowing of strikes and balls as he made! He stood, hands clasped behind him strictly in big league style, white coat spread open in front, and watched intently every batter's move. Once, quite by chance, a foul tip came directly at him, and whizzed through his open coat front, under his arm and out the back. The game halted while both teams gathered round him. He grimaced, flexed his could-have-been-injured limb, examined his precious coat carefully, clutched his breast, and put on agonized expressions. Then with a great show of courage he bade the game go on. The crowd loved it, and screamed all the louder.

Both teams had cheering sections, led by remarkably agile men. There was Ponape Mike, a handsome six-footer, who tied a red bandanna on his head with two knots so that it had a tail fore and aft, and then pranced up and down in front of his section while the crowd whistled and clapped rhythmically. His gyrations reminded us of American Indian festivals we had seen . . . the springy, hunched tread, and the hand motions of a tomahawk dance. Wiry little Goro led the yells for Angaur and amazed the American audience with his muscular agility. He squatted low to the ground, and then bounced up and down at the knees, swinging his torso from side to side as he sprang. It was a calisthenic, or a dance if you will, the most agile movement we had ever seen. It looked simple enough to do, but no American could ever begin to emulate it. We simply do not have joints in the right places! The cheers were always shrill through-the-teeth whistles, together with handclaps in metrical patterns of three (whee-whee-whee, whee-whee-whee, whee-whee-whee-whee, whee-whee-whee).

Takime of Angaur got the first hit, a towering, booming drive out of the park; and the crowd went wild. He trotted around the bases for a home run. In the weeks of practice before the game, Heinie had concentrated especially on Takime for the finer angles in hitting. When Takime got back to the plate after his home run, he shooed off the admiring crowd, looked toward the stands until he located Henry, and then with a sweeping wave of his cap he called triumphantly, "Ho, Mr. Wahl! We did it!"

We could have lost 100 to 1 then; Henry was so completely thrilled by Takime's compliment, and he felt repaid for his weeks of work with the team. Alas, Angaur did lose, 4 to 2. No amount of alibiing that Koror's field was smaller than Angaur's home field, or that the second and not the first squad played for Angaur could stop the ribbing that "Coach" Wahl took from his friends over the loss.

The rest of the day was filled with the admiral's inspection; a program of games and singing by the school children, and the usual Fourth of July speeches. No Fourth of July can be finished without fireworks, and so the Navy chiefs on the base endeavored to manufacture some. They were mostly ship's flares, red, green, and white; but they were as good as any skyrocket ever tried to be. The balls of light soared high above the hill, and then floated down gently to the grass where the native youngsters chased them till the fire died out. The ships in the harbor put on a mirrored display of the flares, too, which reminded us of fireworks across a lake at home. The wife of one of the chiefs had brought several packages of sparklers from the States many months before and had hoarded them carefully in her hot locker. She divided them among the children present, and was paid for her thoughtfulness by the delighted screams and swinging arms of both the small Palauans and American kiddies.

Home we went to Angaur the next day, delighted over our pleasant holiday with our friends at Koror, and with the hit the picket boat had made. It was a feeling of great satisfaction to know that the sleek craft lay snugly in our harbor ready for any emergency or business for which we might need her.

We felt less isolated than before. Now our waits for mail, which was coming to Koror instead of Peleliu, wouldn't be so long. The natives, too, set great importance to the boat. Look how many fish they had caught on our homeward trip from Koror . . . nine large bonito and barracuda. Think how fine it would be to build a barter system with the Japanese laborers in the phosphate. We could bring fruit and taro from the northern islands and exchange them for cloth and essentials from Japan. There were many reasons to be thankful for our "Number One Boat, all Palau Islands."

CHAPTER SIX

Trouble, Trouble, Boil and Bubble

It had been a busy evening, with four guests for supper, and two groups of callers. The LSM was in, and Skipper Richards had brought one of his officers and some beautiful steaks down to our beach house. A big cargo ship had just arrived from Japan bringing the news that the Japanese would take over the mining operations again. There were a half dozen high-ranking Army and Japanese officials aboard, all of whom came to call. Henry was rather harried, and I was hurried.

The company had all gone by ten o'clock, except Pleasants, who stayed to listen to his favorite records of the *Unfinished Symphony*. It was a pleasant relaxed hour. When the lights went out at eleven, we lit a pair of candles and finished our beers leisurely. When Jack finally ambled out to the door, he said, "You poor Wahls. You sit way down here away from everyone, and no one ever drops in to visit you . . . not more than fifteen or twenty people a day. Y'know, I feel so sorry for you, I think I'll just come down about five o'clock tomorrow morning and get you up, so you can enjoy a little company."

"You do, and it'll be your old neck! Tomorrow is Sunday, there's no tug to Peleliu to check on, and I intend to sleep at least till nine, preferably longer."

"Five o'clock, sir! I shall expect coffee to be ready! Well, thanks for the music and the visit. 'Night, Wahls."

Even the rats didn't waken us that night. We were in bed less than five minutes after Jack left, and we literally "died."

The voice and the scratching on the screen by the bed wakened me. It was pitch black on the terrace. The lighter water beyond outlined the silhouette that stood near us.

"Heinie. Hey, Heinie, wake up. I need you."

I sat straight up in bed, startled, and angry.

"Now see here, Jack Pleasants, a joke is a joke! Go away! You're drunk."

"Cecilia, I'm not kidding. Wake up Heinie. There's trouble up."

Henry thought it was a lousy joke too, even though it was five o'clock almost on the nose. But he started moving fast when Jack explained.

"One of my night patrolmen found two natives in a Henderson jeep out on the airstrip. Drunks as lords, with a case of beer between them, half empties. When he got out of his jeep to pick them up they lit for the brush, and he couldn't find them in the dark. He came back to get another one of my men to pick up the jeep; but when they got back, the kids had disappeared with the jeep again. God, Heinie, they're crocked, and they'll wreck that jeep, sure as hell. You'd better help us find them before they get into more trouble."

Henry dressed hurriedly, strapped on his gun, and went out with Jack. There was nothing I could do to help, so I promptly went back to sleep.

They came in at eight, hungry and angry. While they had toast and coffee, they related what they had been doing.

"Boy, at five o'clock we thought we just had a missing jeep. Now it looks more like a crime wave! Wait till you hear." This was Henry speaking. "First thing, we got Tulop out of bed and took him with us to try to find the lost jeep. We figured he'd know where to look in the jungle. Well, we found it about daylight."

"Yes," Jack chimed in as he buttered his toast. "When we got around to the northwest point of the island we found the jeep stacked into a big rock alongside the road. Whoever was driving it didn't even try to back it off . . . apparently just lit out on foot. The half-used case of beer was still in it, and empty cans were scattered all around the jeep. So we looked it over for damage, and finding only a couple dents and a flat tire came back to camp to get someone to go get it."

Henry continued, "When we stopped at headquarters to tell the boys we'd found the missing jeep, Jefferson ran out to tell Jack that one of the office men had reported his jeep missing from the north road where he'd driven during the night to go crab hunting with the natives. When he came back to the spot his jeep was gone. So he bummed a ride back with some of the crowd. They said they came back down the middle road. So they missed seeing the first abandoned jeep."

"My men were out looking for the second jeep then, and were due to report in about ten minutes, so we waited for them. While we were waiting, Mike Rogers came tearing in to say that while he'd been asleep someone had broken into his hut, stolen his case of beer, and had disappeared not only with his beer but his jeep."

"So there we were . . . seven o'clock in the morning . . . three jeeps stolen, a house-break, and heaven knows where they got the first case of beer!"

The men paused to pour second cups of coffee.

"But, Heinie, who on earth can it be? Natives, you're sure of that, and really stinko drunk. But I can't imagine who would break in to one of the huts. What does Tulop think?"

"Tulop's keeping his mouth shut and his eyes open at this point. I think he has a pretty good idea. But he may be waiting to see how much we find out before he commits himself. I don't think he'll hold out on us; but then again I doubt that he'll tattle on any of his villagers. Yep, these natives are certainly drunk, or they'd never have been bold enough to start this reign of terror! Well, Jack, we'd better put the show on the road."

"Yes, Heinie. I have a hunch those culprits will be getting sleepy pretty soon from the sun and too much beer. Then maybe we can catch up with them. First I want to check with Tulop on this knife."

"Knife!" I howled. "Is there a stabbing too?"

"Oh no," said Jack. "When Jefferson first caught the boys last night he managed to take this knife away from one of them before they beat it. If we can get it identified, I think we'll have our man." They put on their sun helmets and glasses and went out. Heinie called back as he got in the jeep, "You might have a sandwich ready for us about noon. I don't know when we'll be in, but we'll probably be starved. 'Bye, dear."

It was an unusually hot morning, sticky, with no wind. Even on the shady terrace it was hard to find a really comfortable place. Mariana, the house girl, came late, still carrying her prayer book and head kerchief from mass. She was gone within an hour, for she stayed only long enough on Sundays to make the bed, sweep the three rooms, and wash the dishes. Quiet settled down and the morning dragged on, made interminably longer by the suspense of the boys' absence. I finished reading the latest stack of magazines, and sorted and straightened the magazine rack; there were some socks to mend, and yesterday's dusty shoes to polish. I tried to start a letter home, but every time a vehicle went by on the road I ran out to see if it was the boys returning.

Finally at 1:30 the jeep rolled into the garage, and Henry and Jack dragged into the kitchen. They were disheveled, hot, and sticky. Their faces had that wet translucent appearance that comes with too much sun. It was clear that they had spent a good part of the morning in the jungle because every uncovered part of their skin was blotched with small red points of irritation from the prickly leaves of the undergrowth which always were flung into the jeep. Their wet shirts clung to their sagging shoulders.

"Well . . . well!, did you find them?"

"Yes, we found them, dear. God, what a morning! Fix us a couple of the coldest beers you have. We're too tired to eat yet."

Pleasants didn't say a word. He took off his shirt, sank back in a chair, and reached limply for the beer can when I brought it. The cold liquid seemed to revive their voices and spirits somewhat, and the story gradually came out.

TROUBLE, TROUBLE, BOIL AND BUBBLE

Tulop had not been able to identify the knife at once, nor could several other young natives, so that the angle of the puzzle was set aside for a time while the search went on for the two missing jeeps. After several hours of driving around the island, off and on the main road at every trail into the jungle underbrush, along old roadways now completely overgrown, behind skeletons of deserted quonset huts, they had found the second jeep at the north end of the island, stuck in the sand where a practice rifle range had been built several hundred yards from the main road. That was two jeeps and two beer cases returned. Now all that was missing was one jeep and two natives.

The search continued throughout the increasingly sticky morning. Every road, trail, and footpath on the island had been traversed. The men worked their way from the north end of the island toward the southern tip. Late in the morning they drove across the village baseball diamond looking around the open area. One trail cut around a marshy spot into heavy tangled undergrowth. Henry had inched through that section once before in search of a lost Chinese cemetery which had been placed there many years before when the Germans had brought some Chinese laborers with them. The cemetery had long since disappeared under the gnarled trees and shrubs. Remembering that the trail was barely passable, he drove the jeep in, and there they found the last missing jeep. There was no incriminating evidence in the jeep, but its nearness to the village led the searchers to believe that the vehicle had been abandoned by the natives who then went to their homes, or some other place of hiding in the village.

Tulop stood a moment, mulling over the problem. "Meestahr Wahl, I think first we try *a bai*. Maybe somebody there."

"Oh, yes, the men's house. Good idea. Let's go."

At the *bai* they found the usual number of Sunday loafers . . . older men sitting on the stoop passing around the various ingredients for betel nut chewing while they chatted, inside several younger men lounging in the broken deck chairs, or sleeping on camp cots.

Among them was sleepy Hideo, who gave Tulop a lead on the ownership of the knife.

"This knife belong to Orotong, I think. Yesterday I see him cut rope with it."

Orotong was speedily sought out at his home. "Oh no, Mr. Wahl. This no longer my knife. One week, maybe two week ago I make trade with this knife to Hideo. See, he give me this fishing line and some money."

Hideo! That fellow was giving us the run around. Now, we're getting close.

But Hideo was not at the *bai* when the three men got there. A systematic search was made through the village, first at his home, and then through other houses, returning in the end to chez Hideo. He was there, sound asleep on the floor; and with him was a younger boy of 18, Sebastian, also asleep. Tulop muttered something in surprise, which Henry could not understand, and pulled the boys to their feet. Hideo had seemed all right when they had talked briefly with him at the *bai*; but he was now pretty ragged, with blood-shot eyes and a sneering expression. Sebastian, too, was definitely hung over, but his manner was bumbling and uncertain. The boys were marshaled into the jeep and taken to the police station, where they were to explain where they had been the night before.

Jack drove the jeep to the jail door, where Henry got out with Hideo, and Tulop, looking grimmer and angrier than usual, with Sebastian. Hideo suddenly bolted, hopped inside the building, and slammed the door in Henry's face. Hot and tired, and almost beyond his patience, Henry flung open the door, grabbed Hideo by the shirt and sat him down hard on a bench.

"Hideo! That you cannot do . . . slam a door in my face! Now I want you to make talk and make talk fast! You tell me where you were last night and what you did! And you be VERY careful how you speak. You remember there are many things I know about this, and some things I do not know. But you do not know what things I know. So you think how you tell me the truth, because if I find you lie, I make much trouble for you!"

All Hideo's bravado suddenly melted away and he slumped against the wall, thinking how to begin talking. At this moment Henry looked up to see Tulop entering behind Sebastian. He closed the door, reached above it and took down a policeman's club, all in one smooth motion. Abruptly he began yelling a stream of Palauan and Japanese invectives and belaboring Sebastian on the head and shoulders. Henry was dumbfounded, for Tulop seldom resorted to violence.

Sebastian cowered under the blows, but finally managed to fend off the club. Tulop dropped it, grabbed Sebastian and flung him over his shoulders flat on the floor in perfect judo fashion. His diatribe had petered out into guttural words and sobs, and tears were running down his cheeks.

"Tulop! What is the matter? Why do you do this to Sebastian?"

"Ah, Meestahr Wahl. Sebastian is my brother. The brother of policeman cannot do these things. He make much trouble for me. Maybe you see how he is bad, and pretty soon I lose my job. Ah, much trouble. But he never make trouble before. I am very sorry, Meestahr Wahl."

"I did not know before that Sebastian was your brother, Tulop. He does not live with you."

"No, Meestahr Wahl. Sebastian stay with my cousin here. Ah, I talk like everything to him! Nobody in my family has trouble before."

"Well, you talk like everything to both Sebastian and Hideo, so we can find out what happened last night."

After lunch Henry and Jack dictated their report of Hideo and Sebastian's confession, along with the search for them from five till one o'clock. This would go into their records and would be used when the village court met the next evening.

"Well, Wahl, I shall take leave of you once more," grinned Pleasants when they had finished. "This time with no dire threats about when I shall return! Maybe you can salvage a little bit of your weekend yet."

"Heck, that's all right, Jack. People wouldn't believe us if we told them we had a seven day and night a week job on a south sea island, with no long, lazy weekends on the beach! Anyway, I think

I prefer it to be a constant job here. Even with the bad days, like today, it's a better way to get to know the people and to try to do a little good."

"Well, it must prove something. You've either got to be crazy, or else really like work of this sort to live on a little old island and spend your Sunday hours ferreting crocked natives out of the jungle! I, for one, am going to forget it all and get some sleep; and I suggest you do the same. Let me know what happens tomorrow night at court. S'long."

The village court at Angaur met whenever they had a problem to handle, and meted out minor fines up to $25, and sentences up to one month. The cases ran mostly to intoxication, operating a still, or brawling. The more serious cases, such as mayhem, would be sent to Koror for trial as well as sentence, and sentences over one month for any offense were served at Koror. Hideo and Sebastian were sent to the higher court.

Though nominally the senior member, Henry sat on the court mainly as recorder, for he felt that it was not his place to mete out village justice. Chief Uherbalau must handle all such matters, for he not only knew the background of all his people, but was the local law and order himself. It would have been a usurpation of power, and an insult to native intelligence for Henry to have insisted on being the court. With Uherbalau as judge, several of the *rubak* as jury, and Tulop as chief prosecutor, the Angaur court meted out its justice promptly and efficiently.

Hideo's name showed upon the court records again, not two months after he returned from serving his sentence at Koror. He got hold of agi this time and went on another roaring drunk, brandishing a large knife and inviting any of the local populace to join him in a little competitive blood-letting. All the villagers went inside their houses and bolted the doors. Tulop soon came to divest Hideo of his weapon and to dump him unceremoniously in the calaboose once more.

TROUBLE, TROUBLE, BOIL AND BUBBLE

Henry was much concerned with the case, feeling that unless the correct methods of treatment were used, Angaur had a potential alcoholic on its hands. There must certainly be some frustration or emotional upheaval behind Hideo's actions. He came to the conclusion that an attempt to appeal to Hideo's self reliance and adult ego might be a good tack. On Angaur, as in other Oriental sections, face saving was extremely important. To treat a man as an individual who could not take his place in the community was the worst condemnation that could be set against him.

The trial progressed, the evidence was presented, and the Number One and Number Two Chiefs were deep in discussion of what drastic sentence should be passed against Hideo. Hideo sat slumped in his chair as he had at the first trial, sullen and faintly belligerent. When the Chiefs became silent, Henry addressed the prisoner.

"Hideo, not many months ago you make much trouble on Angaur. All the people were unhappy and ashamed that Hideo would make so much trouble, and have Henderson people think bad things about Angaur.

"Maybe, Hideo, you must have agi . . . like a baby needs milk. I think putting you in the calaboose is not the answer. If Hideo cannot live with other Angaur people and be happy unless he have agi, maybe we can fix it. While everybody else makes garden, fish, and work maybe we can give Hideo a nice house where he can sit and drink his agi. I am very sorry for Hideo if he cannot take his place in this village like other men, but must be drunk all the time and make everybody unhappy, especially his father and mother."

Henry turned from Hideo to Uherbalau and Axiol. "What do you think? If Hideo cannot be like other men, maybe this thing I talk about is all we can do. I am very unhappy tonight. I do not like to see any Angaur people in the calaboose because it does not give me joy to see Angaur people have much trouble . . . and . . ."

"Mr. Wahl! Mr. Wahl!" Hideo interrupted Henry's speech, tears streaming down his cheeks, his voice choked and broken. "Mr. Wahl, these things must not be. I am a good man. I will work hard. Never will I drink agi again, Mr. Wahl." He paused a moment, and then gave himself the most serious penalty possible. "Mr. Wahl, if Hideo get drunk any more, ever, Hideo will leave his home on Angaur and never more, *never more* make trouble for people on Angaur."

A deathly silence fell. Uherbalau looked at Axiol. They both looked at Henry. Tulop's eyes were wide, but he said nothing. For a man to leave his home voluntarily meant virtual slow starvation. Unless he had relatives on the other islands, he had no place to go, no food to eat, for the Palauans did not open their homes to people outside their own clans.

"Tulop," said Henry slowly, "you tell Uherbalau and Axiol that I think Hideo is very sorry, much too sorry to be put in the calaboose. I think after this we all will be very good friends, and have no more trouble with Hideo."

Tulop translated to the two chiefs, who gave an emphatic *"o oi."* They discussed the matter further and decided that Hideo should be on probation, with both fine and sentence suspended. The court session ended with handshakes all around. So far as we knew, Hideo never caused trouble in the village again.

There were problems of a different nature to be met by the M.G. Representative which no amount of questioning and court procedure could solve. Chief among these was the jockeying for position of the three political factions on Angaur. Originally there had been three separate villages on the little island, living amicably, each with its own chief. When the Germans came to mine the phosphate in the early part of the century, they staked out, in true imperialistic fashion, the land that was to be mined, moving the natives from those areas. This cut down on the village areas, but did not move them. When the Japanese took over after World War I, they enlarged the boundaries of the mining areas and moved the villagers all to the south end of the island. This unnatural constriction placed the three separate clans in one living area. The Japanese also decreed that there should be only one chief to each island district in the Palaus. So on Angaur the "place" and "show" clans began the continuous attempt to better their position into Number

One spot, where their chief would be in charge. This led to the inevitable chicanery, intrigue, and petty jealousies.

World War II had thrown the people even closer and more uncomfortably together, for to live at all they must share roofs and food. Now that the war was over they were resettling in more comfortable houses, naturally grouped by family lines, and were trying to regain their old prominence. The arrival of Americans on the island presented a new facet to the picture.

In each of the three clans, an American had married the daughter of either the chief or the woman through which the direct line to chieftainship ran. It is highly likely that the women were thrown at the white men, for having a white son-in-law meant at that time prestige, wealth, and automatic eligibility for a strangle-hold on the future chieftainship. One of the men was a quiet young fellow who had been in the Navy. Taken with the beauty of the islands and the girl of his choice, and lacking any particular reason for returning to the States, Max Rutherford settled down happily to life on Angaur, working for the construction company at native wages, and raising a family. The other two men, Joe Gorgonia and Ernest Litton, were older men, one in his mid-forties, and the other nearly sixty. Their effect on the village could hardly be said to be salubrious. Joe was a huge, grey, greasy man who lived in the village with his wife for a time, was finally fired by the construction company, and returned to the States leaving a much relieved native girl. Litton finally moved to Guam to work for another construction company, taking his wife and her sister with him. But not before near havoc had been created on Angaur.

When Henry arrived on Angaur to be the resident M.G. representative he met all the men of the village as soon as possible. Tulop, as police chief, began to be his advisor; and he listened carefully to each person with whom he talked, trying to get an accurate picture of the people and their island.

Among the first to visit Henry at his office was Ernest Litton. Henry was later to recall that when Litton came in, the group of natives present had melted away. At the moment he put it only to shyness in the presence of the Americans.

Litton was a gray-headed, thin, consumptive looking man. But he carried himself with a great deal of importance. He shook Henry's hand firmly and said, "Lt. Wahl, we're awful glad you're here. We know you're gonna help these people all you can. Now, as you know, I'm married to an Angaur woman. I've spent over a thousand dollars buying clothes for these people and helping them back on their feet. Since I'm going to spend the rest of my life here, I'm mighty anxious to see these natives get going again. Now I know you want to do the same, and I want to help you in every way I can. I'll help with money, my time, my tools . . . everything I've got is at your disposal, and I want you to call on me for everything." He repeated many times during their conversation, "I'll help you in every way."

Henry was definitely in the neophyte class in handling native affairs and understanding native people; but after a few days he began to sense that there were forces at work on Angaur that were not good. He was first aware that the children were not as friendly or as normally curious as they had been on Koror and Babelthaup, where he had served his first few months in the Palaus. The adults here were reserved; and though it was a natural state of affairs with strangers, there was a definite underlying tension in all their relations with the M.G. officer. He began lying awake at night, going over every part of the day's activities . . . what he had said . . . what he had seen . . . how the natives spoke . . . to try to figure out the reason for the taciturn, almost frightened manner in which the natives were acting.

Trouble broke into the open very shortly. Tulop came in early in the morning to tell Henry that someone had been throwing stones during the night at the quonset huts that served as the jail, police headquarters and village council chambers. Such an effrontery was must unusual, and Tulop was very solemn and much worried in not being able to explain the matter.

TROUBLE, TROUBLE, BOIL AND BUBBLE

"Tulop, I think maybe this is small boys. Nobody would throw stones at you at police headquarters. Just small boys having much fun in the moonlight."

Though Henry dismissed the matter with his explanation, Tulop was not so sure. The following night the jail was again stoned, and on succeeding nights not only the jail but the chief's house. Still the perpetrator could not be found. In about a week Henry was jerked out of a sound sleep by a clatter like that of several small cannon balls skipping over the top of the quonset. No one could be seen on the beach. Again they came, several handfuls of large coral hunks cascading over the metal sides of the house. It was useless to try to find anyone in the dark, for there were other quonsets behind which the culprit could run, and many trees which made wide black shadows at night.

First thing in the morning Henry compared notes with Tulop. No other building had been stoned that night.

"Tulop, you think the Angaur people make stone on my house? This I do not understand, why they do this thing. I try very hard to help these people. Your people do not know me very long. You think already they hate me so much?"

"Ah, not so, Meestahr Wahl, no so. They like you very much."

"Then why does this happen, Tulop?"

A brief hesitation . . . Tulop shifted his eyes to the floor for an instant, and then looked up again. "This I do not know." But the pause had been too long. Henry knew there was much more going on than he had found out in his two weeks on Angaur, and that Tulop knew more than he was telling about the affair.

"Tulop. tell me. What people would do this thing . . . all these stones on village houses, on my house."

"Meestahr Wahl, I do not know. But I do know all my life on Angaur I never know Angaur people to make stone on people's house."

The stoning increased in frequency. Elaborate traps were set, the police established night watches, but the work was so cleverly done that no suspect was found. And the people became more reserved and frightened. The thought processes that Henry waded through were involved, and brought him to a staggering conclusion. If the Angaur people were not causing the trouble, it must be the Japanese or Americans. He immediately rejected the Japanese. There would be no reason for them to make trouble for their homeland at a time when they were on good behavior and when the phosphate was so important to them. Furthermore, they lived in a guarded camp, and it was illogical that they would sneak out of their enclosure to come clear down to the village to throw rocks. That left the Americans. But he could see no reason for a hard-working construction man to get up in the middle of the night, walk a half mile down the road, heave two or three handfuls of stones on various quarters . . . except . . . how about the Americans who had married Angaurese and were living in the village? It was a stab in the dark, but more logical. But what would they gain by such conduct?

In the next two weeks he received a course in human relations and politics that could be gained in no college of sociology. He questioned people every day. Some would warm up, be friendly, talk a little; but they would never make any definite statements. Henry began to learn that every angle had to be checked and double checked, and that after questioning periods were over he must do his own investigating of the same questions before he could accept anyone's story. He knew the people were trying to trust him, but were compelled by some force that kept them afraid of giving in.

Tiny bits of information gleaned from casual remarks began to show that the trouble was in the village and was associated some way with the Americans living there. It might be only a shrug of the shoulders when Joe Gorgonia or Litton were mentioned, or a request to move away from the area where those families lived.

The opening clue came in a roundabout fashion. Jack Pleasants, who with his years of police experience had been working on the problem too, hurried in one morning.

"Henry, I think we have something to work on today. It's kind of a funny lead, I'll admit, but listen. Harris, one of the boys down at my shack happened to mention at breakfast this morning a conversation he had last night after the movie with a couple of the natives who work in his shop. The boys mentioned very casually that if Litton didn't leave the island somebody they knew was going to kill him. Then after awhile they asked several times if Jack Pleasants was a good friend of Harris's. It looks to me as if they were trying to get the word spread around to me, but wouldn't take it on themselves to say it directly."

When confronted with the direct question, Tulop said that he had known about the plot against Litton. "Everybody much afraid of Meestahr Litton, not like him. But he is strong man, we can do nothing. Now somebody too angry, Meestahr Wahl, wants to kill him."

"Tulop, we must make the end of this trouble. But to do this everybody who knows anything about this must tell us. You get all those people who say to Mr. Harris that Mr. Litton will be killed, bring them to the police station tonight at seven o'clock. We will make much talk."

When Henry and Jack reached the police station, just after sundown, they found a group of the most reluctant, restless natives on the island. They sat virtually shaking in their boots, doomed to some horrible punishment. Though they listened respectfully, it took fifteen minutes of the hardest selling job Henry had ever had to put himself over to the Angaurese, and to put them in his confidence.

"Tulop, you tell these men that I am here to protect them from any kind of trouble," he concluded. "That is what M.G. is for. If I am going to help you, I must know what things this man is doing that make you want to kill him. I try very hard since I come to Angaur, but I cannot make the people know that if they come to me I will help them."

Tulop translated this to his villagers, and they all talked rapidly among themselves for a few moments.

"But Meestahr Wahl, if you want to help us, why you tell Mr. Litton to take care of our troubles, not to come see you?"

"Tell Litton! Tell . . . " Henry sputtered, and then regained his composure. This was an amazing revelation, but it must be gone at carefully.

"Tulop! I say no such thing to Mr. Litton. Now, can you and your people tell me what Mr. Litton says to you?"

Now the natives were all vying for the floor to explain what Litton had been doing. After proclaiming to Henry that he was on Angaur to stay forever, and to help the natives in any way he could, he had gathered his henchmen in the village together and passed out the word that he had been given a special commission by Henry which made him, Litton, higher in authority than any other person on the island, with the exception of Henry. The people were to do as Litton directed them. Under no circumstances were they to bring their troubles directly to Henry, but to his commissioner who would forward the information. Mr. Wahl, was a very busy man, indeed, and did not want to be bothered by the small natives for any reason whatsoever. If he found the natives bothering the M.G. man they would get a punishment far stronger than they had ever received from either the Japs or the Germans.

"Many months ago," Tulop explained, "Mr. Litton and Oligreel have big trouble. They talk like everything. Oligreel say to Meestahr Litton, 'You can not talk to me like this.' Litton say, 'You will see if I can talk to you. You make much trouble for me, now I have you put off Angaur.' And, Meestahr Wahl, he go to Peleliu, talk with somebody, and pretty soon Oligreel have to leave Angaur. Number One man Peleliu say so. Ah, this Litton is very strong man. He say we must not go to your house; we do not go!"

"My god, Heinie, you know what that man is doing!" Jack Pleasants was as amazed at the revelation as was Henry. "He's playing both ends against the middle for his own benefit. Just before I came down here I talked to Buck, the manager, about Litton. He said that Litton was the go-between for the natives, but wasn't much good at it. Just after he got married, Ernie went to Buck and said that he had found out that the natives felt very strongly about the mining operation and would do everything in their power to hinder it, perhaps even using violence. Ernie felt that if he could do all the hiring and firing of the natives and weed out the undesirables who might possibly plant a knife in the ribs of an American, then things would run better."

"Tulop," said Henry, "Do you understand what Mr. Pleasants is saying?"

"Yes, Meestahr Wahl. This is not so. Not so! My people want phosphate to be mined, we want to work in phosphate. How else do we make money?: But we also fear Henderson men. Meestahr Litton say Americans are stealing our phosphate. They all make much money; we make none, but work too hard. He say if we kill all Americans we can mine our phosphate and have much money. We do not listen to this. We do not want to kill Americans; but we are much afraid. What do you think, Meestahr Wahl?"

"I think, Tulop, we have found the reason for all this trouble. You tell your people that by tomorrow night all this trouble will be gone."

Reassured, the natives carried the meeting on for several hours, airing their grievances and fears until the whole picture had jelled. In retrospect it was amazingly simple, the story of a diabolical, cunning, power mad man. This unbalanced creature was actually attempting to build an empire for himself and to eliminate the authority of the American Navy from the Palaus. The plan was to make himself the Great White Father of all the Palau Islands. Those who backed him would become the ranking chiefs of the entire area.

The whole preposterous plan might have been a harmless pipe dream had not the threat of violence entered in. It was agreed that for his own safety it was now best to get Ernest Litton off Angaur. Next morning Henry dispatched for permission to have the man removed, and received it promptly. He then called Litton in and told him all the facts of the case which had come to light.

Tears rolled down Litton's lined cheeks. He started to his feet. "Lt. Wahl. These are lies by the Angaur people! I have tried my best to help them. I have spent over one thousand dollars on them. They're a treacherous, dangerous people, and I am being railroaded out because of the lies they have told about me. As I stand before you and Jesus Christ in all the nakedness of my innocence, this is all a bunch of goddammed lies!"

"All I have to say to you, Litton, is that by order of my C.O. you are to pack your goods and be ready to catch the next plane out of Peleliu. You will go to Guam, and there you can state your case before the higher authorities. But you are to leave this island promptly."

Tulop was called in and given all the details of the last few hours. Without a word he turned and sped from the house. In a half hour's time shy, hesitant natives were at our house without bidding pulling weeds from the yards, washing the jeeps, attempting to repair the hot water heater, even sweeping out the quarters. Before the afternoon was over youngsters were playing ping pong on the terrace, and swimming directly in front of the house instead of a quarter-mile down the beach. Then Henry knew he was right.

Two days later, still protesting his innocence, and that he had been betrayed by the people he loved, Ernest Litton departed Angaur.

One week later Litton returned to Peleliu with a senior Navy officer to investigate Henry's operations on Angaur. Henry was sick at heart. The natives disappeared again.

Henry knew that whether he was right or wrong, both he and Litton would get a fair hearing since the investigating officer was one of the most capable and astute men in Military Government. Litton had taken with him a petition signed by nearly half the village stating that Henry was unjust and cruel, and requesting that he be relieved of his duties on Angaur. The subsequent investigation proved that the natives had signed the document because Litton had asked them to. He had picked those who could not read English, telling them that the document stated that whatever happened to him, M.G. would take care of his wife and that the natives approved of this.

TROUBLE, TROUBLE, BOIL AND BUBBLE

The night before he had left for Guam he called his adherents together and made a speech. "Tomorrow I go to Guam," he had said, voice shaking with emotion. "There I will tell the admiral all these bad things that have happened to me. And then I will come back. Then all the people in the Palaus will know that Abe Litton is stronger than M.G. Abe Litton will be the Great White Father of all the Palau Islands when he comes back."

The skeptics had jeered. But when the word was passed only seven days later that Litton was on Peleliu, it was indeed the sounding of doom to the Angaurese. No wonder they had been frightened.

Happily, all his mad plotting was brought before the committee of investigation, and additional information was gained from the natives about his other nefarious activities which had included pandering for his white friends, furnishing beer for native cohorts, and appropriating tools and equipment from the construction company for his own use. Back he went to Guam. Peace finally reigned on Angaur.

Despite the fact that Litton was obviously unbalanced, his native wife appeared to have a genuine attachment for him. Arrangements were made for them to set up housekeeping on Guam where Litton had taken a job. Shortly after Misai had joined him on Guam we received the following scrawled letter.

> Dear Lt. Wahl:
>
> It is wonderful to know that I have a true friend such as you left in the Palau Islands. You have sure been wonderful to get my wife here to me on Guam. Tell all my friends I wish them luck. The next time you come to Guam I insist you stay at my house for old times sake.
>
> Abe Litton

Henry leaned back in his chair and slapped the table as he laughed. "I give up! For a long time I could cheerfully have cut that man's throat and thrown his body in the ocean. But I guess in the last analysis I feel kind of sorry for the old guy. Love triumphs over all . . . er sumpin'."

CHAPTER SEVEN

Henderson Heyday

The blur of faces I had seen at the airstrip the morning of my arrival on Angaur soon came into focus, Americans first because they were our "own people", then the natives because they quickly became beloved. The construction men began to drop in one by one to get acquainted and to see what the "house" had to offer in the way of refreshment. Emerging from the group of two hundred rough and ready individualists were perhaps thirty whom we came to know and to enjoy immensely. Their stories were numberless, and their own backgrounds were studded with world-wide wanderings, diversified jobs, shifting marital attachments, and colorful language. These men we came to know on Angaur were peculiar, not only individually, but peculiar to the industry in which they worked. They were wanderers, often made so by circumstance, but largely by desire to move on to something else. One of the quieter mechanics, who visited us often, said over a beer one evening,

"I think we must be like the pioneers of the early days: always having to see what is over the next hill, the newer world. No amount of security and home life satisfies us. I'd like to think that someday we'll be looked on as the explorers of unsettled parts of the globe."

As explorers of Angaur they were doing a thorough job. Two shifts a day worked round the clock on the business of scooping the gray, wet granular phosphate from the swampy areas in the middle of the island, stockpiling it for partial drying, and barge loading it on to liberty ships for the trip to Japan. They were aided in their job by a group of conscripted Japanese laborers, and by a highly skilled group of natives.

They were men who had been on timber jobs in the Northwest, road construction in Alaska, the Golden Gate Bridge, the Boulder dam, in oil in Arabia, on Wake and Guam. For the most part they were a good natured lot, generous to a fault, and as happy-go-lucky as men come. They were at once our salvation and our cross. Without them we would have had to turn to native food for our subsistence, for there was no way during the larger part of our year on Angaur to get regular supplies from Koror. They were more than generous with their time and material in making us comfortable. It could be argued that if they had not been there neither would we. For the construction men's presence aroused the very problems that Henry was there to manage. To handle the social problems arising from two hundred very individualistic construction men on a small south Pacific island is no picnic. Each day brought its attendant problems of personality clashes or policy decisions. And as we went along we found more and more "characters" among the group.

Meet Wayne Ricketts, for instance. Wayne was a truck driver whose job was to keep down the coral dust on the heavily traveled trucking roads between the beach and the mining areas. As one of the boys aptly put it, "Wayne there wears a Number Two hat and Size 48 pants; he ain't so bright." But he took his job seriously, and lost very little of his fabulous wages at the nightly Ace-Away game. Every morning he drove his truck down to our little boat harbor, which was completely landlocked except for the narrow channel leading to the open sea. There he would pump his sprinkler truck full of salt water in preparation for his morning's work. On this particular morning Mac, the tugboat engineer, a rare individual in his own right, was doing some maintenance work on his tug, the *Helen B.*, when Wayne backed his truck down to the pier, dropped the hose into an unusually low tide, and commenced pumping. Mac dropped his wrench, clambered up on the dock, and rushed over to Wayne. In a mock rage he roared,

"Now Ricketts, by god, if you don't quit pumping your goddam water out of my boat basin, you're gonna pump it dry and the boats won't be able to get in or out! Look at this water this morning! Look how low she is! You've damn near pumped her dry!"

Wayne leaned over the edge of the piling and surveyed the boat basin solemnly. Then without a word he unhooked the hose, jumped in the truck and roared away. Straight to the project manager he went and reported,

"Buck, we're gonna have to get our water someplace else for these roads. We've just about pumped the boat basin dry!"

Buck contained himself admirably, put his hand over his face, and seemed to be in deep thought for a minute.

"By god, Ricketts, that's serious. Tell you what you'd better do. You know where that finger pier's been built out at the south boundary of the boat basin? Well, you back down on that and draw your water from the ocean side. I think that's be a safer deal."

After that Wayne was fair bait for any joke the men could pull on him. Mac was the leader, for he had a riotous sense of humor, and a sincere manner that could fool anyone when he wanted it to.

Wayne saw the ships leaving every four or five days loaded with the phosphate rock, and it puzzled him considerably. He knew his company was here to mine the stuff, and that it was being sent to Japan, but its use was something he couldn't figure out in the space under his #2 hat. He spoke of his puzzlement to Mac one evening as they lay on their bunks cooling off.

"Mac, this phosphate stuff we're sending to Japan. What's it used for?"

"Well, Wayne, I'll tell you, this stuff is what they use to make atomic bombs out of. You know the Japs were here before the war for about thirty years. Well, I figure they were tryin' to get that old atomic bomb figured out before we did. Hell, they thought they had a bird's nest on the ground here, havin' all this phosphate so easy. But they were dumb bastards, you know that, and they couldn't figure it out."

"Yuh mean we're still lettin' 'em having the stuff, even now that they're beaten?"

Mac warmed to his subject. "Oh, hell no! They can't use it for atomic bombs. But it also makes good fertilizer. And now that we're watchin' Japan real careful we only let 'em make fertilizer out of the phosphate. You know . . . they take this to Japan, let it dry awhile, then add an equal amount of sulphuric acid; and that makes what they call super phosphate. They tell me that a ton of that super phosphate will make three tons of food, where the ground would produce only one before. So you see it's potent stuff."

"But Mac, why don't the U.S. use it for atomic bombs? It must be worth a helluva lot in the States."

"Well, yeah, it's worth about $5000 a pound. But Angaur's too far to ship the phosphate very cheap, and besides we've got deposits in the States they can use right now if they need 'em. But if you could get any of this home it'd sure be worth a fortune to you."

The next morning Wayne began keeping daily contact with the company chemist, getting the reports on the percentage of phosphate in each new pit. The news spread around camp that Ricketts was saving phosphate to take home, and everyone helped the legend along a little. The chemist padded his figures of the worth of the raw phosphate.

In the dark of late evening Wayne would slip out to the latest "bonanza" and fill his pockets and shirt full of the wet, gooey, muck-smelling mass. Carefully he would wend his way to the company kitchen where he turned it over to Fritz, the baker, and the two night cooks, who were in his confidence. They molded the phosphate into brick shapes and baked it in the big ovens, with the solemn understanding that they would be cut into the big money when Wayne got home with his suitcase full of "atomic bricks." He really left with a case of the bricks; but how far he got in trying to get it to the atomic interests stateside we never knew.

Mac had been half accurate in his story. The phosphate rock was being sent to Japan to be made into super phosphate. And the Japs had been on Angaur since the beginning of the first World War. In fact the Palaus had been the headquarters for the whole Japanese mandated area, with Koror a capital city of an estimated 20,000. When we saw pictures of buildings, gardens, and well dressed natives we often wondered just how much rehabilitation we were really bringing them. The Angaurese had enjoyed a higher standard of living than their island neighbors because they had had a good many years' work in the industrial mining activities. But the Palauans as a whole had not been particularly happy under the domineering Japanese, and were eagerly rebuilding their economy under the tutelage of the American forces.

When the current war ended the Japanese phosphate mining machinery and the plant were total wreckage, for they had undergone heavy Naval bombardment when Angaur was being softened up for the American landing. Phosphate had been forgotten when the Americans made their bloody landings and built a bomber strip. The military camps had covered most of the island, leaving in a crowded area those natives who hadn't gone to Babelthaup for safety.

It was to the quonset camp left by the Army that the American construction company moved in June of 1946 to begin the reconstruction of the mining facilities and to start a supply of phosphate rolling again to Japan, the logical market for the fertilizer. America has ample supply of her own, and the cost of shipping 7000 miles to the States would be prohibitive. Japanese soil was in desperate condition from overcrowding and overfarming, and the superphosphate presented a production aid in getting the Japanese nation back on its feet.

The Henderson Construction Company rolled into its job in typical American fashion. With terrific energy they polished up the deserted camp, rolled their equipment in off ships and planes, scrounged pieces of equipment and parts on deserted Peleliu, and soon set up a new record of pouring out the raw phosphate. During the first six months over 80,000 tons of ore were shipped to the ports of Japan. They worked two shifts daily, under the brilliant sun in the day, and by the light of giant spotlights at night.

And in between times they sought the pleasures of relaxation typical of any all-male society. The Ace-Away game was a crowded

Admiral Andrus, Senior Medical Officer, Marianas, Admiral Pownal, Commander Marianas, Mr. Causey, and Henry.

Phosphate rolls up the conveyor and . . .

pours into a ship's hold.

spot from six to eleven in the evening and from four to seven in the morning, at which odd time the night shift had a bout with Dame Fortune. Run by a weather-beaten, shrewd-eyed traveler of the world who sported two diamonds set in his front teeth, the Ace-Away business flourished. The three dice rattled against the table boards with scarcely a breather, and some men, like Pleasants, built themselves a separate plush account in the Bank of Guam, while others whose wages were as much as $700 a month left the island in debt.

They relaxed in their bunks catching up on the bi-weekly supply of personal mail, magazines, and hometown newspapers. A few men nurtured flower beds in the resistant sand outside their huts. Practically all of them owned hounds, until we worried for a time lest the dogs be getting more meat from the mess hall than the men themselves. The men swam in the surf, hunted sea shells for necklaces and bracelets to be sent home, and gathered in the mess hall for coffee.

But when occasionally a beer ration came in from Guam the lid blew off the island and, as one of the men put it, "All hell broke loose in Georgia." Roars of glee and anger could be heard all over the island. Never did the men spread their ration over a period of a week or so. They drank every bit of the beer in one sitting . . . one, two cases per man in a few hours' time. And the explosion hit the village with such major effects that Henry and Tulop spent sleepless nights whenever there was beer in the Henderson camp.

Technically we had only three rules to enforce in the matter of native-white relationships. Everything in the book forbade giving liquor in any form to the natives because they simply could not handle it. No white man could enter the native village socially without a pass from the M.G. officer, and lastly, no Americans were to be in the village after ten o'clock in the evening. On the face of it there was a great amount of leeway, and the various types of social intercourse to which a man has compulsion could be carried on without too much trouble. Of the group of construction men perhaps ninety per cent had no desire for intimate social contact with the natives. The other ten per cent went whole hog. To a group of men who had pocketfuls of money, few hobbies or mental exercises, and few recreational outlets, the native girls turned snow white in a remarkable short time. Most attractive by any comparison, the Angaur girls quickly developed a desire to conform to American standards. But they learned the standards only from the movies they saw nightly in the construction camp, and from the word of the men themselves. A form of prostitution was the result. This was a natural turn of events, and since it happens in every community in the world there was little Henry could do to curb it. However, when pregnancies resulted, or the Cissy Incident, Henry and Tulop lost no time in bringing the full force of the law against the offenders.

Cissy was our first housekeeper. We thought it humorous to have a house girl with the same name as mine, Cecilia, and made much over it when introductions were made. She was a slap-dash housekeeper, and though she spoke the best English of any native woman on Angaur, did only as she pleased in spite of clear instructions. This we could pass over, for we knew her brand of English was largely the bedroom variety. She was a voluptuous, sullen-eyed girl who had grown wise in the ways of American military and construction men; and she would play with any of them. The fact that she was married didn't deter her a bit, though there were rigid native tabus against promiscuity after marriage. She knew all the uses of the native vine which could be made into a contraceptive, and of another which made an aphrodisiac.

The island reeked and roared with beer one spring night when, about midnight, Tulop came running up to the screen by our bed.

"Meestahr Wahl!" he whispered agitatedly. "Meestahr Wahl! Much trouble! Cissy and Henderson man much drunk. Cissy's husband say he make much trouble for American!"

Henry rolled out of bed, dressed hurriedly, and followed Tulop to the village.

Cissy's house was a shambles, the front door broken down, the few chairs and the bed overturned, and telltale beer cans scattered throughout the two-room quonset. Both Cissy and her husband, Olikong, were drunk, she on beer, he on agi; and both of them were so incoherently angry that it took some time to get the facts of the case from them.

Barnes, a young construction man of playful intent, had brought a case of beer with him to Cissy's house just at dusk, while Olikong was out talking with his friends at the *bai*. Barnes and Cissy had locked the door and proceeded to make merry with the beer and the bedroom.

When Olikong returned about ten o'clock he found the door latched and heard raucous noises on the inside. Knowing too well his wife's habits he departed in a rage to a secret supply of agi to build up his courage in order to handle the situation. About midnight he drew his sharpened knife and roared into his own house, smashing down the door in a melodramatic fashion.

This hullabaloo brought Tulop to the scene in time to see Barnes disappear toward the construction camp in a cloud of coral dust. Both Barnes and Cissy had been happily drunk, but the sight of Olikong's gleaming knife had sobered Barnes considerably. He screamed to the Henderson police for personal protection. His struggle with Olikong had frightened him thoroughly. He had managed to rip Olikong's knife from his frenzied hands, thereby avoiding bloodshed.

Tulop and Henry took Olikong to the Henderson police headquarters to identify Barnes. He did so with much vituperation and flashing of eyes. Barnes offered to give the native's knife back to him; but Olikong declined the offer with sinister words.

"Oh, no, you keep this knife! I get another knife. Sometime I give you this new knife. Nice new knife. Maybe six o'clock in the evening, maybe midnight, maybe in jungle . . . but I give you this new knife." He made his words more graphic by fierce slashing gestures across his stomach. Barnes was most happy to take the penalty of dismissal from his job and return to the States at his own expense to get away from Olikong.

In village court the next night Cissy was banished from Angaur, and allowed to go to another island where some of her relatives lived. Olikong was awarded a divorce from his unfaithful wife, but was fined for his drunkenness and misdemeanors.

Here we saw an excellent example of a clash between two cultures, with serious detriment done to the natives. By American standards the natives' code was exotic, promiscuous, and somewhat immoral. There was no tabu concerning promiscuity among the unmarried group, and if children were born of these attachments no stigma was attached to them. They were taken into the home of one of the couple's parents in a most humane manner. But a brother and a sister would not stay in the same room if no one else were present; and a father would not stay in his house if only his daughter were at home. In a land of free and natural sex laws there was a rigidly enforced tabu against sexual relations with one's mother-in-law.

In the olden days, before the impact of other cultures, the penalty for adultery was death. Now the codes are not enforced by such stringent action though there is still a great deal of force behind them.

Consider the chaotic impact on this social structure when a new, dominant national group comes in, having no concept of the social tabus. Being aggressors, what they want of the women they buy with money. One native woman sees her friend breaking time-honored codes, and, instead of being punished, accumulating fancy dresses, luxury items, and money, all of which have been either scarce or unheard of. This honorable woman is certainly prone to jump the traces herself. Such liberal treatment of the women in return for something so casual as sex was chaotic to the native code on all the islands where Americans were situated. We saw three specific instances on Angaur where respectable married women became camp followers for the tangible gains, and became ostracized by the village because of their actions.

Not only does the native suffer because of these conflicts; American prestige drops accordingly. The natives are part of a strict class-conscious society based on hereditary nobility. The American is placed ahead of the highest nobility and treated accordingly. Yet the American was in no means discriminating in his choice of native women; and the natives began to wonder what kind of people we Americans were who broke the time-honored class rules. To attempt to make this white man understand his obligation was one of the major problems facing the M.G. representatives.

The aftermath of the Cissy Incident brought to light an entirely different group of construction workers, and the most amazing of the lot. When Barnes went to Peleliu to catch the transport plane for Guam he found all the seats on that flight taken. He was forced to wait three days for the next plane. He sweated two of the days out on Peleliu, then came back to Angaur for a day to pick up some of his gear he had carelessly left behind in his rush to get away. The natives knew immediately that he was back on the island, and word reached Olikong in a matter of minutes.

That night in the dark of a back road, Harry, another construction man, similar in appearance to Barnes, was stabbed by a native. He fortunately fended off the blow and was bleeding only from a long slash in his forearm when he reported reluctantly to the Henderson doctor.

Jack Pleasants called Henry into the case to try to identify the native, and the longer the case continued, the more confused it became. The victim contradicted himself thirteen different times regarding the sequence of events, the appearance of his assailant, his height, weight, and type of clothing, and even the sex of the knifer. It became more and more apparent that he was trying to hide something. When he was confronted with Olikong he made the only positive statement of all his testimony. This, definitely, was *not* the man who cut him. At this point Henry and Jack were certain by the American's manner and statements that Olikong had been the stabber, that Harry knew it, and that he wanted the thing hushed up quietly and quickly.

The case began to unravel when Jack and Henry were driving

Harry back to the construction camp from his interview with Olikong. They passed one of the new office workers strolling down the road to the store. He was a pudgy individual, pink faced, round hipped, who walked with a definite swish. Henry waved to him and was greeted in turn by a dainty flutter of fingers.

"Now who the hell is that guy?" Pleasants perked up.

The abused Harry replied, "Well, his name is Bitsy; but *we* call him Mary."

"Migod, don't tell me we've got another queen bee on the island!" roared Pleasants. But his keen policeman's brain figured this to be a new angle on the case, and the questioning started anew. It was finally brought to light that Harry had been involved in various acts of sexual perversion, and that Olikong had been approached in the dark of that back road. Insulted not once, but twice, by the construction men, Olikong made good his threat to use his knife, but on the wrong man.

So here was a group of the "girls" flourishing in the midst of a rough and ready gang of construction workers. How they had filtered into the group we never knew, but that they were operating in full force was certain. The first "queen bee" had been sent back stateside because of some little matter concerning the handling of money. After he left, one of his staunch admirers stamped into Henderson police headquarters and harangued angrily at Jack, "Mr. Pleasants, I just want you to know that I don't appreciate for a minute the way you treated poor Harold!"

As these things became known to the more masculine members of the camp little time passed before hulking six foot bruisers would trot up to each other and mimic in a high, falsetto voice, "Say kid, could I buy you a beer?" It was the momentary rage for everyone in camp to mince, speak in effeminate voices, and in general behave in a manner that would have horrified a total stranger. One of the favorite and most amazing occurrences was for a big brawny rigger to yell down to a crane operator in a sweet, petulant voice, saying "Ki-i-id, would you pass me up another piece of steel, puleeze?"

Oddly enough, with all this horseplay at the mess hall tables and on the job, the real perverts never took offense or lost their composure, as far as we could see. They were inordinately jealous of each other, and so wrapped up in their own group that they paid little attention to the rest of the camp outside of working hours. If one of them could not explain to his friend a lost half hour there was a serious tiff, and all the actions of jealous, domineering women boiled up. Added to this odd group were a few exhibitionists who showed up during the months of large turnover of personnel in the camp. They bothered the native women in the gardens during the daytime, and roamed into the village now and then. Usually, their actions were soon uncovered and they were sent back to home base.

When the construction men knew that they would be folding their tents shortly and starting stateside, what discipline they had maintained fell to pieces. Few of the men seemed to care whether school kept or not, and the resultant carousing in the village, and lax behavior in their own camp reached an alltime high. Tulop was the only native on the village police force by that time, and was worked night and day to keep watch over his people, and to keep their tempers smooth.

On several occasions Pleasants had come to us stating that the natives working for the company were stealing from the men in the huts.

"Heinie, the men say there's clothing missing, and Cookie says half the silverware is gone from the mess hall. We've seen some of the native girls who clean the huts carrying sheets, and a bunch of junk they've no doubt picked up where they work. Now we're going to have to search the village if this thievery isn't stopped."

Outright stealing as such is practically unknown in these islands, and it was most difficult for us to believe that the entire working population was robbing the construction camp on a wholesale basis. Matters worsened as the days went by, and the whole affair was brought to a head when one of the outgoing men lost his trunk with all his clothing and personal papers.

Pleasants insisted on the search of the village. Tulop was most upset. "Meestahr Pleasants, none of my people have this trunk. This thing I know. If you make all my people show you everything in their houses you make them feel too bad, like you think they lie to you. This they do not do."

But, determined to check every possibility, Jack directed the search through the village. As Tulop had predicted, no trunk was found, and the people were resentful and offended to think that such a shameful program would be forced upon them. The boys did turn up, however, quite a few pairs of underclothing, old and new clothing, and towels with the laundry mark torn out. Whenever the natives were asked how they came by these items, which were like nothing they could buy at USCC or the construction company store, they answered that Jerry had sold it to them. When they came upon the fine new pair of summer worsted pants which Olikriil said Jerry had sold him for one dollar, Henry and Jack decided it was high time they had a conference with Jerry.

Jerry was one of the most comical, yet the saddest character we had run across in our travels. We met him first one spring morning when we went to the camp post office to pick up the mail that had accumulated for us while we were at Koror. I sat waiting for Henry in the jeep when a short florid faced, balding chap of about forty came up to me and said, "Do you have plenty of sheets at your place?"

"Why, er, yes," I answered. We have our own supply of sheets. Why?"

"Well, we have a good supply now, and I just wanted to be sure you had everything you needed."

I thought everyone knew that we got only our food from the construction company, so I couldn't quite figure this chap's angle. "Yes," I said again, "We take care of that ourselves. We just got back from Koror this morning and took all our dirty clothes to the laundry."

"Oh! Then you must be Lt. Wahl's wife. Well, Mrs. Wahl, I'm Mr. Beemer, and I came out here to Angaur to help Mr. Shultz clean this camp up. Yessir, we're getting things squared away just fine. That's a Navy term, isn't it? I left the States one month ago, yessir, one month ago this very day. Came out on a special plane that stopped at Johnston Island and Kwajalein. There were several high ranking officers aboard with me, and we made tours of each of those islands when we stopped. Now if there's anything you need you just let me know."

Ye gods, I thought, here's another B.T.O. Oh, Henry, hurry out of that post office and get me out of this predicament. What do I say to him now! I was always acutely uncomfortable when one of the talkative characters teed off on me, but I always wished afterward that I'd heard more.

Jerry was a "bull cook", the lowest paid rating of men in the camp. His "Helping Mr. Shultz" consisted of cleaning up the ground, collecting dirty linens and taking them to the laundry, and then seeing that the beds were freshly made. He soon had the animosity of every man in camp. The laundry manager took an immediate dislike to Jerry and stated loudly and frequently, "That jerk had already lost two of his marbles, but, by god, when he came out here he lost the bag they came in!"

But his job was to clean up the camp and that he did! He had a crew of Japanese workers whom he didn't understand, and who obviously didn't understand him. He stayed with them all the time they worked, pointing jerkily and emphatically at what he wanted weeded out or swept up. The camp did take on a spic and span look very shortly. Whatever we said against poor Jerry later, it must be admitted that he worked like a man possessed, day and night. He first brought the wrath of Hut 15 down upon him when he carefully instructed his workers to "pull out all those weeds and shrubs; they're keeping the light out of this hut." Unfortunately those weeds were coconut seedlings, and other carefully transplanted flora of the island of Angaur plus some precious flower seeds mailed all the way from home to one of the garden-loving workers! So intent was Jerry upon pleasing everyone that he went into a hut one morning and woke up two men just settling down from the night shift to ask them if everything about the camp service was satisfactory. The two bullies threw him out bodily!

Mr. Beemer's complexion was splotchy; and if he weren't already unflattering enough in appearance, the sun made him sadder by giving him a miserable burn and a heat rash. His poor bald head gleamed and blistered, and he took to wearing a red handkerchief around his neck to stop the perspiration. But he was every cheerful.

"Mrs. Wahl," he said enthusiastically one morning when I stopped for the mail, "you know this is the most wonderful experience I ever had. To travel around the world like this is something not many people get to do. Why, the training I'm getting on this job will be good for getting me any kind of a job in a good hotel back home. Why, I could even work up from laundry and baggage work to a managership!"

Jerry became an efficiency expert at folding and storing sheets. Almost any time we took our dirty clothes to the construction camp laundry he could be found there explaining graphically and vociferously to the Japanese workers that *ten*, not nine, folded sheets must go into each pile. He effected a new plan of folding together sets of three or four of the Guam Navy News as they came so that each man would get a whole set without walking down the line to hunt each one.

One night the tug boat came back very late from Peleliu with the mail, and I drove down to see what the lifeline had brought us while Henry entertained our dinner guests. Jerry held forth alone in the office when I walked in, and he gasped, "My goodness, Mrs. Wahl, you're a sight for sore eyes! I tell you a white woman all dressed up is a wonderful thing to see. You are *positively* beautiful!" Now "beautiful" is something I had never nor ever could have been called. I figured he'd been away from home too long, so I grabbed the mail and beat a hasty retreat. A few days later we had a most ravishing platinum blonde guest who turned the heads of every man in the camp. When we went into the mess hall for breakfast with the camp manager, who also had fallen for her charms, every mother's son in the hall gaped wildly and fed his ear for the rest of the meal. After we had seen our guests off at the boat basin we encountered Jerry. Thinking the sight of the gorgeous guest would have been a treat for the lonesome Mr. Beemer, I said, "Well, Jerry, did you see our pretty guest?"

"Mrs. Wahl, I want to tell you something. I saw her. And I think you are still by far the most charming. You are an intelligent, lovely woman, and I'll take you instead of that blonde any time! Now don't you tell anyone else I said that, because I've gotten to be known as a sort of Walter Winchell around here, and everything I say gets all over camp. This is just for you!"

Well, maybe he's harmless, after all, I thought, and went home to tell Henry about my unprecedented flattery.

Not two days later Henry and Jack Pleasants were seeking out Jerry to ask him a few questions about the sale of clothing. Jerry was hurt beyond expression to think we would even harbor such a suspicion. Sell clothes to the natives? Definitely not.

But the boys felt a search of Jerry's belongings would be in line after the questioning. What a revelation it was, not for the quantity of goods he had squirreled away, but for the mental processes that were indicated. He had a large rubber stamp with which he carefully stamped everything he had with his own name. There were a dozen or more towels, the company laundry mark carefully scissored out of the corners. Jerry had trouble explaining that. A neat pile of undershirts came next, laundry marks carefully and symmetrically cut out in circles.

"Now, Mr. Beemer, have you anything else of suspicious nature in your belongings?" Pleasants queried.

"Honest to god, Mr. Pleasants, that's the only thing I have."

Further search brought forth a pair of trousers from which Jerry had neglected to eradicate the name of one of the construction men.

"Damnit, Jerry, now this is the last time. We're trying to help you stay out of a jam. We don't want to turn you in. Have you anything else?"

"As I swear before God Almighty, I haven't another thing that doesn't belong to me . . . I don't believe!"

Continued search of his quarters brought forth more personal items, with other people's names marked in.

"Anything else, Jerry?"

"That's AB-solutely everything I ever took . . . I think."

Buck, the manager, washed his hands of the whole affair, and stated picturesquely, "That guy is phonier than bird crap in a cuckoo clock!"

The boys locked Jerry in the jail and looked into his case further. He had been selling articles of clothing for a few pennies. He had sold at one-fifth of cost articles he had brought from the States. He had gone to the company store and bought such items as shaving cream, toothpaste and toothbrushes, carefully packaged them and sent them to New York. A dispatch was sent to Guam to hold all packages from him and investigate them. Nothing of a condemning nature was found, but one item turned up which roused our curiosity. Ten pounds of saltpeter carefully tied and labeled was the most peculiar thing we found. That got Pleasants.

"Now Jerry, what in the hell was this saltpeter for?"

Jerry blushed, grasped his hands behind his back, and dropped his head on his chest before he said in a small voice, "I won't tell!" And he didn't!

A check of Jerry's personnel file showed that he had a psychopathic discharge from the Army and that he had held over a dozen jobs in the past two years. Jack and Henry began to feel sorry for Beemer, and Jack decided to let him have the run of police headquarters rather than to keep him cooped up in a hot cell. Not ten minutes later Jack went to get something from his locker in the private quarters at one end of the building. A stack of his underwear was missing. Search found them carefully tucked away in the bottom of Jerry's suitcase. Jerry good naturedly shrugged his shoulders and turned them back over to Jack. Every evening thereafter Comfort would go through Beemer's belongings to sort out and return to the various items Jerry had accumulated during the day. And every day Jerry would dolefully wander through the police barracks picking up anything that appeared saleable to him, and stacking it neatly in his bags.

Pleasants made the reports which would start Jerry toward haven in a military hospital, and therapeutic treatment when he returned to the States, and returned to the Henderson shelves all the supplies Jerry had spirited away.

Jerry left on the first special plane that came to Angaur to transfer the Henderson personnel to Guam. His bags had been packed under Jack's supervision and sent to the strip ahead of him, so he could hardly have concealed many items on his person. He came to each of us and shook hands solemnly, thanking us for all we had done for him, and saying he hated to leave this paradise of the Pacific. Face red, and perspiration dripping from his bald head, he mounted the steps of the plane and turned to wave at the crowd as had each man ahead of him. At that moment someone in the crowd yelled, "Tell 'em where you got it, Jerry!" Everyone roared and Jerry roared too, as he bowed deeply and stepped into the dark interior of the transport.

Along with these various "characters" marched a group of solid, intelligent, generous Americans. These men made friends with the natives, enjoyed their society, and gave the Angaurese great benefit by their acquaintance. Red Mills was one of these. The chief mechanic for the company, he trained several of the natives in his shops and in the field. Two of the young boys learned so well they qualified to go to Guam for on-the-job training sponsored by the Navy and USCC. Joe Mrar worked with Jonesy, the head garage man, and by his inherent intelligence, and good training, became the finest boat mechanic we had ever seen. When Mills left he told us he could recommend four of his native workers to stand against any American mechanic he had ever known. Many of the men, generous as the typical construction man is, gave away most of their clothes and belongings to the natives when they were ready to return to the States. Rogers and three other men spent their free hours constructing a motor boat from spare parts and pieces from junk heaps. When they left for home they presented it to Aniichi, their native confrere who had worked with them all along. After the whole construction company had left, several of the men corresponded frequently with native friends, and one man who had enjoyed the small native Catholic chapel sent a pair of images for the altar.

These men held the deep respect of the Angaur natives, for they had tried to understand the local customs and had revered them. They had treated the natives as intelligent human beings, helped them to learn good American ways, and left their women folks alone. The natives spoke deferentially to these Americans: "Thank you very much, Mr. Rogers." "Ah, good morning Mr. Mills." Always the formal title. But they sluffed off the nicknames of the men who had given them trouble. "Hi Buck, Hi Baldy." "Hallo Cookie, what you say?" Not only did they treat these finer men with respect; they gave unstintingly of their meager possessions to show their appreciation to the Americans. Scarcely a well-liked man left the islands without a bag full of handwoven cigarette cases, purses, or place mats, or several of the salad sets or monkey men whittled from ironwood.

On the Sunday before the special planes began to wing into Angaur to take the construction men to Guam, the natives gave an all-out feast for the whole company. It was to be a fish fry, and many pounds of fish had been brought over the day before from the good fishing grounds off Peleliu. Someone had slipped up when the fish were placed in the Henderson reefers, for they were not cleaned. Early Sunday morning the natives discovered that the fish were spoiling, and, being uncommonly careful about their seafood, discarded the whole lot. The Japanese workers were delighted to have the half-soft fish; but the Angaurese were left in a quandry as to what to feed the Americans. One of the villagers came forward and offered one of his few pigs for the feast, and the rest of the villagers bought it from him in order that the Americans have fitting fare. The trays were made up separately, a helping of roast pork, a whole boiled lobster, several crab shells filled with that minced, gently seasoned delicacy, plus taro, tapioca in its various forms, and bananas, more than any one man could eat. The children had spent a good many hours on the reefs and beaches spearing and trapping enough lobster and crab to go around. And the women of the village had worked most of the night preparing the food.

When the construction men were stuffed with the native feast they were led to the center of the village where stood the old Army movie stage. There the women and girls staged a program of native dances, some which we had not seen before; and the young men played their harmonicas and guitars. It was the finest thanks the natives could make for the Americans who had taught them their ways and given generously of their clothing and knicknacks, but also for the Americans who had left unsupported white children in their village, harassed the women, and schooled young men in drinking, carousing and petty thievery.

Toward the last of June the special planes began to roar over Angaur and settle down on our long strip to be loaded with office supplies and personnel. Each day the gala crowd at the strip was smaller, the merry insults, and the *See you in Frisco*'s fewer. The company manager and Chief Uherbalau shook the men's hands as they filed past to board the plane. And then the planes taxied the length of the strip and roared back over our heads as we all waved madly in farewell.

We had all looked forward to the peace and quiet that would settle over the island when the men were gone, though we knew we'd miss the close friends we had made among the men. We'd miss their daily visits, the mid morning coffee, the cribbage games, the late steak supper, and the evening record concerts.

When the last plane raced over us, so close it drowned out all other noise, yet completely removed from us in its intent to

Away they go! Nobody left but "us natives."

rise above the ground and be gone, there was a fleeting moment of loneliness for the people of our own kind, a sense of being left behind. But when the C-54 circled high above us and we turned to our jeeps to find Tulop, Mariana, and a truckload of the natives smiling at us, we were home again among our people . . . just us natives.

CHAPTER EIGHT

The Phosphate Problem

The rumor that the Japanese were coming back to mine the phosphate had snaked through the Angaur village early in the spring. No one seemed to know where it had originated, for Henderson was still not sure whether their contract would be renewed, and the M.G. Unit had had no news whatsoever on any possible change on Angaur. But the rumor was there, ugly and frightening to the natives who came to Henry in great consternation. Tulop's eyes were wide and dark again, and his forehead wrinkled when he asked,

"Meestahr Wahl! Chief say somebody tell him the Japanese come back to Angaur to mine phosphate. Is this so?"

"Tulop, you tell Uherbalau M.G. knows nothing about this. But we will tell the Chief as soon as we have any word. Mister Buck says maybe the Henderson Company will stay."

"But Meestahr Wahl! How about this thing? If Japanese come back to Angaur again do American leave and let Japs take islands like before?"

"Oh, no Tulop! That would not happen. The Americans have come to these islands to help the people. The United Nations say now that the Americans are to take care of all these islands. If the Japanese come to mine the phosphate they do what Americans tell them to do. No, Tulop. M.G. would not leave."

"I do not understand these things, Meestahr Wahl. U.S. makes big fight against Japanese so they are no more on all these islands. U.S. say they win the war. But then maybe they let Japanese come back again. Meestahr Wahl! We beat the Japanese. Why we now give them this phosphate?"

"Well, Tulop, sometimes you very angry at a man, want to make fight against him; but you do not want to kill him, just beat him. This is so?"

· *110* ·

THE PHOSPHATE PROBLEM

"Oh yes, I know this."

"Well, this is how it is with the Japanese. America was very angry with the Japanese and wanted to beat them so they would not beat us. But when we beat the Japanese we made the fight too strong. Many Japanese cities now lie flat. And all Japanese people are flat too. They have no food, houses, no clothing. Now we want to be sure the Japanese will be our friends and fight us no more. So we must help them to get food, houses, clothing so they can take care of themselves. This is why we have been sending phosphate to Japan. You see this?"

Tulop nodded his head doubtfully. "Yes-e-e-ess."

"You and Joseph ask me many times what about the Russians, when will they come to these islands. One reason we must make the Japanese our friends is so they not want to fight with the Russians against us some time. Now if Japanese come back to mine the phosphate it would be to save the money the U.S. has to pay the Henderson men to do the work. Japanese do the work with Americans watching them and make not so much money they owe America for this phosphate."

But Tulop couldn't quite fathom the American logic in the matter. The Japanese dogs were down; let them lie! "The Japanese no f_____ good, Meestahr Wahl! F____ the Japanese!"

Our eyes popped at this epithet, for the four-lettered Anglo-Saxon word that Tulop had tripped off his tongue so readily was hardly an acceptable parlor word in the States. But, like most of his people, he felt so strongly about the possible return of the Japanese that whenever the subject came up his eyes snapped and he spit out the worst phrase he knew. "Meestahr Wahl, my people do not like the Japanese. %$#&* the Japanese!"

The rumor became fact late in May when the big Japanese cargo ship, ARIMISAN MARU, sailed into our port to test the loading of dry phosphate from the now completed conveyor belt. She brought as passengers a party of Army brass who had come down from the SCAPJAP headquarters to check the facilities and effect the transfer of the mining from American to Japanese hands. Headed by Major Sherwood, and Shinkichi Minami, the managing director of the Phosphate Import Association, the group carefully looked over all the mining equipment, estimated the supply of fuel and parts that would have to be sent in, mapped the phosphate areas of the island and outlined their plan for mining through those various areas, and planned how the six hundred Japs who would eventually come to Angaur would take over the Henderson camp, install their own kind of cooking equipment, and crowd their men into the quonset huts. The Army major and the sergeant who were to become the first liaison men between SCAP and the Navy settled in the Henderson headquarter house and began to get acquainted with the problems they would meet.

The natives were in a high state of tension. When it was discovered that no plan had been made for the natives to continue working in the phosphate their anger boiled over, and they came in a group to talk to Henry about it.

"Meestahr Wahl, Chief say Angaur men work in phosphate for many years. When they work for Henderson they make much good money. Now Henderson go home and the Angaur people work no more. When the Japanese come back to mine phosphate and the natives cannot work, Chief say his people will have much trouble, be very angry. They will talk like everything, and maybe somebody will hurt the Japanese. Meestahr Wahl, what you think? Angaur people can work in phosphate?"

Henry told the men that he would speak to the officers from SCAP and see if it could be arranged that the Angaur people keep on working.

"Meestahr Wahl, if my people can work that would be good. But, also, there would be much trouble if Japanese were boss over my people. Angaur people have Japanese for boss before. They do not like this very much. What do you think we can do about this thing?"

The oversight in not planning to have the natives continue with their jobs was discussed with the party from Japan, and steps were made to set up jobs for them and a fund from which they would be paid. It was heartily agreed that a touchy situation would arise if the Japs came back in boss positions over the natives. All the men agreed that the natives should be put into jobs where they had little or no contact with the Japanese or where they supervised work in the shops or dock area.

We knew the problem of fraternization, which had been a major one in the year previous, would disappear entirely when the Japanese returned in force. They came without families; but the native women would have nothing to do with them, threatening graphically that if any Japanese approached one of them they would fix him so he couldn't bother anyone else! The rule that the native women were not to be in the Japanese camp was easy to enforce, and the only time they were seen anywhere near the area was when the moved along the road skirting the camp to their gardens at the far end of the island.

The gardens, however, became an area which needed constant vigilance, for the Japanese, no longer kept in a stockade, looted the island for any fresh fruit they could find. It was easy to understand, but impossible to condone. The workers were living on what was known in Japan as a miner's ration, 1750 calories a day. This was some 300 calories more than the average citizen at home in Japan was getting, but the men were still starved for fresh things. And seeing the bananas and papayas growing and ripening was more than they could pass by. But the natives had such a constant struggle against nature to keep themselves supplied with foodstuffs that they needed every bit of fruit the trees could produce. Tulop and his villagers set up watches at night around the gardens, and the Japanese who were caught were threatened with a return to Japan.

They were not the only ones who were alarmed. The newscasts on the Armed Forces Radio from the States told faintly of the protests that were being made by elements of the British Empire. Australia and New Zealand were howling that SCAP had not notified anyone of their return of the Japanese to Angaur.

The mail brought clippings from friends at home who saw the word "Angaur" in the article and thought it might be something we were interested in. Interested! We were vitally involved.

"Good lord," Heinie worried, "this is no place for a junior officer. I wish there were a nice big three-striper here for policy making. Why, the slightest incident could whip up an international situation. Listen to what this article from the Chicago SUN says."

> A foreign office spokesman said today that General of the Army Douglas MacArthur apparently did not consult the Far Eastern Commission or the British government before authorizing the Japanese to operate a phosphate rock project on Angaur Island, in the Palau group. Asked whether Britain was satisfied with the U.S. decision, the spokesman replied at a news conference: "The authority apparently was given by the supreme commander before raising the matter in the Far Eastern Commission or through diplomatic channels. Press reports of the decision . . . represented the first intimation the British Government has received on the question."

"Boy, we'll have to watch things darn carefully. Any little trouble between the natives and the Japs could have a party of investigation here on the first available plane."

"What do you mean?" I asked.

"Well, look, joe. Say one of the Japs can't resist a bunch of bananas some night, and the native catch him with it and beat him up. Or say there's an accident on the job in which a native gets killed by a machine operated by a Jap worker. I'd naturally have to make official reports on these things. Someone just looking for a reason to get Japan out of these islands again could hop on that and claim infractions of the peace treaty laws and an investigation would be on. But if our police force works well, and we can try to understand the natives in their pleas for proper royalties for the phosphate and mining only non-gardening areas, then things should run pretty smoothly. I believe the Japanese are eager to please the authorities and will do everything they can to make this project a success."

THE PHOSPHATE PROBLEM

When the last Henderson men left and the Japanese took over the phosphate works the authority had not yet come for the natives to go to work. They were restless without work, or the nightly movies, or the Henderson store to patronize. Now the three major family factions in the village began to get on each others' nerves, and verbal feuding broke out.

Max Rutherford's mother-in-law decided that her daughter's son should be primed for the next chieftainship of the village, since the royal line passed through her. So she played politics among all the groups, making most of the villagers annoyed at her scheming. Charlie Eduardo's group, which was closest related to the Chief's group, claimed that Carlos, pious Carlos who strolled up and down the roads with the beatific expression of a church elder, and his group were not interested at all in the welfare of the village, only in their own selfish ends. And harsh words were spoken among many families.

This resulted in a general, healthy moving day. Scarcely a day went by without a native coming to Henry to make arrangements to move his quonset to another section of the village, or to buy a deserted quonset on another section of the island and erect a new home for his family. The quonsets were sold "on the books" at one dollar a running foot, an average house costing about fifty dollars. Led by Joe Mrar, a group of eight families moved to a remote quonset camp at the south tip of the island and worked it over, repairing houses, the water pump and storage tank, and connecting electric lights with the village system.

The young men of the village got out the clumsy old village truck, which Charlie Eduardo and his boys had pieced together from scrap piles, and drove up and down the streets singing and shouting merrily as they cleaned up piles of dead coconut palms and unruly shrubs. The women cleaned and swept the yards and the village cemetery, and the children gave the school yard an extra thorough weeding and sweeping. The whole village sparkled.

They watched the general confusion that reigned in the Japanese camp when the mining operation changed hands. Whether by Henderson design or by accident, twenty-four hours after the Japanese took over, not a single vehicle in camp was running. Jeeps and trucks stalled along the roads, and the American sergeant was run wild trying to get the Japanese to get them back in running order. Apparently unaccustomed to American equipment, the Japanese workers and officials ground gears, jerked jeeps into motion, and puzzled for long hours over the boat engines that would not start. Faced with a recalcitrant motor they never seemed to think to check the carburetor or the starter mechanism; they just took off the engine hood and began tearing the motor apart. It wasn't long till all the boats were crippled too.

The natives just smiled, and watched, and waited. Tulop repaired his pipeline of information in the Jap camp and mended political fences. No matter how often he muttered to us, "%$#&* the Japanese," we knew he was an astute politician and was getting along fine with all the officials. When the go-ahead signal came for the natives to return to work they slipped quietly into supervisory jobs in the shops, at the dock, and over the many vehicles. In a matter of hours jeeps were purring, and the LCMs and barges roaring in and out of the boat basin.

While the natives had been idle they had made much talk at village meetings and small gatherings about the future of the phosphate and their island.

"The Japanese say to me," said one *rubak*, "that they come to mine phosphate to the very edge of the village. If they do this thing we will have no good place to move. Before the war we live in three villages on all parts of Angaur. Now we must live too close together in one village. This does not make peace among our people."

"And what if they mine the phosphate where our one taro patch lies. What do the people do then?" queried an old man who had seen the swampy taro patches disappear one by one into the grasping maw of the crane shovel.

THE PHOSPHATE PROBLEM

"Many times somebody tell us we get money for this phosphate on our island. But nobody sees this money. If they take all the phosphate from Angaur and give us nothing what do we eat, where do we live?"

"Somebody say we must maybe move to Peleliu, maybe Babelthaup. But Angaur is our village, our island. Nobody likes to be taken from his home."

"When the German and the Japanese mine our phosphate before they make much trouble for us. Then there was much phosphate on Angaur. Now, not so much. Pretty soon all garden space on Angaur will be made into lakes from phosphate mining. Then we have much trouble again. Uherbalau, what you think we can do?"

Tulop came to Henry with the report of these conversations and questions. "Meestahr Wahl, my people make much talk about phosphate money. Nobody gives us this money yet; but they say we will get it. When, Meestahr Wahl? When we get this money?"

"I do not know, Tulop. Army men from Japan say to me that this money is owed to Angaur people; but nobody has seen it."

"Meestahr Wahl! Chief say this money could make much trouble. Maybe the money come some time and every Angaur man gets his part. That is much money now; but what happens to that man's children and grandchildren when phosphate is all gone and no more money comes. My people talk much about this, say that maybe if we get some money every year to use for school, for village, for roads, maybe this would be better."

"I think Angaur people think very good, Tulop. How do you think you can keep money coming to Angaur from the phosphate after the Japanese dig no more."

"Meestahr Wahl, Joseph, and other rubak think about this. Meestahr Wahl, why you not take this money to States with you when you go. You buy stocks and bonds. Every year you send money from these to Angaur people. This way we have some money every year."

· 117 ·

Stocks! Bonds! There is nothing these Palauans are not acquainted with in the world of finance and politics!

Henry urged the natives to write a letter to the Army officials at SCAP and to the M.G. headquarters to see if their situation could be clarified. Uherbalau and the leading *rubak* of the village gathered together in several long sessions and wrote passionately in Palauan the history of the phosphate mining on the island, and the problems and troubles with which they had been beset. Tulop and Joseph brought the letter to Henry. They could translate it into English, they said, but not so good. So maybe Mr. Wahl could get someone to help make the words better.

From Peleliu, where he was waiting to catch an Army plane for Guam, we brought a fine young Army doctor, an Hawaiian-Japanese who served ably as interpreter for the document. Fortunately a visiting field party from Koror was stopping at Angaur for an official check of the village and medical facilities, so the navy officers served as witnesses, and Tulop and Joseph read the document aloud, phrase by phrase, for translation.

Word by word the story unfolded, a tragedy of conqueror nations taking over islands, and the same time their helpless people, and using them ruthlessly. What of the integrity, what of the basic rights of the native people to their own land? Little, or nothing! Our knowledge of the history and environment of the Angaurese grew greatly that day, and all of us sitting in the living room-office of the quonset by the sea found a new basis of understanding for these native people.

Here are sections of the letter from Chief Uherbalau, Chief of Angaur Island to the M.G. Officer on the subject of the mining of phosphate in relation to the people of Angaur.

> I know that you are very busy in your work on Angaur; but I would like to present this letter concerning phosphate on Angaur to you. In 1908, when I was aged 31, I became Chief of Angaur, taking the title which was previously held by my mother. I have served as chief for 39

years. My mother was involved in the troubles over the phosphate; as a result I took over the job as chief. My mother has passed away, and I felt a great deal of sorrow about the whole situation. The Germans forced my mother to resign her position. I have always tried to figure out how to do the best for my people, to make them live comfortably, to be wealthy and to make Angaur the best island in the Pacific. The Americans are the fourth nation to occupy this island; and, judging from my experience, the Americans have no racial prejudices and have tried to enlighten the natives in the ways of the western world.

I do not know the exact month and day, but it was approximately 1908 when the first German ship came to Angaur. My mother was then chief, and since the Germans said they could not talk business with a woman they wanted one representative for the chief and four other natives with whom they could talk business. They went aboard the ship, and the natives were told they were being taken to Koror. When they got to Koror the natives were told that the German government and the German phosphate mining company were going to mine phosphate on Angaur. The people were given 500 marks and five pieces of Palau money (small, glass type beads). The five natives said, "We cannot accept this money because we are not the chief and we did not know why were brought here." However, the Germans forced the natives at the point of a pistol to accept the agreement and the money. "Even though you protest, the Germans are going to mine the phosphate," said the Germans.

The Chieftess said that if the Germans would give a certain per cent of the proceeds to the persons who own the land she would agree to let them mine it. The Germans became angry at this and said, "As of today you are no longer chieftess." So Uherbalau was made Chief, and was then sent to Yap. . . . the Germans did as they pleased, cutting down the trees, building new property, and exploiting as they saw fit. The natives noticed the exploitation and tried to get rid of the Germans, but an old man told them it was no use and not to do anything.

The Germans mined here approximately five years until November 9, 1914, when the Japanese Navy came and occupied the island. "If we are going to have the mining done," the natives said to the Japanese, "let us do it properly on a tonnage basis. This land really belongs to the native people." Lt. Ogino, the head of the Japanese force, said, "No. We have conquered the land from the Germans, therefore it belongs to the Japanese. And if you are going to keep bothering us or making trouble we will shoot you all or put you in jail." Each time we approached the Germans or the Japanese about mining our lands to tell them that it was rightfully ours they said, "This land belongs to *our* government." We, the Angaur people, are disturbed about these things, and our heart weeps to think of them. We are most disturbed over the problem of what will become of our people when this little island that belongs to us has all been mined.

This is the second time the Japanese have come here to mine the phosphate; and I have talked to the Military Government officer previously about this condition. The Japanese in the past mined very many of our taro patches and we now have very few. If the same plan continues, what are we going to do, and what will be the future of our livelihood. We request that the Military Government Officer see that the people of Angaur are paid the royalty due them on the phosphate mined here.

/s/ Uherbalau

The translated document was sent to the proper authorities up the line, and photostatic copies of maps of the island were made marking the village, the old mining boundaries used by original German and Japanese agreements, and the proposed moving of those boundaries. Before the summer was gone definite rulings had been passed protecting the living areas of the island from the mining operations. And encouragement came from the headquarters at Guam that the royalty money would be coming through, in a form the natives could see, before the year's end.

But still the threat of mining the taro patch remained. According to tests the area under the south end of the airstrip and under the lone taro patch adjoining the strip held one of the best percentage deposits of phosphate on Angaur. The American visitors from Japan voiced the average opinion in the matter. "Why, the whole island grows green! What difference does it make where the taro is planted, and the other gardens. Can't they just be moved to another area?"

To the casual observer all the tropics look lush and productive. Again we had to bring up the point we had learned early in our stay: the limestone and coral islands of the area were really marginal gardening land. A garden is grown in one spot for a year or two, and then that land must lie fallow for four years, storing up enough energy for further growth. The pesky underbrush must be painfully grubbed from the rocky soil before the tapioca roots and sweet potatoes can be planted. Gardening on Angaur was no easy business of sitting on the front porch and hearing the sweet potato vines grow.

The concern of the natives was real, and understandable. After a summer of careful watching to see if the surveyor's stakes came close to the disputed area, the natives wrote one of the most beautiful, moving documents we saw. This time they translated it from Palauan through Japanese to English themselves, and presented the finished form to Henry. He was moved, as I seldom saw him, when he read it.

"This is a beautiful piece of work! Think how many hours of labor it required to translate it through Japanese, via slow dictionary reference, to English."

The subject of the letter was "Petition for Protection," and it said in part,

> I will tell my thoughts concerning our dwelling, that you might know it. I am very concerned with the phosphate digging in Angaur. I do not say that there should be no digging of phosphate at all, but I pray that where there is not being digged ought to be left, and only in the water they should dig at all. For if they would dig it all so that no soil would be left, where will we raise our food? The present birthrate is good and the population is increasing. We have some taro patches, but not from the best kind. And out of these we can not bring forth enough food for many people.

Therefore I ask to help me with your authority, while you are living with us. Arrange it that all the edges of land with some bush, and where we have already planted some food might be left to us and not be digged. Now in the next days they intend to dig phosphate, where we intended to cut and to clean the bush and raise food. I would appreciate to have your help in telling the Commanding Officer, that he might have mercy with us and help us to keep the soil for our use, where not yet has been digged phosphate.

We surely cause work and trouble to you with this petition, but I need your help and protection. I appreciate to get your information very soon.

/s/ Uherbalau

CHAPTER NINE

Just Us Natives

Peace! It was wonderful! After the large group of Americans left, the island settled down within its seams and the pleasant days moved by without great incident. It was perhaps our easiest, best remembered time on Angaur, for we were together constantly, Henry and I; and we saw more of the natives, who relaxed with fewer strangers among them. They had more nearly accepted us now, and visited and talked more freely.

We inaugurated a series of Sunday evening "at homes," making our house open to all the people of the village who cared to come. It was mostly the younger group who showed up, all spit and polish and manners at first, and then relaxed by the gay music from our phonograph. We tried each week to insert one or two favorite American selections of light opera classics into the concern. The natives listened carefully and politely; but they clamored for the cowboy, Hawaiian, and schmaltzy records on our shelves. Several of the boys played guitars, and they were fascinated by the "hot" guitar records we could play for them. They drew near the loudspeaker, tapped their feet, and shook their heads in wonder at the cascade of notes that flowed from the unseen instruments.

Joe Mrar was the acknowledged youth leader of the village. He managed the baseball team, taught the young girls the line dances they performed at native parties, and played the mouth harp in accompaniment. It was Joe who marshaled the youngsters in and out of the house on Sunday evenings, and he who led some bashful girl to the center of the floor to begin the American type dancing to "Old Dan Tucker" or "Here's To the Ladies." A young Coast Guard couple had been on Angaur for some weeks early in the year, and they were the envy of all the local young set because they could jitterbug. It didn't take the lads long to pick up this American fad.

Most of the village youngsters between six and twenty piled into our house on Sunday evenings. All the chairs were moved into the bedroom-music room, where the record player was placed on the "throne." The boys and girls sat on the bed, on the floor, in the chairs. Some bolder individual would pick up a late magazine, and soon all the small fry would follow his lead. They lay flat on the floor, magazines spread out in front of them, pointing and chattering over the graphic art of America. The magazines changed hands continually, becoming more dog-eared every week. Whenever they found something they couldn't understand they brought it to Henry for explanation. The girls hunted out the fashion magazines, the catalogue, and the pattern book and discussed dress styles and luxury items like any country club set.

We tried to have some new item for the group to see every week: an illustrated book on Big League baseball, about which they were so curious; the set of colored pictures of American scenery which a western oil company had distributed and which gave the Angaurese an idea of the many kinds of climate and scenery we have in the States. One week we borrowed a projector at Koror and showed the villagers all the color slides we had taken in the islands. It was great sport for them to see themselves objectively in the pictures. Often we made a tub full of lemonade, or passed candy from our latest box from home.

Singinari's favorite tune was "I am just a luttul ba–arfly with a beer bottle for a home." We found it on a V-Disc left over from the Army days on the island, and played it till everyone knew the words and tune. This was followed in popularity by a highly rhythmic instrumental recording of "The Elks Parade", and a Burl Ives record of "Little Mohee." Mariana didn't speak English too well, but she made it clear one Sunday night when we played the selection four times that, "This is my song, Mrs. Wahl. You teach me my song." So we wrote down the words and recited them till she and her friend, Fumiko, could repeat them. During our latter days Singinari took a fancy to "Till We Meet Again" and asked to have the words. He sang, "Smile the while you kees me sad adoo," most of the time he piloted the boat, making our imminent departure even sadder.

The evenings seemed to grow in popularity, which was gratifying to us. When we were preparing the house for Henry's relief officer we arranged to have the native men paint the floors while we were on a trip to Koror. We returned to find that the paint, as sometimes happened to the old wartime paint left on the islands, hadn't dried at all. After several days of bunking with the Army major we finally had to go home, even though it meant taking off our shoes and tiptoeing stickily back and forth. We suggested tentatively to Tulop that this Sunday there be no party. But on Sunday night the crowd started filtering in about seven o'clock, and we wound up with the record number of fifty-five! The magazines stuck to the damp paint, sand ground into it, and the floors were never the same afterward. But it was worth it.

Singinari and his crowd of young men spent hour after hour rebuilding an old command car that had been left on the junk heap. They pieced together bits of canvas for a top, and then carefully folded it back in the fashion of a convertible. On the days when the junker would run they drove majestically up and down the island roads, Singinari at the wheel wearing one of his wardrobe of nautical caps, the rest of the boys lounging in the back, feet propped up, hats pulled down over their eyes. They might have been any group of stateside teenagers in an old Model T Ford. They needed a name of some sort, so we privately dubbed them "The Young Men's Yachting and Agi Society."

Henry set up the plan of village work to be executed during the layoff period. The men were to paint the village store, police station, and school house, replace the supports under the several village storage quonsets and M.G. units, and clean up the village. The work progressed nicely, and the village took on a new look. But we sensed an undertone of dissatisfaction among the old men who were doing the work. After several days of this Tulop came to Henry with a message from Uherbalau that explained the unrest.

"Meestahr Wahl, Chief say everybody in village make talk about working, fixing village buildings. These people say, "We make much work for Angaur village, but we get no pay for this work. We would like M.G. to make pay for work we have done and for all other work."

"Oho! So that's the trouble. M.G. pays a few village people who do work for M.G. and everybody else wants to get some money too. Everybody wants to get into the act! That so, Tulop?"

"Yess, I think so, Meestahr Wahl. My people have no money now that they do not work for Henderson Company."

"Well, Tulop, I know the people think much about where their money will come from. But they worry too much. Now you tell the Chief and the people that if they want pay for village work they can have it. But you tell them also, Tulop, that if we do that they will have to begin paying for all things that they have been getting for nothing. They must pay for running water, for electric lights, for these houses you moved into after the war, for the village trucks, for boat rides to Koror."

"Oh!" Tulop was surprised at this tack, evidencing the fact that the villagers had not thought about the other side of the picture, the fact that they had any more fittings of civilization than the people of the other islands of the group.

"I think Angaur people are spoiled by the Americans, Tulop. They have many things the other islands have not, but yet they want more. In my country there is an old story about a dog who had a big piece of meat in his mouth. He was running to eat his meat when he came to a pool of water. When he looked into the pool he saw another dog, a big dog, with a bigger piece of meat in his mouth. He thought of his piece of meat, but he wanted the bigger one, so he dropped his piece and jumped in the water for the other. And he came out with no meat at all, and was a very wet dog. You know this story, Tulop?"

"Yess," Tulop grinned, catching on to the parable immediately.

"You tell Uherbalau these things, Tulop, and I will write a letter to all Angaur people explaining this. We will make what we call in America a "pep talk."

The letter summarized all the points Henry had mentioned to Tulop, and was effective in its simple phrasing and illustration. He climaxed it by saying, " . . . Angaur is a small island with not many people. But Angaur people are the most healthy in all islands; they have the best food, best houses, best roads, best school and hospital, and more money than anybody else. But that is not enough! Some people yap, yap all the time because they are expected to keep up and maintain these things that belong to all people on Angaur. These are not good thoughts. People should work for each other and keep this island the best island with very happy people, with good medicine and schools.

"All these things can be had and kept without outside help; and there will be no outside help. All Angaur people should know that they have many things that have not cost them one penny, which is not true any other place in the world. People with good heart and good mind should know this without having to be told. But if the people want to think only in money, only of themselves and not the village, pretty soon all these things will fall away. People who think together and work together are happy and strong. People who think only of themselves and are selfish and greedy are a weak people, and do not last long. Many small sticks make a strong club; but the sticks by themselves are easily broken . . . "

As soon as Tulop had translated the letter and posted it on the village bulletin board there was an open meeting of the villagers. They came in a body that same evening to say that they wanted to work for everyone on Angaur, that Angaur was indeed Number One Island, all Pacific.

These were easier days for Tulop, too, for headquarters had finally authorized three additional policemen for his force. They came reluctantly from Peleliu, for they had heard many stories about the return of the Japanese and about what hard work it was to be a policeman on Angaur. But they soon found things to be running smoothly, found relatives to live and eat with, and gardens to share. So they brought their families to Angaur. They were well trained policeman, Ichero, Edelok, and Ngueous, whose difficult name was pronounced Nee-wee-ose, and they reported very formally every evening. When the one on duty knocked at the door Henry always went to answer.

"Good evening, Mr. Wahl," the man would say, waiting for Henry to ask the question.

"Good evening, Ichero. Everything okay?"

"Everything okay, Mr. Wahl! Thank you very much. Good night." With a formal, snappy salute he would turn and disappear.

The first thing on our schedule in the morning was the nine o'clock radio communication period with headquarters at Koror. We could usually be lazy till radio time, and then dash to the kitchen, down a glass of grapefruit juice or a can of Toddy, roll out the jeep and hurry down to the radio shack in the old Henderson camp where there was a twenty-four hour supply of electricity. One of my greatest pleasures was to take over the radio schedule when Henry was too busy to handle it. The radio job I had had during the war had given me enough training to handle the equipment with ease; but learning to sling the Navy spelling, which used a specific word for each letter of the alphabet, took a little time and quite a few trip-ups.

"Nan Dog King, Nan Dog King, this is Nan How George calling Nan Dog King. How do you read me?" we would begin.

"Hello, Nan How George. This is Nan Dog King. I read you three by three. How do you read me?"

"I read you five by five, loud and clear. I have one message for you. Shall I send it now?"

"Send your traffic. We have negative traffic for you."

Date and addressee heading over, I was ready to struggle into the message proper. "LSM 921 has completed loading operations, has completed loading operations. X-ray initial. Departs for Koror, departs for Koror 1630, that is numerals one-six-three-zero, king time. X-ray initial. Major Anderson, that is able-nan-dog-easy-roger-sugar-oboe-nan, will be passenger, will be passenger, to catch plane for Guam, to catch plane for Guam. Long break, and over."

"Nan Dog King, this is Nan How George. How do you read me?"

The morning and the three o'clock afternoon radio schedules were the manner in which we transacted official business with the Navy headquarters at Koror, and passed any unofficial messages to each other. We frequently heard humorous conversations from ship to shore, or from the garrison force at Peleliu to Koror.

"Say, Harry," came the voice from Peleliu, "put Chief Brownell on a minute, will you?"

"Roger, he'll be here in a sec.". . . (long pause) "Brownell speaking. Whatya want, Bill?"

"Say, Chief, you got any potatoes up there? Real potatoes? We're darn near starving down here. Haven't had a fresh vegetable for six weeks now."

"Well, we're down to dehydrated spuds too. The LSM is due in from Guam this week. How you doin' for eggs?"

"Eggs? What are they? We're back on wartime rations down at this dump. What does that supply officer want us to do, starve to death?"

"Well, I'll look around, and if I can find anything for you I'll send it down on the next native boat. Anything else?"

"Roger, thanks a million. No, no further traffic. Peleliu out."

"Nan Dog King out."

When a storm was brewing we made special contact with Koror, and through the crackling interference kept abreast of the latest weather reports. We sent headquarters our departure and estimated time of arrival reports for the boat when we started for Koror, and we kept track of the arrival and departure of visiting phosphate ships. Though we now had a Navy call signal we were still called affectionately by the station name that the Henderson Company used when they handled the station, "Stinky One." "Stinky One, the skipper would like the report on vital statistics on tomorrow's radio." Or an informal message from a Koror friend, "Hey, Stinky One, I hear we're going home next month. What'll you bet I get sent first?"

Moses, net fishing

In these leisurely July and August days we did have time to take our coffee to the terrace after dinner and lounge in the comfortable canvas chairs, watching the sunsets and the fishermen inside the reef.

JUST US NATIVES

When the tide was low in the evening the shallow water was dotted with natives who were dressed in loincloths or shorts, and who carried long bamboo spears with head of steel slivers. The water was so still at low tide that it seemed more a lake than a bit of ocean. fifteen or twenty supple men usually were scattered along the waterfront, moving through the clear water so easily and quietly that scarcely a ripple moved behind them. When one of them spotted a fish ahead, he poised momentarily like a bronze statue, spear poised level with his shoulders. Then a flick of the wrist let fly the long javelin-like instrument. The instant the spear hit the water its owner ran after it in a noisy splash that disturbed the whole quiet evening.

Old Tomas was one of the best fishermen. He seemed to bounce along on the balls of his feet in slow motion through the water. His body was still hard and youthful though his years approached sixty. There seemed to be only a split second between the time he snapped his wrist to loose the spear and the instant he drove it into the sandy bottom to impale his fish, and reached in the shallow water with his free hand to bring the fish up to the bag slung over his shoulder. There was great excitement the night Tomas speared two fish at one throw.

Striking sunsets were not an everyday occurrence as most tropical publicity leads one to believe. Usually the sun slipped into the sea behind the roll of clouds that marched by our western front day and night, leaving a brief blue cast on the island, and pale pink clouds in the east. But once or twice a month there would be a rare display of cloud colors and formations. A clear, brilliant red sunset sometimes foretold storms in the vicinity. It was hard to believe that such a magnificent range of vibrant reds and purples gave portents of typhoon weather. There was the pink variety of sunset, too, which tinted the buildings, the water, the clouds, even the sand with dainty Eastertime pinks and lavenders. Small gold flecks of cloud drifted above the horizon for a few brief moments of glory on these evenings. Occasionally below a clear blue sky a fan of clouds rose from the horizon. They seemed to hang above a whole range of islands lying to the west of us. Mirage-like, they were real enough to make it seem urgent to boat over to see them. The whole circle of the horizon was rimmed with clouds on the nights of wondrous sunsets, ranging from the intense, vivid colors surrounding the sinking sun to delicate tints in the far eastern range.

The display of color never lasted long; and we found ourselves hard pressed to get the camera equipment out of the hot locker, figure the amount of light, set up the tripod, and make an exposure for our collection of color pictures. Within a half hour after the disappearance of the sun complete dark would be upon us.

The boundaries of day and night meant nothing to the natives so far as fishing was concerned. They suited their type of activity to the tide, the moon, and their pantry. On moonlight nights the young people would be out most of the night catching land crabs for which their younger sisters and brothers had set traps during the previous day. All along the road rimming the island they had secured halved coconuts to the base of trees, marking the spot by a branch placed on the road pointing to the tree. When night came the young folks set out in groups with much laughter and fun to the various corners of the island. The concoction the natives could make of minced crab meat, coconut milk, and a chopped green shoot, similar to chives, was pure ambrosia. They blended the mixture and then put it back in the crab shell. It became quite a contest among the Americans at native parties to see who had the biggest pile of shells when the meal was done.

Often when the fish were running well, or the need was great, the old men sat off shore in their outriggers through the night, hauling the fish in with a hooked line. None of them used rods. They could haul in a sixty pound fish on the line, hand over hand, almost as rapidly as it could have been reeled in by the finest sporting equipment. Their hands showed no cuts or line burns. None of the Americans could handle a line in this manner without shredding his palms.

A fine specimen of a sailfish

The big fish . . . the sailfish, the marlin . . . necessitated a different technique. They were caught, unbelievably, by one man in his outrigger, with only the line and the hook. When the fisherman latched on to one of the big babies, he could only tie down the line and ride out the fight, letting the fish pull the light boat along until he was exhausted. We saw one morning a magnificent 141-pound marlin which had been brought in after a two-hour jet-propelled speed ride. Such a fish as this made good eating throughout the village for several days. The fish would be smoked or cooked immediately, and then eaten at leisure.

Small fish were cut up for bait, or used whole. But the big fish bit on a hook that had a lure instead of bait. The lure was fashioned from the stem of the spider lily plant. The bulbous plant which grew profusely on Angaur was dug up and the underground stem cut in four or five-inch sections. The flesh peeled off these sections in the manner of birch bark, and was a glistening white satiny texture. The native cut a zig-zag edge on his lure, and then wrapped it carefully around the hook, making a dainty skirt to hide the sharp points. When this concoction was pulled through the water behind a boat it sparkled in the reflected greenish light and attracted the fish easily.

Quite the most exquisitely beautiful form of fishing to us was the spear fishing with flares inside the reef during the night. On the nights when there was little wind the surf rolled over the reef in a muted roar, and the small waves whispered against the beach at the edge of the terrace. In the dark of these nights we would be wakened by a soft orange glow which crept into one side of the room and moved across our line of vision, making long shadows of the feathery ironwood trees, till it slipped around the partition into the next room. We would prop ourselves sleepily on one elbow and watch an outrigger move slowly by. At the prow of the boat would stand a native holding aloft a large gasoline flare which made a silhouette of the outrigger, the statue-like light bearer, and the second native dipping his paddle into the water. The mellow flare, the quietly floating boat, our half awake state made it an unearthly experience, a dream, a picture from a medieval period. An etching, perhaps, of the Lady of Shalott floating down to Camelot. Only the soft voices of the natives, blurred as they drifted in to us, brought the scene into the realm of reality.

When the storms came the waterfront was a different place than the quiet, picturesque spot we usually enjoyed. The whole world burst into sound and motion. The surf roared over the reef like a continuous freight train through an echoing canyon, and the water inched ominously closer to the edge of our terrace. No gentle murmur of rain on the tin roof was this, but a torrent of noise pounding on the quonset. Tree branches and screen blinds banged against the house, and the gusts of wind whistled through the trees, shaking the building to its very foundations.

Really stormy days we spent jailed in the house trying to keep things dry and wondering uneasily if this would be a real typhoon.

JUST US NATIVES

To venture out was to get soaked to the skin despite ponchos and helmets. But the nights were worse. Even with the screen canvases down, the rain misted into the room across our faces. In the inky-black room, huddling close to Henry, I felt that each gust of wind was heavier, more devastating than the one before, and that the wind's direction was surely shifting again. I began to plan, as I kneaded his shoulder or hand, what things I would quickly throw in a bag if we had to take to the typhoon shelter on the ridge . . . as much warm clothing as possible, the letter file, the camera and film and the slides. And the copper teapot and silverware, if possible, said my housekeeper's heart.

But the storms passed, never reaching full typhoon capacity, though they may have been damaging. A sudden rain squall on a quiet night could have equally startling effects, for we would have to run for the screens to let down the canvases. One such squall broke just before dawn one morning, bringing the rain in force through the kitchen screens at the south end of the hut. We both hurried out to cover the openings and were stung on our bare shoulders and backs by thousands of icy needles of rain.

Heinie screamed as he fumbled with the hooks, "Gee-suss! It must be all of seventy! I'm freezing."

We raced shiveringly back to the bedroom where we got a blanket from the hot locker, tossed it over the bed, and clung to each other under it to get warm. That was the only time we used a blanket on Angaur, though a gray, rainy spell could bring a few degree's change in temperature that seemed more like twenty.

Our days were by no means lazy after the departure of the construction company. There was always the work of keeping the village reports and activities up to date, of supplying fuel for the water pumps and the light generator and overseeing their repairs, of spraying regularly to keep the mosquitos and flies at a minimum. Now began weekly trips to Koror for mail and supplies. The bi-weekly Navy transport planes no longer came to Peleliu, and there was only a weekly PBY service from Guam to Koror bringing mail and visitors. Going to Koror meant losing two or three days of every week from our work and pleasures at home. We must go very early on Monday morning, or, if the tide was not right, on Sunday, in order to get mail on the outgoing plane. The PBY came in the midafternoon and departed Tuesday morning at eight. The mail wasn't sorted till suppertime Monday, so that meant staying till the next day. It was surprising how little of the week seemed to be left after we spent one day going, one day returning, and one each in preparation and recovery.

The trips were a joy, for there were never two alike. Usually we carried between thirty and forty natives and Americans, plus all manner of mail and cargo. Once we took a thoroughly frightened goat from the Angaur herd to Koror. Our biggest crowd was fifty-five, and we held our breath all the way home. Not one more fly could have come aboard. The only unpleasant part of the trips for me was the always present threat of sunburn. I never could stay on deck long, and even at that had to wear long slacks, and a buttoned-up, long-sleeved shirt to keep the sun's reflection on the water from blistering my skin.

We traveled in a small world all our own. Its boundaries seemed to lie just beyond the horizon around the Palaus. There was no distance greater than the sixty mile length of the group of islands, no other ocean than the blue Pacific within the reefs surrounding these abrupt hills. Indigo blue water, boiling into white froth in the boat's wake; the sky studded with cotton candy clouds; the hills ever covered in shiny June-green foliage; long-tailed snowy tropic birds soaring over the tree tops. This was our world, with home waiting at the southern end of the trip, and smiling brown-faced people whom we loved. The pleasant days are the best remembered.

Nor were we completely alone. The Army major was settled in the old Henderson headquarters, and we exchanged visits several evenings a week, listening to the baseball resumes coming over the short wave radio, playing competitive solitaire, or talking business.

JUST US NATIVES

As soon as our boat began the Koror runs we had a steady stream of company. We had sung Angaur's praises so long that the Koror folks seemed eager to come down south for vacations.

We had time now, and reason, to see more of the Japanese group which was settling down to the business of mining the phosphate. Studying the group of men was a baffling process which led us, day by day, to feel that "inscrutable" was certainly the word to describe them.

When the Henderson Company was on Angaur the Japanese were seen very little, for they were workers who were interned within barbed fences during their off hours. But when the officials of one of the large Japanese combines came to Angaur in the late spring we met a different group of men. Keen conversationalists, analysts, technicians, they whipped the bowing, scraping group of workers into trotting action. We enjoyed several evenings with the group, for some of them spoke English well, and they joined in learned discussions of economics, the war, and literature with much gusto.

They entertained the Henderson officials and the Wahls on the large ship on which they had come in May when the change over plans were made. One of Japan's remaining large transports, the Arimisan Maru had been on the silk run to New York before the war. She had once been a lovely ship, as evidenced by the paneled salon, the etched glass shades for the wall lights, and the wide decks and stairways; but she was rough and battered now. The meal was excellent and unusual, featuring delicious paper-thin strips of smoked salmon, and canned tangerines, with many dishes of cold roast beef, cold asparagus, cabbage, peas in the pod, all accompanied by Japanese beer and saki. The ship's officers and the visiting officials sang their college songs, which sounded sentimental, various popular songs, and some lullabies which sounded more like marching songs.

Buck felt that he must return this meal, which he proclaimed to us was a bunch of crappy food. "I'm gonna show these Japs what kind of food they ought to eat. I'm gonna have my cook and a couple of his men take steaks and french fries out to that old Shushu Maru and cook 'em up the first real meal they've probably ever had."

This second feast was an affair of spine-crawling social torture. The Japanese galleys were not built to handle the hot cooking of steaks and french friend potatoes, and many hot words emanated from that area while we all waited in the salon. Buck growled around, and went below to the galley to stir things up. The crew bobbed politely, like a tubful of Halloween apples, and the high ranking officials sat calmly with cold smiles on their faces. finally the meal was under way and Buck undertook the job of master of ceremonies. He made many official speeches, thanking everyone in the room for one thing or another, and then he tried to whip up a little camaraderie. "Come on, dammit, somebody do something, even if it's wrong. Mr. Wahl, you start a song." Someone would finally start an American song, and before he could get everyone to join him, Buck would interrupt.

"That's no good. Come on, somebody else, like I always say, DO something even if it's wrong. Mr. Shinami, you're the head of this Japanese group. You do something."

The suave Shinami, who had lived ten years in San Francisco, who was head of the group from Japan, rose quietly, gave a curt, polite speech of thanks for the "elegant meal so kindly served us by our American friends," and sat down again. His was an air of tolerance for the foolish antics of the Americans who, in this meeting of two societies, had come out on the small end in manners and *savoir faire.*

The skipper of the ship was a grinning little scoundrel who sent his crew surreptitiously ashore during both his visits to Angaur to pick fresh fruit, and to dig up coconut seedlings recently set out carefully by the natives. He was independent as a hog on ice, and held up loading operations for days when he didn't want to bring his ship in near the shore. But he made many jokes and seemed

JUST US NATIVES

most affable and eager to please when we met him. He was one of the Orientals we never could fathom.

The men who took over the managerial jobs for the new mining setup were industrious in their work and almost introverted in their living habits. They came occasionally for official calls on Henry, or upon our invitation for an evening of classical records and refreshments of cake and coffee. They seemed hungry for both.

Dr. Kyakawa was one of the most interesting to know. He conferred with the native dispensary head whenever a village emergency was too serious for the local man to handle. And he brought to Henry each month an exquisitely written report in careful columns of the health and illnesses of his workers. He spoke English with much effort, and it was sometimes embarrassing for us to wait out this translation without jumping in to help him with the words. One evening when he came down for permission to call on a sick woman in the village we were playing records. His eye lit up with immediate recognition at the selection. The doctor asked many questions about the music we had. Did we like classical music? Did we have many records? Did we enjoy Schubert's "Unfinished Symphony?"

Yes, we replied, we considered that symphony one of our favorites. He must come some evening and hear it with us.

Not two evenings later he appeared apologetically at our door carrying his old records of the symphony which had been recorded some years before in Germany and issued with Japanese labels. This was his present to us, he made clear, for letting him listen to the fine music.

After that we invited him, and any of his confreres who were interested, for a concert every few weeks. We served coffee, and cake or pie, and were amazed at the zeal, in exception of politeness, with which every man cleaned his plate and cup. They put all the sugar and cream possible in the coffee, making us realize that their diet was short on sugars. When the music began they settled back in their chairs, closing their eyes, and listening intently, mov-

· *139* ·

ing only to mark time, or to change expression in appreciation of the music. True American music interested them greatly, and they asked again and again for "Rhapsody in Blue." The story of the "Nutcracker Suite" as portrayed in Fantasia held their interest, and they followed the music carefully as we described it. And they howled delightedly at Jerry Colonna's "Casey at the Bat," particularly when it was accompanied in pantomime by old right-fielder Wahl.

But with all the understanding that is possible in the common language of music we never felt we knew any of the men well. They did not talk of their families or lives at home unless they were specifically asked questions, and then they answered politely and briefly. We found it next to impossible to get any feeling of Japanese postwar philosophy, or to find out if they only tolerated us, or genuinely liked us.

The workings of the Japanese mind became even more baffling to us when a group of workers attacked one of the officials one afternoon. It was the first such upheaval we had had, and Major Bruce wanted to make an example of the men so that such an incident would not happen again. The culprits were lined up in a row at the police station, and Henry and Major Bruce, with Tulop and Mr. Takazawa, the manager of the workers, questioned each one of them. To a man they pleaded guilty without being questioned at all.

It was decided they should be sent to Koror to the high court of the islands where they would stand trial and be fined or sentenced. Subsequent questioning brought out the fact that the men had been arrested for a crime, therefore they were guilty of it. That was the beginning and the end so far as they were concerned. Authority had suspected them, and authority was supreme, therefore right. After weeks of slow questioning and growing confusion the light was finally thrown on the fact, as admitted by one of the minor officials, that the man who had been attacked had willfully taken the beating as a face saving gesture to cover the error in judgment made by his immediate superior.

JUST US NATIVES

How then could we begin to understand this race of people whose philosophy, whose very way of life was completely different from anything we had ever known? It was a tantalizing puzzle we were unable to solve, one which made us resolve, if possible, to spend some years in Japan in order to work with and study these people.

Most of the examples of Japanese we saw on Angaur were sad ones. The workers came off the ships from Japan carrying perhaps one small package of belongings. Search for any contraband items found only one set of clothing, a few paper bound books, a toothbrush, perhaps some needles and thread. The men made their own tabiis and thonged sandals. And they laboriously pieced together garments the Henderson men had discarded in the trash can until one pair of shorts might look like a patchwork quilt of pieces an inch square. Many of them wore only a G-string during working hours.

They seemed to have no understanding whatsoever of American equipment. The stalled vehicles and wrecked jeeps and trucks were strewn all over the islands for weeks. Operations dragged to a virtual standstill, yet the men seemed to be swarming over every working area. Enterprising Major Bruce discovered that the Japanese workers needed almost constant supervision. If his back, or the supervisor's, was turned work slowed down or something went wrong immediately. It took a great deal of explaining, jacking up, and threatening to get the work going.

They were a hungry looking lot of men, these Japanese. Though they were rationed more food than their families at home, their diet was heavily unbalanced toward rice and potatoes. They nursed along a scrubby garden which provided more sweet potatoes and a few green things, but not enough to feed all seven hundred men. The Japanese were not allowed to fish in the native fishing areas, and though the new major sent them out in one of the boats almost every day, the catch was inadequate. From time to time they got portions of meat from the major's reefers, meat which had been so long in cold storage it acquired an old, reefer taste. It is presumed that they trapped wild chickens in the jungle area of the island.

NUMBER ONE PACIFIC ISLAND

A very peculiar fact was the sudden drop in the canine population after the Henderson men left. Every other construction man had had a dog, a fat, sassy dog which was fed from the mess hall every time it begged for food. When the Americans left we worried considerably about the problem we thought would arise when these dogs no longer had a source of food. We feared they would overrun the island, and become bothersome in the village. But strangely enough the dogs didn't bother us. We paid little attention to their absence for several weeks till it suddenly dawned on us that scarcely a dog could be seen in the camp area. So sure were we that the hungry Japs had been having dog stew that we became alarmed every time our own fat, simple hound was missing for any length of time. The pack of dogs would have had to be killed; it was a vastly more humane end they came to feeding some undernourished men. Whenever we drove into the Japanese area and stopped long enough for Rosco to bound out of the jeep, several men would whistle to him, stoop to pet him, and start walking off, calling to him as they went. Surely they just liked pets . . . but one never could feel quite sure.

But always they seemed eager to please. They bobbed and hissed whenever they greeted us, and smiled agreement to every pleasant word. One night we stopped by the radio shack to listen to the weather report; and while we waited for the news we decided to sweep out the building. We were barely aware that a jeep drove by from the Jap office, paused in front of the screen, and went on. In a few moments Mr. Takazawa came trotting in, all smiles, followed by two briefly dressed, sleepy workers.

"I beg your pardon, Mr. Wahl! I'm very sorry that because of my neglect my men did not clean this place. Your wife should not do this cleaning. I have here two men who will clean this building for you. This area is to be kept clean by our men. Thank you very much."

Takazawa seemed to be everywhere at once. As Japanese Government manager for the workers he was the go-between for the

· *142* ·

JUST US NATIVES

company and the Americans, whether it was the Henderson Company or the liaison officer who came later. He caught a "barrel of hell" from the Henderson men every day, for they did not like the Japs and made no bones about it. Takazawa probably was called more kinds of a descendant of a female dog than any other man on the island. Through it all he seemed to remain calm, pleasant, almost apologetic. He was the only one above worker level kept over for the new setup, and it fell his lot to explain the system to his countrymen, as well as assist Major Bruce in all quarters. Takazawa had excellent technical training and had done engineering work in Japan and China for some years before coming to Angaur.

He accompanied any group who came to call at our house as interpreter and spokesman, for his English was good. It was from Mr. Takazawa that Henry received one of his most prized mementos of the Palaus. Takazawa came down one evening in late September with a plain looking book which he presented to Henry.

"Mr. Wahl, I wish to thank you very much for the kindnesses you have shown me on Angaur. I will return to Japan soon after you leave Angaur, but I will not forget you. This book that I have can explain only in part my gratitude to you. It is a very old book, which Mr. Shinami found when he was in Australia, and it pertains to these islands. Since you have talked with me of how interested you are in the history of the Palau Islands and their people, it occurs to me you would enjoy having this book."

Henry was quite moved that Takazawa should give him one of his few private possessions, and such a rare one. He protested that his friend should keep the book, but Takazawa insisted. Underneath the brown paper protective cover, we found a book which had been published in 1803 in England, the story of a British vessel commanded by Captain Henry Wilson, which had been shipwrecked off the Palaus in 1783. The log of the ship, the sojourn in the islands to build a new ship, and the return to England with the son of the high-chief accompanying them were all put down in detail. Excellent steel engravings of Palauan scenes, natives, and native utensils and accouterments were included throughout the book. The wonderful title page read:

> An Account of the Pelew Islands,
> Situated in the Western Part of the
> Pacific Ocean;
> Composed of the Journals and Communications
> of
> Captain Henry Wilson
> and some of his officers
> Who, in August 1783, were There Shipwrecked
> In The Antelope
>
> A Packet Belonging to the
> Honourable East India Company
> by
> George Keate, Esq. F.R.S. and S.A.
>
> To which is added
> A Supplement
> Compiled from the Journals of
> The Panther and Endeavor
> Two Vessels Sent by
> the Honourable East India Company
> To Those Islands in 1790
> by
> J.P. Hocken, of Exeter College, Oxford, M.A., London
>
> Printed for Captain Henry Wilson
> By W. Bulmar and Company
> Cleveland Row
> Sold by G. and W. Nicol, Booksellers
> to His Majesty
> Pall-Mall; and J. Asperne, Cornhill
> 1803

JUST US NATIVES

The natives were as interested in the old book as we, and they asked again and again to hear more details of the story. They nodded their heads in recognition of the early native names, of LeeBoo, the chieftain's son; and they studied the map with Henry to ascertain which island had been the scene of the British camp. On our next trip to Koror we made a side trip around the now deserted island, pointing out the coves and sandy beaches tucked between sharp cliffs where the shipwrecked, frightened crew must have found refuge during the storm of so long ago.

Takazawa seemed to be one of the intelligent type of Japanese who were making a go of the phosphate mining and of their postwar rehabilitation. On the other end of the scale was the most amusing Japanese on Angaur. He was a happy little fellow who helped Johannes, the native cook in Major Bruce's kitchen. Johannes dubbed our little friend, "Inski, the bull", for everything he did seemed to be backward, and he was utterly clumsy. We saw him once a day when we stopped by the kitchen to pick up a loaf of bread, some butter or canned supplies, or to get Johannes to take us to the reefers to get a piece of meat. Inski simply knocked himself out trying to please us. Johannes would give him the keys to the meat reefer and he would run ahead of us, unlock the door, open it wide, and start pointing to one item after another.

"This? This?" he would question in his meager knowledge of English. "Maybe you like this. Good biff!"

I would point to a carcass of lamb. "I think I would like some of this, Inski. You cut in half . . . so. Only one leg I want. You cut here, and here."

"Oh, yesss!" He would haul the carcass out on the ramp, raise his big cutting knife and whack away across the back of the frozen meat. Never could we make him understand that it was one leg of lamb we wanted. We always were presented both. By no amount of pointing or gesturing could we get across that it should be cut apart. Apparently that would not be ample. We finally gave up and took to roasting both legs, every time we chose lamb, and taking one to the Major.

Then we would go to the fruit reefer, Inski ahead of us on a dead run. He never walked. I would point to an unopened crate of oranges.

"Some of these today, please, Inski."

To our horrified amusement Inski set down his knife, doubled his fist, and . . . BOP! BOP! . . . beat on the slats of the crate till they gave! Then he proudly extracted a pan full of oranges, checking each one to see if it was all right. Moldy ones he simply threw over his shoulder through the open door.

One day we stopped by the kitchen just before dinner time to pick up a warm loaf of bread and a pound of butter. Inski met us at the door on his usual dead run, holding out the carefully wrapped bread and butter before we could even ask for them. The most pleased look of absolute originality spread all across his round face and bared his three gold front teeth. He giggled and bowed again and again as we thanked him.

During early September a party of American women geologists from Tokyo visited us for several days. They were keen individuals, the best company we had had, and they howled with us over our stories about Inski. When we went down to have dinner with the Major one evening, Miss Esther greeted Inski in Japanese, and the poor boy nearly fainted from sheer excitement and bobbing up and down. Such service as she got that night! The Major's claim that Inski did everything absolutely backward was undoubtedly true when he first began to work. But he learned more than almost anyone on the island during his dining room and kitchen apprenticeship.

This same slow improvement was apparent throughout the company of Japanese workers. Bit by bit the phosphate dryers were put into order, and the amount of rock run through them daily increased. The conveyer belt loaded the phosphate into the holds of the ships with fewer hitches. The garage had only a few vehicles waiting for repair or overhaul, and the harbor was no longer jammed with boats out of commission. Under Major Bruce's watchful tutelage all these kinks slowly smoothed out in the phosphate works.

JUST US NATIVES

The natives were by now back at work at various jobs in the phosphate, but wherever possible not working directly with the Japanese. They were generally relaxed about the Japanese being on Angaur, but they kept a wary eye out for any signs of difficulty. Their individual income was assured again, and that did a great deal toward making things peaceful. And from the many letters traveling between Henry and Koror and Guam, we began to gain some assurance that the royalty monies for the phosphate would be seen, not only heard of. None of these things ever fully settled themselves while we were there, but a momentary peace fell on Angaur.

CHAPTER TEN

Rough Sailing

No sooner would matters quiet down in one corner, giving us a false feeling of well-being, than the bell would ring for the next round of difficulty elsewhere. The picket boat seemed to be the center of troubles of one kind or another. After the famous Fourth of July run to Koror she made only two trips before she was out of commission again.

We were never free of treacherous seas in the Palaus for more than a few days at a time. When a storm blew up off the Philippines or in our own area, the sea would be monstrously rough for days afterward. When the seasons changed, twice a year, there might be weeks at a time when it was not considered safe to take the boat out of the basin.

Executing the entrance to the boat basins was always a breath-holding affair. Singinari would take the wheel, Tomas and one other crewman would take their places on either side of the boat at the forward end. The two directed Singi right or left till he was in position to start his run. He watched the waves, throttled the boat down till she seemed to poise in the water, took a quick glance out the windows behind him . . . then jabbed the throttles forward, gripped the wheel and raced us in on the crest of the wave. Even the boat seemed to take a deep breath and relax once we were through the breakers. Coming out of the basins was even more of a hazard. Several times we rode the first wave, mounted the second barely, and . . . whamm . . . went crunching deeply through the third, completely drenching everyone on deck, water spraying in through every window. Once the cross breaker rolled out from under us too soon, and we dropped like an elevator with a broken cable that seemed fifteen feet to the trough of the new wave, landing with a vibrating thud.

Wiry Singinari's skill was remarkable; he felt his way through all manner of waves, and sensed the exact timing for speeding or inching the boat through perilous waters. Tomas knew every reef and type of weather in the islands, and was an incomparable pilot.

Late in July the boat crew was sent to Peleliu first thing one morning to pick up some Army visitors from Japan. There was a stiff breeze blowing in the west, and the water was quite choppy, but nothing particularly unusual. The entrance at Peleliu is an obstacle course of shallow water set with nasty boulders and sunken barge sections, and wind blowing at an angle across the harbor mouth. To enter smoothly it was necessary for the boat to ride the crest of a wave at full speed for fifty feet until the boat cleared the shelf and reached the dredged channel inside the entrance. The boys misjudged their speed that morning, and the wave rushed past them, leaving them at an angle in the trough, and dashing the hull against a submerged boulder. Only their skill righted her and carried her into the harbor.

For the second time the boat was towed home to Angaur, this time to a long-faced welcome, quite the opposite of the first joyful arrival. There was serious damage, and the boat had to be beached for major repairs to the rudders and screws.

Again the natives went to work, this time repairing the old marine railway the Japanese had had on the Angaur beach. The boat was then run up the narrow rails on blocks, above the tide, for repairs. After several weeks the rudders had been repaired and the screws straightened, the plywood stern replaced, where the rudders had broken through, and a complete repaint job from Koror. Henry's ears grew redder at each word as we took the message.

"Designate picket boat government property. What is present operating condition of the boat?"

By the time I had finished copying the message for the files, Henry was pacing the floor. "I knew it! I knew from the beginning it was too good to be true, that the natives would never be able to keep the boat even if they did do all the work. Well, I won't have it!" he stormed. "Headquarters has no right to try to take the boat away from the people who fixed it when the Navy was ready to tow it out to sea and sink it. Who did the work? Who scrounged the material? The natives did!" He banged his fist on the table.

"If I get orders to send this boat away from Angaur, I'll raise hell in Guam, Honolulu, San Francisco, and any other place along the line where I might stop on the way home!"

The boat was not commandeered. But we were never certain from that time on that the Angaurese could keep it. Each time we went to Koror Henry made his stand clear, probably to the boredom of our friends there. But they could not know what a major part of our life the boat had become. Spending almost half of two days each week going between Angaur and Koror, we naturally became attached to the vessel itself, disregarding any feelings on the moral issue involved.

September was the trochus month, and everyone set out to get as many of the shells as possible to be shipped to Japan, where they would be sold for button making. The children had a month's vacation from school, and the old folks were gone in their outriggers day and night to the good fishing grounds in the bay of Peleliu. Singinari took the picket boat over one morning loaded with food and a gay crowd of young people, for a day of fishing. But they weren't in sight by dark, and we could see no lights out on the water for an hour thereafter, though we kept a close watch on the point at the north end of the island. Just about dusk a chilly, steady rain set in; so we concluded Singi must have wisely put in at Peleliu for the night.

A rainy night was one of the few times when we were home alone, and we settled down to a pleasant evening of selecting our favorite records for a concert. I was curled up cosily on the combination loveseat-phonograph table, records on one side, player on the other, a pan set just so to catch the rain that dripped off the overhead beam, and a book in hand. Henry had brought his favorite reading chair in from the living room to the bedroom/music room and was quietly reading. Nights like this always sent my thoughts off on wild journeys, and we had just finished a discussion of what we would do if we saw a distress flare off the horizon. We agreed the best thing to do would be to send an answering flare up from our stock in the office, radio Koror with the information about general location, try to radio the ship in distress and, weather permitting, get out the boat and set out to find the ship. Satisfied with the answer to that never-never problem, I changed records and returned to my book.

Henry's back was to the beach, but I faced that way, and it was I who saw out of the corner of my eye the red and white balls of fire drift lazily down over the beach, reflecting in the water. A cold fuzz zipped up my back and arms and centered on top of my head, and I yipped loudly.

Henry looked up. "What's the matter, joe? Another rat?"

"Flares!" I gulped. "Honest! Right straight out there off the reef. Lo-oo-ok, there's another, red and blue this time!"

"M'god, the picket boat's on the reef! Hurry up. You take one jeep and get Tulop and Joe. I'll get down to the boat basin and see what I can do."

We were half undressed, but we bothered only to put on our boots, and to don ponchos to keep us dry. I grabbed my rain hat and tossed Henry his pith helmet as we ran through the living room toward the garage.

Tulop had seen the flares too, and I met him on the road in the village going after Joe, so I hurried after Henry to the boat basin.

There, in the beam of our jeep headlights we saw the boat safely moored at her usual spot, loaded to the gunnels with the most sodden, chilled bunch of young people we had ever seen, and at least three hundred pounds of every kind of fish the ocean offered. The youngsters were shivering from head to foot, for a squall after dark in the tropics can make one cold clear through. Singinari explained cheerfully, "We were all so very cold, Mr. Wahl, and we had so many fish. We thought it would be good to have the village truck come to get us. Nobody would know we were here, so we shot two flares so you would all see us." Henry and I were much too relieved to find the boat all right to be annoyed. But Joe Mrar was furious.

"Mr. Wahl say these flares for trouble only. You made a very big mistake to frighten us all so. Never again you use this flare gun unless trouble is very bad." He warmed Singi up verbally with his raking over the coals until Singinari stepped up to Henry and said that he was very sorry he had caused so much trouble.

I took the jeeploads of girls back to their homes, and then went back to watch the fish being loaded on the truck. There were great strings of them: tuna, barracuda, small ones I couldn't identify. There were longusta and crab, and one big old turtle. There would be much cooking and eating in the village that night. The fish were already cleaned and ready to cook; and we wished it might have been daytime so we could have taken a picture of this record catch.

What we thought would be a catastrophe turned out to be a gala occasion; we left the beach with a token gift of beautiful fresh fish. The picket boat rested secure and glistening at her pier. And we went home to dry ourselves and drift off to sleep with the soft drumming of rain on the metal roof.

Early in October we had one wild trip which tested the seaworthiness of our boat. The months of shifting winds were upon us again, and we had scarcely gotten to Koror with the mail when a storm set in and we knew it would be a couple days before we could safely go to sea again for the trip home.

The next morning the Angaur radio came faintly through stormy interference with the report of a flare-up between the Japanese and the Angaur natives.

"Damn it," Henry worried, "It seems that every time I get away from the island we get trouble. I hate to take you on this trip, but the boys think we can make it, and I may need you to help me write a report on this incident. We'd better start in an hour."

ROUGH SAILING

It was soon obvious that the passage down the center of the islands, inside the reef, was too windswept from the southwest to be safe. So we cut through Malakal Harbor to the east and sailed down the east side, in the protection of the islands. When we left the shelter of Peleliu and with the gale blowing between that island and Angaur, it became obvious that it would be impossible to angle directly across. Manuel came up from helping Singinari at the wheel. "Mr. Wahl, we cannot go to Angaur like other times. Sea too strong. Maybe big wave hit us on side . . . no more boat! We must try to get behind Angaur, where the wind is not so strong."

By skillful dodging of the mountainous waves and short tacks to take advantage of any decrease in the wind's intensity, we worked our way across the seven miles of treacherous open sea to the leeward side of Angaur. We had a relatively safe run to the west until we cleared the north end of the island. Then it was nip and tuck as Singinari fought to keep the nose of the boat into the wind and yet work his way far enough to the southwest where we could chance a fast U-turn which would bring the wind to our backs and drive us into the boat basin. Several times he tried to turn, and the plywood craft heeled over until those of us hanging on the handrails atop the cabins could touch the water with our feet.

"No! No good! Too strong!" The natives gasped and shook their heads. But they grinned reassuringly when I looked at them. We struggled to straighten out, and Singi tried again. After several attempts we made it, and, pushed by the wind, streaked for the boat basin.

When we finally tied up at the pier at Angaur, seven rocky hours after leaving Koror, almost the whole village met us. Major Bruce rushed down and said breathlessly, "Say Wahl, we're glad you're here. We had lookouts all around the island, and all the small boats ready to help you, though they probably couldn't have gotten out of the basin. Boy, we worried about you!"

· 153 ·

Henry laughed with relief. "Brother, that's an understatement of how we felt about ourselves! Now about this trouble; what happened?"

"Well, one of your boys was accidentally killed when a Jap driving a big truck backed into him. The natives were a little upset about it, and threatened some violence. But everything's quiet now. They're waiting for you to see the boy and attend the funeral. And then we'd better get to work on the report. Ready to go?"

CHAPTER ELEVEN

Tell Me a Sea Story

We parked our jeep on a rise above the boat basin to watch an LSM slip around the point of Angaur one day in March. The "M" from Guam might be loaded with food, with mail, or with much needed repairs for the houses at Koror; but all I wanted to see on that ship were my three trunks of clothing and household gear which had been a month on the way.

Henry was inclined to be less hopeful. "Don't get yourself in an uproar, joe," he cautioned. "If I know the Navy it'll probably be weeks before that stuff turns up."

He squinted at the ship bobbing along our western sea front for a few minutes. "We've never beached a landing craft in this harbor before. There's a six-foot tide when it's in full tomorrow morning. We'll have to arrange to have her come in then."

It was just dusk when we sputtered out to the LSM 938 in a small, open LCVP. The lights of the ship glowed softly against the water as we drew near and circled in front of the lowered landing ramp. A number of the crew and some native apprentice-seamen sat smoking and talking, legs dangling over the edge of the ramp, which opened like a drawbridge. They jumped to grab our lines as we came alongside in the small boat. I gripped the outstretched hand that came my way and jumped over to the ramp, thankful that I didn't have to climb a ladder over the side in the near-dark. Henry joined me, and we were taken by the deck watch into the well-deck of the ship.

It was like walking into the end of a lidless shoe box. The ship's jeep stood at one side, and a motor scooter lay disassembled next to it. Midway of the deck to our left the circular conning tower rose about thirty feet, lights shining from the portholes and from the topside. The walls of the deck rose ten feet on all four sides to the narrow rimming deck. There was one stack of cargo boxes covered with tarpaulin and lashed to the side of the well deck. But obviously most of the ship's cargo had been unloaded at Peleliu, for we could see the length of the deck to the lines full of dungarees and skivvy shirts and sheets, all buttoned or tied in knots to the line in true male efficiency. My boxes and trunks were nowhere in sight.

We were greeted at the center of the deck by the officer-of-the-day, a young, curly headed chap who looked as if he ought to be about a junior in college. "Good evening, I'm Ensign Vawter. What can I do for you?"

We introduced ourselves and said we would like to see the captain of the ship.

He led us into the close, muggy heat that never left the interior of ships in the tropics, and headed back toward the wardroom.

"Just a minute. I'd better check the doors here." He moved ahead and closed a couple doors into the officers' and crew's wash rooms. "Coast's clear now," he grinned. "We don't get women visitors aboard often, and the boys kind of get careless in their manners. Watch this ladder now."

The Navy always refers to stairways as ladders, and in this case they were right! It was so steep I had to proceed slowly sideways, hanging grimly onto the chain guard rail all the way, and trying to keep my skirt tucked between my knees so it wouldn't blow up into my face. How these sailors can bang down these ladders as if they were casual steps! On the lower deck we crowded into a tiny passageway outside a screened door. Mr. Vawter stuck his head in the door and said, "Captain, guests to see you."

We filed into a cabin that seemed very little wider than the passageway outside. Immediately before us was the dining table, now used as an office, for it was strewn with report sheets. Stretching out from the bulkhead opposite us were two tiers of bunks. This was the living, dining, and worker quarters for the three ship's officers; and a more compact spot I'd never seen. It occurred to me that no submarine could have more crowded quarters.

The man who rose to greet us was a jolly, roly-poly individual. A big man who carried his two hundred seventy pounds well, he seemed privately pleased about some secret thing. He was fortyish, with a receding hairline and a tropic-tanned complexion that matched his khaki uniform. His shirt clung to his shoulders and back, soaking wet. He extended a warm, beefy, hand in greeting. This was Lieutenant Richards.

"Sit down folks, and make yourselves comfortable." he grinned. Glad to have you here. Everybody got a chair? Vawter, how's to getting these folks a cold drink. What'll you have, folks? The ice box is behind you, and you can see the choice of the house."

He sat down in his chair at the head of the table, tilted back and reached in the sideboard behind him to hand out glasses and a bottle opener. The cokes were passed around and we drew a long, cool sip which made the sticky little room seem cooler. Every drink the skipper swallowed seem to appear immediately in perspiration on his shirt; but he took little notice of his discomfort and only bothered to wipe his damp brow occasionally.

We chatted for a time about his beaching the next morning to load quonset material for Koror. Without moving from his comfortable position Captain Richards reached for the ship's phone, pushed a buzzer with one fat thumb, and spoke into the instrument.

"How's to sending Schultz down here with the map of Angaur and the boat basin."

Shortly a trim sailor knocked at the door and handed in the required chart. The men pored over it, noting the width of the entrance to the boat basin, the recorded depths of water, and the tide depth.

"Okay," concluded Richards, "We'll bring her in at 8:45 in the morning. If you'll have some of the natives there to help us tie up, it'll be fine. Now, how about another drink? No? What's the matter, you guys sissies? I'll have another one, Vawter."

I nudged Heinie. "Ask him about the trunks now."

"Oh, yes. Captain, would you check your manifest to see if my wife's three trunks and boxes are aboard?"

Richards reached behind him unerringly to the chest of drawers and brought down a manila folder full of shipment listings.

". . . Mmm, not on the ship now. Let's see, we put off about a dozen boxes of personal gear at Peleliu today. Where's that list? Oh yes, here it is. Let's see, Harrold, Crafton, yeah, here we have it, Wahl, that's you, isn't it? By gosh, we left it at Peleliu. That was the direction on this sheet. If I'd known you were over here, I'd have brought it direct to you."

I sank back disappointed. Now I'd have to wait till the Henderson tug could bring the boxes, and just hope that someone at Peleliu would remember where they were and see that they got aboard.

Every man off duty at the construction camp, half of the native population, and the Wahls were on hand first thing the next morning to watch the ship beach in our boat basin. We lined the hill facing the entrance to the dock; and some of the men even hurried out to the end of the finger pier which had been constructed of metal barge sections. Forty feet across to the north began a limestone and concrete seawall, running parallel to the beach, and reinforced with old tanks and twisted steel beams. To enter the harbor was tricky, even in a small boat, for there were shallow spots just inside; and when the sea grew rough breakers rolled and broke directly in the mouth of the little harbor. The tide was full six feet that morning, adequate to carry an LSM onto the beach and leave her high and dry. And, much to our relief, it was a quiet morning at sea.

We watched the shoe-box ship cast off from the buoys and cruise into position a half mile out from the beach. She poised like a track man about to sprint for a broadjump, measured the wind and the drift of the tide, adjusted her position a bit to the south, bounced a time or two, and then started slowly toward us. Straight as a die she came, closer and closer till the prow split the center of the mouth of the harbor. Then when we thought she would stop and float gently on in, she seemed to race for the beach at a speed that would carry her right on up the rise and into the construction camp. The men

Rosco, Buck Harlan, Cecilia, Lt. Richards

made a general, nervous movement to the side. But just as the tip of the ship began to touch sand she quietly came to a dead stop, crunching gently against the sloping beach. We could stand on the finger pier and touch her side, so closely was the 938 parked in our beach lot.

Skipper Richards grinned as he stood in the top of the open conning tower. He spoke to a sailor standing by, who relayed an order through a microphone. Lines came spinning down from the bow of the "M", and the waiting natives grabbed them and tied up the ship. The ramp slowly ground down, and one of the men carried down a wide plank to bridge the narrow margin of water the high tide left between the ramp and the sand. We trooped aboard to renew our acquaintances of the previous evening.

The 938 was beached at Angaur several weeks while the natives dismantled and loaded quonset material and food from the warehouses. The crew seemed to enjoy our small island, and we most certainly enjoyed them. Paced by the jolly Richards they were the happiest crew of sailors we had ever seen, and the best behaved. Henry had had trouble with men from other ships that came to Angaur. Boys came ashore and tried to force themselves on native women, or broke into village homes, and ended up by being restricted to their ships. Even the skipper of one ship was guilty of misbehavior. He brought his crew ashore one night for a party where the natives performed some dances. And as soon as he found out that Henry would not "fix him up," and his fellow officers too, with the native girls, he arose huffily and snapped, "All right men, let's go." This was a behavior we could never understand and one which would not win many friends or constructively influence strangers. If someone came prowling through your back yard at home, walked in your back door, took pictures of your house and family, and grabbed at your daughter, you'd most certainly have him thrown in jail. But, in too many instances, Americans abroad among the natives seem to take such action for granted. So it was a pleasure to have a well behaved group nearby. These men from the LSM worked well together, and, given the initiative to make their own decisions, took pride in their ship and kept an efficient schedule.

Their days with us were not too busy, so they roamed about the island, brought their beer down to our terrace and spent the afternoons swimming, or lolling in the canvas deck chairs. They fed small portions of beer to our two puppies, Rosco and Heathcliff, and studied the canine reactions, oh so scientifically, of course, but with many howls of enjoyment! They dismantled and rebuilt their scooter bike and the ship's jeep a half dozen times, and tried them out on our smooth roads. They reveled in the fresh bread and pastries turned out for them by the old Dutch baker in the Henderson kitchen, and they trooped into the dining hall at the camp to eat the fresh food the construction company somehow always had.

But they had their problems too. The burly old Chief who looked as if he'd been weaned on salt water and Navy beans got beered up with the construction men and unfortunately turned up on duty in that state. He was promptly restricted to the ship.

One noon as we went aboard with the skipper for dinner we walked up the ramp just in time to hear one of the men coo in dulcet tones over the intercom system, "Dinner is now being served on the lower floor for all sailors. All those who wish to join us for dinner, please come below to the dining salon."

A grin split Richard's cubby face from ear to ear; but it disappeared as quickly as it came. "Who said that!" he bellowed, as he strode toward the communications center.

"Well, I fixed his hash, all right!" he said as he joined us a few minutes later in the wardroom. "That kid is going to yell 'Chow down. Chow down' the Navy way for the next thirty days. Jewett, how's about buzzing the galley and telling Spam we're ready for dinner?"

Spam was the colored mess attendant who always stood quietly by during our meals on the ship. Buck Harlan discovered that Spam was from his home state of South Carolina, and asked him every time he saw him when we were going to have "cawn bread and buttermilk, and good old turnip greens."

"When we all get back to Sahth Caalina, Mr. Buck," Spam would laugh back.

One afternoon during their stay Captain Richards came into our house, his face an angry red. With barely a greeting he lowered himself into a chair and rasped,

"Somebody give me a beer. Now I've seen everything! Mygawn, these dumb seamen they give a man nowadays. I walked on to the ship just now and there sat the seaman guard handing his .45 pistol to a Jap who had just come aboard with some repaired jeep parts. I saw red! I grabbed that gun and said to the kid, 'Is this thing loaded?' 'Yessir,' he said, surprised-like. Without reviewing the case I bellowed at him, 'Thirty days restriction and sixty hours extra duty for you! Good god man, don't you know any better than to hand a loaded gun, any gun, to a Jap? You don't ever know what they're going to do! The war ain't over for a lot of these Nips. Now you do some thinking about that kind of stuff!' Oh me! What'll they think up next."

He shook his head, and enjoyed his beer for a minute, and then he grinned at Heinie, "Well, loo-tenant, how's about telling me a sea story?"

"Tell me a sea story." That was Richard's byline. Whenever a lull came in the conversation, or the beer cans were empty he would lean across the table, and, chuckling from his fat belly to his high hairline, would beg coyly, "Tell me a sea story." He could tell better stories than the rest of us put together, and he would only start a wild round of fabrication so he could go us one better.

Richards was to retire from the Navy in a few more months after thirty years' duty. He knew the Navy through and through and had loved it, especially the submarines in which he had seen duty for most of his career. He was an old Chief Motor Machinist's Mate who had become an officer during the current war, and he knew his business. But when he had reached the top age for submariners he had been moved to an LSM, where he was finishing his Navy days. The "Ms" were poor substitutes for subs to him, but he took his assignment in good faith, and we never heard him gripe about his job except to bemoan a recent cattle run when he'd hauled a whole load of cattle and pigs to one of the islands. Since that time the ship had been bothered by pesky flies that seemed to come out of the steel bulkheads.

The ship's wardroom was always open to us, and we had dinner with the officers almost every other day. We'd invariably find Pleasants or Buck already there screaming over a defeat at Acey Ducey or cribbage, for Richards was a past master at those old Navy games. Or they'd rumble down the ladder just as we finished our canned fruit and coffee. The skipper would have Spam find the boys a chair, ply them with cool drinks and start the ball rolling with, "Tell me a sea story, Pleasants."

The two off duty officers returned our noon visits every afternoon or evening, leaving one aboard as O.D. They came down and swam, lounged lazily reading on the terrace or "sacked out" for a few hours' sleep in our extra bedroom. The two junior officers were a delightful pair. Fortunate victims of an interrupted education late in the war for Navy officer training and a year's cruise, these two young fellows were seeing as much of the world as they could and taking to their diversified jobs of engineering and meal planning under the tutelage of the skilled Richards better than most dry land sailors. Jeff Jewett had been in V12 training at the University of Colorado; and we'd have made money, he and I, if we'd been working all the hours we sat and talked about beautiful Boulder, the University, and Flagstaff mountain. Jeff and Bill Vawter talked about the dates they were going to have when they hit home, and the smooth clothes they'd buy when they got out of these uniforms.

They brought down their food packages from home, and we fared on the caviar, fancy cheese and tinned tamales which a thoughtful mother had packed several months before. There was always an accumulation of ship's officers and Henderson officials for supper; and we would rustle up steak and french fries, or whatever else we could manage on our temperamental stove, plus fresh vegetables, and ice cream contributed by the Henderson men.

At last the deck was loaded with material for Koror, so full there was scarcely room inside the ramp for the jeep and the motor bike. We rolled sleepy-headed out of bed in the dark of early morning to watch her pull away from the beach. The skipper was concerned lest the ship, so heavily loaded, be too securely set in the sand. So we anxiously watched his preparations for departure. The ramp was hauled up, the lines cut away, and true to Richard's efficient form, the 938 slipped immediately away from the beach and straight through the channel entrance. "We'll pull out at 6:40," he'd said the night before. And at 6:43 that morning they cleared the boat basin. All the natives who could muster up a reason to go to Koror had wangled passage on the LSM, for they seldom had a chance to ride anything but the small boats. They had come aboard the night before to curl up on boxes, and they now called and waved to us as they departed, as if we'd never see them again. It was still inky black night, and as soon as the ship was away from the shore we could see only her running lights. But by the time she was out in the stream and headed north toward Koror, fingers of light began to run up in the east; and we watched the 938 roll off our stage just as a golden sunrise burgeoned across the sky. We knew they'd be back in a few weeks; but we had no idea that our next encounter with them was going to be a rugged two days of rough sea riding.

As the departure date for the construction company approached the men had a great deal of time on their hands. They sat around dreaming up things to do, usually mischievous. When they conceived the idea of taking a small boatload of men up to Koror for a sightseeing weekend we fell in with the idea most enthusiastically. Henry had business to attend to at headquarters, and the men hadn't seen any of the northern part of the Palaus.

Buck came down to the house about three times a day to go over the details. "Now, let's see, Mr. Wahl. I just wanted to check over these plans with you. Now, bygod, we're going to have ourselves a time, and nothing's gonna stop us. The cooks are fixing us up enough food for Saturday and Sunday. Now if you'll just loan us this gasoline stove of yours, it'll go on the boat fine. I've checked a cot for every man out of the supply warehouse. You're sure we can stay in that empty quonset?"

Henry assured him that arrangements had been made at Koror for the men to bunk at the BOQ annex, empty at the moment, that they would have a trip around the island and through Malakal Harbor to see the sunken ships, and that they were invited to the Officer's Club for cocktails before dinner on Saturday night.

"Now, by george, that's pretty good planning, I'd say. Oh boy, a wee snort before dinner. We'll have a fine old time. This'll be almost as good as bein' in South Carolina and havin' cawn bread and buttermilk and good ole turnip greens. Now, let's see, I'd better just go over these plans again . . ."

There was enough food loaded on that LCM, the morning of the trip, to take us all the way to San Francisco. Buck had commandeered half the supplies in camp, it seemed . . . roast turkey, roast beef and pork, boiled eggs, bologna, apples, oranges, onions, boxes of bread, butter, coffee, canned juices. It was piled high in the front end of the flat-bottomed landing craft, and we all laughed as we set out that gray Saturday morning about "going on safari, old chappy. Into deepest, darkest Koror, don't y'know. Think you'll bring back an elephant, old boy? Oh rawther! A pink one, I believe! Haw! Jolly fun, what?"

"Now, men," Buck reminded them for the hundredth time, "I don't want you to forget. When we get to Koror, Mr. Wahl's gonna see that we get a ride around the island. We'll move all this stuff into that empty quonset, and we'll eat when we're hungry and drink when we're dry, as they say. Now when we go up to that officers' club before dinner I want you to go slow. I know you ain't had anything to drink for awhile. But we can't drink 'em out of house and home. Now, tomorrow morning we'll take the boat out and have a tour of Malakal Harbor. And after we clean up this food tomorrow noon we'll start back to Angaur at one o'clock. Now, I want every last one of you to be down at that dock at one o'clock, and I'll leave behind any bastard that don't show up."

Most of the men tuned out, for they'd heard this song before. They enjoyed the unusually smooth, leisurely trip to Koror, munching on the ample food, and watching the scenery float past.

When we tied up at Koror shortly after noon, the gray clouds that had shielded the sun all morning were dropping down close to the green hills around us. But the threat of rain was quickly forgotten, for we were next to our old friend, the LSM 938. And sure enough, there was Captain Richards, sitting on the ramp with his chair tilted back against one of the big steel doors, a perfect picture of a man relaxing on his own front porch and watching the world go by.

"Well, well, well," he called, not stirring from his comfortable throne, "I see you southern folks decided to come up north and see the world. Well, see the sights all you want. And when you're done, if you want some real visiting, I'll be right here where you left me. I don't like this island like I do Angaur. You'd better get going, boys, or you'll get rained on!"

The afternoon became grayer and grayer as the men were driven over the bumpy roads to see the old Japanese installations, the piles of bottles near the ruined Japanese brewery, the deserted machine shops, the bombed bridge to Malakal, the old seaplane ramps, and the twisted steel of the hangar ruins.

By the time the truck loads were heading back to their bunkhouse, a steady, sullen rain had begun, whipped up by a gusty wind out of the northeast.

We could hear much gay banter from across the road at the annex where the men were cleaning up to go to the officer's club. We could well guess what they were saying. Who cared about a little old rain when they could sit in the club and guzzle a real whiskey for a change. That rain would sound mighty good on the roof, accompanied by the tinkle of ice in a glass. And in an hour or two it'd be clear again, and maybe they could slip back down the road to where that native restaurant is, and drum up a little trade.

But the rain didn't stop in an hour. It didn't stop all night. By morning the skies had opened and a steady, cold downpour had set in. The construction men slept late, trying to get over the excess of liquid refreshment they'd taken on the night before when there was nothing else to do. The wind rose higher and colder and began to swing around from east to south. Rain misted through the screens of the houses on the hill where we sat listening uneasily to the gusts of wind whipping through the trees. The squalls were so heavy that the bay below us was hidden from view most of the time.

"I dunno," said Cap Hacker, the man who had piloted the LCM on our trip up the day before. "This looks pretty bad. If the wind dies down we may be able to make it home. Buck says we got to get back to get ready for the first plane that's due this weekend. If 'twas me, I'd stay right here." Cap was a perfect picture of a taciturn New Englander, weatherbeaten, wizened, with pale blue, hard eyes. He put on his poncho and stood outside the BOQ annex for a long hour, watching the direction of the rain, and shaking his head.

Henry checked with the radio shack. There was no storm warning from Guam. But the barometer was falling. As he came back up the hill he met Santiago, one of the skilled boatmen. "Santiago, how long you think this storm last? You think we can go home today?"

"Mmm, I don't know. Maybe two, three days, Mr. Wahl. This not so good, this storm." He squinted a practiced eye at the misty bay, and at the trees bent before the wind, which by now was from the southwest. "Yess, I think two, three days."

At noon, however, the rain slowed to a drizzle, and the wind died down. Sudden activity was begun in the annex. Buck came splashing across to the Pipers, where we were staying, with a big box of fruit juices, bread, and onions.

"We're gettin' ready to go, Mr. Wahl. Couple of my boys are too damn sick to stick around any longer. So we figure we'd better get them started home. God, but they've got hangovers. I guess it's all those pork sandwiches they ate after their drinkin' last night. The doc had to come up and give 'em some pills awhile ago."

"You think we ought to risk it, Buck? This may only be a lull in the storm."

"Well, that's what Richards, down on the 938, says, but I figure we can make a run for it. Oh, Mrs. Piper figured you could use some of this food we didn't eat. No use taking it back with us. It'll just get wet in this rainy weather." He sloshed out into the muddy road again, and we could see him taking another box of food up the road to one of the couples he'd visited the night before.

It was nearly two-thirty by the time the sodden, sickly crowd had gathered at the dock. A couple of them had to stop by the 938 to tell their old chum, Richards, goodbye, and the ones who were sickest were brought down last to avoid a long wait in the wet boat. The tarpaulin that had covered the LCM had become so heavy with rain during the night that it had split down the middle. Pulled back across as smoothly as possible, it still left large gaps where water would come in.

The rain had begun again. Cap Hacker paced up and down the pier, his eyes squinted into a thin line, his mouth clamped on a wet cigarette. He muttered swear words to himself in a stream, and every few minutes raised his voice to yell angrily, "Goddam it, let's GO! We'll never make it home before dark if we don't GO!"

Two of the men had cached a bottle of liquor among their things, and now were roaring drunk. They staggered onto the slippery, oily deck of the boat, and had to be caught before they slipped over the side. Finally everyone was aboard, and we eased out into the bay. Henry was extremely nervous. He took off his glasses and put them in his shirt pocket for safety, and then buttoned his poncho and pulled his helmet tightly down on his head. His eyes jumped from man to man, watching the two rambunctious ones, trying to figure out what Hacker was thinking as he grimly wheeled the boat through the channel, watching the flapping tarpaulins over the forward end of the craft.

I stayed with him on the small deck for fifteen minutes, leaning into the wind, wiping the salt spray off my face, and hanging on to the wheel house as tightly as I could. The flat bottomed boat spanked through the water, fighting to make headway. The exhaust was muffled as the waves came above its outlet, and then it sputtered loudly when the boat lifted nearly out of the water. Soon I decided I'd only wear myself out on the deck. And the men with hangovers were seasick before we were a hundred yards out of the boat basin; so the deck was a most unpleasant place to be. I tried to settle down among the baggage on the bottom of the boat where Amanya, and several native men sat frightened. Here we could see nothing, but could feel the rude shocks the boat took every time it hit another wave. The tarpaulin flapped with every bump of the boat, letting chilling spurts of water in on us at regular intervals. It poured down the back of our necks and got in our faces. The native men climbed on the front of the boat, hooked a leg over the edge, and hung precariously by their knees while they tried to tie the tarp more securely; but it kept slipping out of their hands.

We huddled close together and tried to shut out the sound of the wind, and the bucking boat, and the horrible off-key singing of the two drunks. After almost an hour of fighting into the wind the men on the deck began to talk excitedly. A couple of the natives were called up to the wheel house. I was curious and uneasy enough that I moved up where I could hear them and see how we were getting along.

When I got my bearings I gasped. We had gone only a little more than a mile in all that hour of bouncing and bucking. Now the square nosed craft wouldn't turn into the southwest wind around the channel buoys. It shook and stamped like a horse refusing a jump.

Henry looked grim as he shouted to the natives and to Cap, "Joseph, you think we had better turn back?"

Joseph didn't hesitate in his reply. He knew every reef and every wind in the Palaus, and he yelled his answer above the increasing wind and rain." Yes, Mr. Wahl! We *must* go back!"

Cap only nodded his head in answer to the same question. He was using every ounce of his strength to keep the boat under control.

"Then we go back. Couldn't make the boat channel by dark at this rate. We'd never get across those ten miles of open sea from there to Angaur. Better go back than have to beach on one of those deserted islands along the way." Henry seemed relieved already. And even Buck, who had hoped till the last that we could make it, was a shade less gray when the decision was made.

The boat swung around, back to the wind, and fairly skimmed back to the Koror boat basin. We were a sodden, exhausted lot, and the bravado of the two drunks had disappeared into green-faced queasiness. The cots were settled again at the annex and the whole lot of men fell quietly to sleep. The food they'd given away was rounded up again, and more coffee was brought from the hill.

Richards sent up bread and meat. Since most of the men had only one set of clothing with them, and no bedding, they slept wet and miserably cold, and were reduced by morning to a bored, shivering group.

Storm warnings were out by Sunday night, and a twenty-four hour radio watch put on for further storm news from Guam. The wind whistled and moaned all night. Puddles of water gathered in all the usually waterproof houses, and the bedding became soggy and cold.

All day Monday, and all day Tuesday it rained, hard gusts of biting rain, driven by a heavy wind. The wind swung back to the southeast, and though it never passed a velocity of forty knots, we weren't sure it wouldn't increase more. They were uneasy days, for there was little to do but watch the barometer and listen to the wind. It's a good thing, we all laughed shakily, that this is where the storms make up. Think what it would be if we were up at Yap or Guam where they really hit. Being this close to the equator we get only the inception of the storms, and not their full force. But whenever another gust rattled the tin roofs we all fell quiet for a few moments.

The LSM, loaded and ready for a field trip to remote Sonsorol and Tobi Islands, didn't budge out of the harbor. The trip was postponed from Monday to Tuesday, and then to Wednesday. The rains slowed late Tuesday, and Captain Richards and Lt. Standish, the station officer in charge of the field trip, decided that even with heavy waters the trip would start, rain or shine, on Wednesday morning. Since they would pass Angaur they consented to take us all home, leaving the LCM in which we had come to be brought home later by a native pilot.

Once again we gathered our things together for the trip home. Much relieved at facing the trip on a ship instead of the small boat, we trooped aboard early Wednesday morning. The sky was overcast and still brooding, but what did we care, we would be home in five or six hours, the time it took the LSM to thread through the narrow barrier reefs and run down the west side of the islands.

We had no sooner cleared the reef and hit the open sea than the storm returned, doubled in fury. It was like being lost in a Wyoming blizzard. The spray that blew across the decks might have been stingy, icy snow. The whole world was a gray, howling mass of spray and water.

And the LSM, breadpan that it is, bounced like a cork in the angry waters. The din was constant: engines growled, pushing the boat forward by fits, wind whistled through the conning tower and the ropes, water pinged against the metal of the ship. She would jerk along to the crest of a tremendous wave, poise momentarily, bobbing up and down as if she were getting ready to jump to the top of the next breaker. Then came the lurch forward, the try . . . and the miss. We seemed every time to fall short of the next crest and fall into the trough of the wave, every bulkhead in the ship vibrating, bangle-bangle-bangle-bangle-bung.

Anyone standing must then grab for the nearest solid support, and hang on, knees flexed to take the jolt. Most of the passengers took to their bunks immediately, and scarcely raised their heads except to be seasick.

Twenty-eight hours we were at sea, not five or six! We came banging down the west side of the Palaus, visibility zero, steering by compass and radar. Henry tried to forget the rocking boat by manning the radar for Captain Richards. We had been scheduled to pick up English Elliott and some additional supplies for the field trip at Peleliu; but the breakers completely obscured the boat entrance to the harbor when we came close enough to make out the beach.

Dr. Deming, the Navy doctor from Koror on the field trip, took to his bunk early in the day, dragging a galvanized pail as near his side as possible. Henry made the mistake of trying to read a magazine during the morning, and was rocky for half the day. Every bed in the wardroom/bunkroom was full, and the chairs at the table banged and scraped occasionally when someone staggered in to rest a few minutes. Lunch time came and some of us tried to sit at the table and eat. But lunch was stew, highly seasoned hunks of carrots, potatoes, and meat with large blobs of fat attached. The plates went away hardly touched.

All except Richards'. His humor and appetite seemed to improve conversely with the weather. He rocked along the deck, grinning at everyone, greeting the sad-sack construction men. "What's the matter, man? You don't feel so good? Just a little rough, not much of a storm."

He came dripping into the wardroom at chow time, peeled out of his slicker and helmet, and sat down at the head of the table, wiping the salt water from his face. His plate was filled twice, and he cleaned up the other parts of the meal, which none of the rest of us remembered because we didn't even dare to look at them.

But he kept in constant touch with the pilot house and knew exactly the ship's position all day and night. He may have rested for a few hours during the night, but it is doubtful that he slept. He watched the Catholic missionary, a Spanish Jesuit priest, who lay crumpled up against a forward gun tub the whole day, so sick that when night came he called Lt. Standish and said that he had consigned his soul to Heaven, for he knew he would not recover. The Captain watched the weather instruments, and his men, and the Henderson passengers who tried to sleep on tables in the chow hall, on the deck, in the gun tubs, anywhere they could find a little protection from the rain.

We rolled along the west front of Angaur in the mid afternoon when the rain lifted enough for us to see the beach. Our eyes, and a talk with the Henderson radio operator, told us the breakers were entirely too high for a small boat to come out to get us. Captain Richards relayed this to Buck and Henry.

"I think I'll stick around for a couple hours till the tide is mid-high. We might be able to run you in then if the water quiets down a little more. How's that with you?"

That was fine, and our hopes rose. We got our gear together, and then lined the upper deck rails to watch the island first from one side of the ship and then the other as we cruised in circles till late afternoon.

But the high tide was no smoother than the low tide had been, and the ground swells rolled past us and broke with terrific force against the rocky western edge of Angaur, spray rising so high it reached the top of the conveyor belt, sixty feet above the water.

"Sorry folks, we don't go in." Richards called down to us from the conning tower. "We couldn't possibly hold steady through those ground swells. What we're going to do tonight is go over here between Angaur and Peleliu, where there's a reef we can drop our anchor on. Come morning we'll see how she goes. Might as well relax and everybody have some chow."

"Well, dearie, we might as well hunt ourselves a bunk. It looks as if we're going to be rocked to sleep by the waves tonight." Henry joined me, and we watched the beach and our own little quonset disappear as we headed northward toward Peleliu again.

"Are you going to try to eat supper?" he asked as we slipped down the ladder to the wardroom.

"Sure. Why not. I didn't eat much this noon, and I'm pretty hungry now. I've slept enough today that I probably won't want to look at a bunk tonight."

"Say, I don't believe you've been sick, have you? I used to think every time you got queasy on a bus that you'd never make a sailor. But, by golly, you've done all right. 'Youse is a good girl.'"

"I know it," I laughed back. "Just between us I'm darn proud of myself. I really couldn't let myself be sick in front of all these men, could I? But, boy, if I were a sailor, I bet I'd have a tired stomach all the time."

A few hearty souls gathered at the supper table, but most of the crowd took to their bunks again. The food went down in a hurry; everyone seemed determined to get the nourishment from it without seeing it or smelling it. None of us could remember afterward what we had eaten.

The captain sat for a few minutes to chat before going above decks. He was concerned over the large group of construction men who had no place to sleep.

"We could go back to Koror," he said, half to himself. "But I don't see much use in that. Maybe I'll just end up taking you all on the field trip. You'd like to see Sonsorol, wouldn't you, Pleasants?"

"Good god, no! All I want to do is get off this tub. What if the water's still heavy in the morning? What'll we do then? I got work to do, and besides I'll bet those bastards taking care of my pet monkey have teased him silly."

Richards laughed heartily. "Well, nobody's sorrier than I am that we're stuck here. I wanted to get this field trip over with so's I can get back up to Guam. I'm due to go home any day now. And I hate to waste this much fuel. Oh me, so it goes, Meesus Wahl!" His eyes lighted on me, and he used the phonetic title he'd heard Tulop use so often. "Meesus Wahl," he twinkled, leaning toward me, "How's for you telling me a sea story?"

"Well," I began, trying to brace myself against the rocking of the ship, "once upon a time there was a red headed girl who lived far from an ocean. She read a very, very interesting article one day on typhoons, which made the 'eye' of the storm seem a dramatic, romantic experience. And she said to her husband, 'My, that sounds fascinating. Sometime I'd like to see a typhoon.' And then she grew up and came to the Western Pacific. There she found way too much water, and not enough land. And when the winds began to blow in from the ocean against her little house on the beach she clutched her husband and thought, oh dear, if we have to go to the hills, what shall I pack real quickly? The copper and silverware, or Henry's files, or warm clothes? And after being tossed around at sea in a rocky old boat in a storm that didn't even approach a typhoon, she thought again of her wish and . . . well, she changed her mind!"

The captain rocked back in his chair and howled delightedly, his stomach shaking like the proverbial Santa Claus. The rest of the men joined in the general fun, and finally the party broke up in order to get everyone bedded down for the night.

Tied up in about sixty feet of water over the reef between Angaur and Peleliu seemed at first a nice, quiet promise for the night. The rain had slowed to a drizzle, and the winds to a breeze. But the heavy ground swells following the storm gave us a rocky, rolling night. We lay directly in the face of the rollers, which gave us the feeling that an angry, exhausted mother might be rocking the cradle of her obstreperous child. Jerk, roll! . . . yank, push! . . . Jerk, roll! We finally went to sleep, Henry and I, in the upper bunk of the chief's quarters which had been assigned to us. We decided to double up so one more person could have a place to sleep. The bunk was too narrow to accommodate us in straight sleeping fashion, so we curled up, Henry at the foot and I at the head. We spent the night pushing feet out of faces and trying desperately to keep from rolling out of bed. The exhausted construction men slept fitfully wherever they could find a place to land. Those who had been sickest found benches on the deck or curved spots in the life boats, where they could have fresh air and a modicum of comfort.

When we went up on deck at six-thirty it was a clear, calm morning. A roseate gray dawn was breaking, and the air smelled fresh and washed. We made our way up one of the ladders to the forward end of the ship and sat watching the sunrise lighten the dark trees and rocky coast of Angaur. It seemed a peaceful end to the hectic twenty-four hours we had spent since we left Koror.

"Oh, I'll be so glad to get home and get some clean clothes. I feel as if I'd slept in this slack suit for a month." I scratched my legs comfortably where the salt water spray had dried. "Surely we'll be able to land this morning, Heinie. The waters look pretty calm along this coast."

"I don't know about landing. I talked to the skipper while you washed up. He says communication with Angaur says the breakers are still too high to beach."

"Say," I interrupted, "That black, circular front cloud south of us is coming *this* way. I thought it was the storm moving away from us."

"Yep, I'm afraid so. Looks as if we're in for more rain."

We had scarcely spoken before the cloud rolled over Angaur, obscuring it with slanting rain. In a few minutes it was upon us, ruffling up the water and stinging our faces. We hurried below.

Richards was all for going back to Koror this time. But Reed Standish was not to be put off on the field trip. And the Henderson men were getting weary of looking at Angaur and not being there.

Standish joined the group at breakfast. "I can get this crowd ashore, Captain, if you'll let my native men take one of those whaleboats off the ramp. As soon as this squall is over we can take two loads over the side of the ship into the whaleboat, and then row for the north landing beach where the Army made its landing during the war. I'll need a little rowing practice with the natives; but it can be done. Then we can get this damn stalling over with and get on our way."

It was agreed, and while Reed gathered his men together, and got the whaleboat ready to launch, the ship cruised up and down along the north coast of Angaur, figuring the wind and the tide, and contacting the Henderson people on the island to come meet us.

Reed did a really beautiful job of handling the boat and directing our quasi-rescue. The whaleboat was lowered over the ramp, and brought around to the leeward side by the native crew who, after a few minutes' practice, could row well together. Ropes were dropped to secure the boat while half of the construction men climbed carefully over the side and down the ladder.

Just as they were ready to pull away a near catastrophe developed. The painter line caught on a flange of metal on the side of the LSM. This anchored the small boat directly under the engine exhaust outlet of very hot water. All the men scrambled to get away from the scalding water, yelling and swearing. This brought the ocean pouring into the other side of the boat, and she nearly swamped. The panic lasted possibly thirty seconds, and then Red Mills managed to get his knife out and reach under water, wrist watch and all, to cut the line,

They rode free then. But we had drifted nearly a mile during the loading and detaching of the boat. So they had a long, miserable pull to the beach. By this time most of the workers and natives on Angaur had rushed to the north beach to watch the rescue. There were men to take the lines of the boat when it came alongside a natural rock landing, so they didn't have to beach the boat in the sand.

Soon Lt. Standish was back with his native crew, and the rest of us donned oily, dirty life jackets and gripped the rope ladder tightly while we swung awkwardly down to the boat. It was a long jump from the ladder to the heaving boat, and I hung fearfully over it, waiting for the two craft to coincide their rocking.

"Jump!" yelled Standish, holding out his hands to me. I took a deep breath and leaped down into the boat. I landed right in the lap of Chief Uherbalau, who had preceded me, and we both laughed shakily.

The LSM had sat in closer to the beach this time, and she towed us even nearer till the tow line broke and we were on our own. Reed immediately took the tiller, and started yelling to his crew. "SRO-ose, SRO-ose," he called, all the way in, pacing his oarsmen.

We were gratefully pulled ashore to the midst of a chattering group of natives and construction men. They took our gear and hurried to the jeeps, and we started to follow.

One step, two steps, whang, bang! I seemed to be falling. The ground rocked up to meet my feet, jolting me at every step. I looked at Henry for an explanation and found that he had the same cross-eyed look that I was feeling. We were land sick! Sicker and rockier than we'd been on the LSM during any of those wretched, wet, stormy twenty-eight hours on our way home from Koror.

He took my arm. "And you were the little girl," he laughed as we staggered together toward our jeep, "who wanted to see a typhoon!"

CHAPTER TWELVE

In Tropical Climes There Are Certain Times of Day...

The village of Angaur, during the middle of the day, was like all the sleepy villages of the world. Under the biting rays of the sun the coral burned blindingly against unshaded eyes. Dust rose in the footsteps of the children who jogged home from school. Chickens scratching in the dirt, and dogs seeking the shade became languid. Through the warmest hours, and into the afternoon a few of the old gaffers could always be found in the shade of the boathouse talking and sharing their betel nut or napping by their outrigger canoes. One of the most delightful sights was Antibus balanced on his back on the narrow outrigger part of his boat, reading a Honolulu Japanese language newspaper.

This was the hour of the day when Henry and Tulop, released from their usual busy demands in the village, sat comfortably under the banyan tree in the back yard talking over the day's problems and searching into each other's philosophy. Here it was that Henry learned much about the Palauan society, its history, and its philosophy. And Tulop drew his information about America, and, more important, about M.G.'s and Henry's plans for Angaur, which he passed along to his people.

They discussed, for instance, the eating habits of the Palauans. The feast fare which we saw occasionally was, of course, extra special. The lobster, crab, fried chicken, and smoked fish; all the forms of tapioca from glutenous "tapioca bananas" through large stick balls to sweet, crisp julienne strips fried in coconut oil; the starchy taro slices; and bananas, oranges, soursop, papaya, and

IN TROPICAL CLIMES...

A native outrigger canoe

pineapple . . . this wide variation could hardly be expected to show up on the every-day diet. Since we saw little of the inside of the native homes or cook shacks, we turned to Tulop for information. Two meals a day seemed the customary habit. At noon, after the morning's work, they ate smoke fish, taro, maybe a little tapioca or a fresh banana. They ate no breakfast, but often carried a small basket with a little smoked fish, a piece of taro, and a banana to the gardens, or in the canoes, or on the Henderson job. The big meal was in the evening, fairly late, after they had washed and rested, and when coolness slipped over the island. The diet was substantially the same, but in larger quantity and variety in the evening. It was then that the pungent, nostril-tickling smoke wafted up from the cookhouses, the chatter of youngsters quieted, and Mesau, the proud young father, strolled along the beach with his baby son in his arms, watching the spear fishermen in the lagoon.

The native health was excellent, primarily because they kept the village spotlessly clean. Garbage was collected twice weekly, papers burned, and *benjoes* (outdoor toilets) well screened. There was little incidence of tuberculosis or of venereal disease. Colds would reach epidemic proportions whenever they started in the village. Some people laid the excellence of the natives' teeth, and their good health in general, to the presence of phosphate in the drinking water.

From health and food Henry and Tulop might turn to religion for a topic of discussion. We were curious to know something about the reaction of the Palauans to Christianity, and of the native religion *Modekngei* which still was the dominant force in the less sophisticated areas.

Nominally, Angaur was about ninety percent Catholic. But a very small number, perhaps forty-five or fifty, attended church services on Sunday mornings. The Catholics on Angaur had been interested in getting a full-time priest on the island; but since the war was so recently over missionaries were not yet returning to the area. So they had to be satisfied with the circuit rider type of religious leadership. The Jesuit missionary came down from Koror every month or so; and in the meantime Elena led the services. Few marriages were solemnized in church; Henry had seen two such ceremonies. Tulop was evasive about the reasons, but implied that once a couple was married in the church there could be no divorce and that nobody felt sufficiently strong about it to take the irrevocable step. Divorce was certainly possible in the native society, and infidelity had once been a serious charge. The advent of the Americans modified this somewhat, and though there was much promiscuity among the unmarried young people, and no stigma attached to illegitimate children, marriage was monogamous.

Beside the Catholic church, Christianity had been brought to the Palaus by the Lutherans. This church was represented by a German pastor and his wife who had been in the area thirteen years, and had undergone great hardships along with the natives during the war. When asked about the influence of Christianity in the islands, the couple stated that perhaps half the Palauans professed Christianity, and that this group was divided equally among Catholics and Protestants. But of the actual members professing Christianity perhaps half actually were influenced by it in their daily lives. He felt, and we concurred, that the people accepted only those parts of the dogma which they held compatible to their own society, as do all other peoples!

Modekngei, the native religion, means "to join forces" or "bringing them together" as nearly as we could figure out. It centers on Babelthaup, which as yet has felt less of the forces of Western civilization. Formed of a rather complex mixture of nobility, economics, and witchcraft, its proponents were people quite conservative in their way of life and thinking. Though they were not antagonistic toward outsiders they still clung to the principle of Palau for Palauans. The members of the sect seemed to belong to the ruling classes in the various villages. One good advantage in the *Modekngei* system, as seen by Americans, was that a premium was put on virginity up to a certain age. They did not seem to favor a first hand knowledge of the facts of life until girls were in their late teens. But one of their methods to achieve this end was a tiny bag of herbs worn inside the neck of the dress. The sect had its holy men who served as combination medico-ministers, for they set bones, forecast future events, made food offerings, and worked to appease the gods so they would do such things as overcome sterility in women. These few facts were all we were able to learn about *Modekngei;* and since our stay was so short, and our contact with

Johannes and Tumiko are married.

the Babelthaup people so brief, we are reluctant to make statements that might be accepted as authoritative about the sect.

There seemed to be a certain healthy fear of the supernatural. Even Tulop evinced this when he said to Henry one day in some excitement, "Meestahr Wahl, last night at jail, we have ghosts!"

"Ghosts? How do you think that, Tulop?"

"Last night when I go to the jail after eleven o'clock to see if the prisoners are okay we hear very funny noise. Somebody makes steps along the floor from front to back of jail. I shine my flashlight all around, but there is nobody! Everybody is much afraid."

"Maybe a dog ran under the quonset, Tulop, and his tail bumped against the floor."

"No, I see no dog! We hear the noise again. Somebody walks, Meestahr Wahl! Ss-ss, ss-ss, ss-ss, we hear his feet slide on the floor. But there is nobody there. Ah, this is very bad."

"What did you do about it, Tulop?"

"I ran away!"

"You ran away? What about the prisoners?"

"They ran away too!"

The Palau money was another item about which it was difficult to get information or to see. We had heard about the native currency from the time we came to the Palaus; but whenever we professed an interest in it, even to Tulop, we got the manana answer as to when it would be shown. The story came from one source that the bead money originally came from one island at the very north end of the Palau group, where the Portuguese had first landed. The people of Kayangel, the northernmost inhabited island of the group, so the story went, had had all of the money at one time, but had lost it through trading with the other islanders. Joseph, the Angaur storekeeper, told us that the money was so old that no one knew where it had come from.

Our curiosity grew and grew; but the only pieces of money we saw were small turquoise colored beads, or curved pieces of obsidian-like mineral worn singly on a string around the neck of the wives or daughters of the village *rubak*.

IN TROPICAL CLIMES...

"Yes," Tulop would say, "That bead that Mariana wears, that is Palau money." Period! No further explanation. Henry finally realized that the people were undoubtedly afraid to show the money because they felt the Americans with their fondness for souvenirs might induce the people to give up some of their pieces. Accordingly he decided that before we could ever see it we must convince the Angaurese in some subtle way that our only interest was to see and photograph the currency.

Shortly before our departure Tulop announced that Uherbalau would be pleased to show us his Palau money. He readily agreed to our taking pictures. So we lost no time in hurrying to Uherbalau's house for the long-awaited inspection.

Uherbalau brought out a string necklace about fifteen inches long on which were placed curious beads and bits of mineral pierced

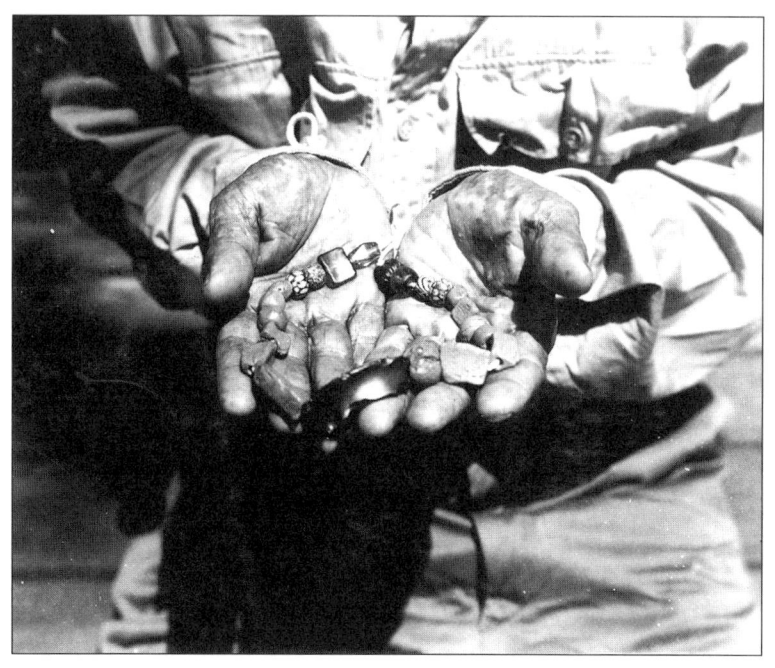

Palau money. Its source is unknown to the people. Its value is hereditary, the pieces are owned only by the Rubak (nobility).

· *183* ·

for stringing. Intrinsically they would be worth little or nothing, but here in our hands we held the wealth and prestige of Angaur. What ever Palauan owned that handful of money would be the Chief of Angaur. The most valuable were saffron-colored clay-like pieces which looked as if they might have been roughly molded into curved, three-sided pieces and baked in a home oven. There were lumpy pieces of turquoise-like rock, the aforementioned black, glassy pieces, bits that might have been broken bottles washed up from the sea and worn smooth by the sand, and the only true beads . . . the Chinese porcelain type with an overlaid design and the turquoise with a silver inlay.

Henry looked at the rather simple construction of the so-called cash and asked what was to keep other people from getting pieces of their own or making pieces just like these.

Tulop translated from Uherbalau that during the Japanese times the Japs had tried to do that very thing, thinking to build a very lucrative trading system. But their plans went awry because they did not know that every piece of the money is known in the Palaus. If Uherbalau has, say, fifteen pieces, and were to get five new ones, they would not count; for the people know all fifteen, and knew, furthermore, that that is all Uherbalau truly represents. So the scarcity created the value in part, and a shipload would not change the present status quo.

The men do not wear the money, only the women, which may be an outward sign of the matrilineal society. As nearly as we could ascertain, through talking with Uherbalau, Tulop, and Joseph, and observing the people, the money was no longer generally used for trading purposes, except in the remoter areas of Babelthaup. It seemed to have reached the heirloom stage, where it represented only prestige and authority.

One generalization that might be made about the native moneys of the Pacific is that its value is directly proportionate to the difficulties attached to its procurement. The Yap money, best known of Pacific monies, and so completely different from the small beads

IN TROPICAL CLIMES...

Chief Uherbalau with his three grandchildren

of Palau money, came from the Palau islands and was transported by native boat to its present home, some two hundred fifty miles away. A natural question is why the Palauans have not used the same huge pierced circles of limestone for their basis of trade. But the Palau money apparently came from elsewhere than the Palaus, accounting partly for its value. The man who learns the whole story behind these native monies will have a real insight into the sociological background of the people.

We saw the string of Palau money only once, and felt greatly privileged at that. But Henry talked many times with Tulop about its value and uses and ownership as they sat under the backyard banyan tree.

Often the men's talk would be punctuated by hilarious laughter which made me so curious I would call to them from the house, "What on earth are you talking about out there? Let me in on the joke!"

"No joke, dear, just man talk. Go 'way woman!" Henry would answer while Tulop giggled.

But later in the day Henry would say, "When you called to us this afternoon we had gotten around to another discussion of sex, and I was recalling the party on Christmas night, before you came. I said to Tulop that it had been a beautiful moonlight night and that I thought it had been a good time for nocturnal celebration and amorous affairs, or as I said to him 'much play and much push.' Tulop said, 'Oh yes, Meestahr Wahl, every time big party with full moon, I think maybe in nine months, seven, eight babies come every time.' But what we were laughing about was what Tulop said to me after the big party. Boy, that was quite a celebration."

Christmas Eve had been blessed with clear skies and a bright moon. All the village had taken on an air of celebration, and the ironwood trees were decorated with many bright strips of cloth tied to the branches. There was feasting, and dancing, and a fair amount of liquor was available. Henry stayed out of the village purposely so the people could enjoy their annual celebration without being hampered by strangers.

At midnight most of the villagers, Henry, and many of the Henderson men gathered at the church for the Christmas service. The entire inside of the church was banked with hundreds of flowers, palm fronds, and ironwood branches. Strips of cloth and paper in many colors were stretched across the ceiling. And Joe Mrar had rigged up a portable light plant to furnish light for the usually dim chapel. The services were handled by Elena. All the familiar Christmas carols were sung. And all the American men so far from home at holiday time were noticeably touched when they came to "Silent Night, Holy Night."

However, Henry saw evidences of a fair amount of liquor, and went home from the services convinced that he had better sleep with his boots on. The services had only deterred the buildup of exuberance. And it was only natural that a certain amount of energy would find its way into less desirable channels before morning. Sure enough, three times during the rest of the night he was called on by householders to put some of the more rambunctious celebrants away until they had cooled off sufficiently not to annoy their neighbors.

Christmas Day was quiet during the sunlit hours; but when evening came, and another bright moonlight night, the feasting and dancing were resumed. This night Henry was afforded a rare privilege in that he was the only American invited to the village party. He was particularly pleased because he felt that it was a sign that his initiation period was over, and that he was on friendly enough ground with the people that he could be a part of some of their social life.

The old plywood hospital wing which was the village *a bai* was as gaily decorated as the rest of the village. Long tables were set out at one end where the delectable seafood, chicken, and fruit were served. Soft drinks were consumed in great amount. Only the first few were chilled, but the folks seemed to like the sweetness of the drinks rather than the coldness for which Americans drink them.

After Mrar played several selections on his harmonica, Singinari and Takase had entertained everyone with their guitars, Cissie sang "Tokyo Musame" and some of the other Japanese songs she liked in her low, vibrant voice. Then the line of girls performed their rhythmic clog step to the tune of "Old Lang Syne," singing nasally, and waving their handkerchiefs as they shuffled off the dancing floor.

Then the dancing began in earnest. One of the young girls took a branch from the table, where it had been used for decoration, and sprang on to the open floor where she began dancing alone. The group began clapping in rhythm and singing, "Ka day kee moh ny, nee mohny, nee mohny, nee day day kee mohny, ne moh ny . . ." (Phonetically spelled as nearly as could be understood.) This was their "man friend and woman friend" dance, as one of the girls translated it, or their dance of love. Springing cat-like nearer and nearer one of the boys, and rocking from side to side on the balls of her feet, the girl used her hands to display the charm she possessed, which would make the boy of her choice want to sleep with her. Both hands placed on one side of her face to pantomime sleeping, moved down, pointing out curvaceous bosoms, slipping seductively over her supple figure. All the while her torso rocked nearer the floor. Suddenly when it seemed she could squat no lower without falling she sprang up and to the side, pointing the branch back and forth in teasing motions, while she began the pantomime of her charms again. The boy joined her and they did the same dance facing each other. Then the branch was passed by the boy to a second girl in the same manner, and so on through the group.

Henry had seen the natives perform a travesty of the dance at parties where many strangers were present. The general form of the dance was followed, but with many catcalls and much raucous laughter. It was the procedure at these parties for the girls to invite one of the Americans to dance by the thrust of her branch in his direction. Then all the Americans hooted and clapped while their confrere took to the floor and attempted the same motions the natives had been dancing. It all looked wonderfully easy from the sidelines; but the American suddenly discovered that his backbone had no give, that he didn't have muscles in any of the right places, and that the swinging, rolling motion was a marvelously intricate pattern. He usually retired as quickly as possible to nurse sore legs, after pushing the branch off on another native girl.

But tonight Henry realized that he was seeing the natural form of the dance, and that he was privileged. The primitive beauty of the natives' wonderful muscular control, and the perfection of their dance movements was a thrilling thing to see. John Telei was sitting nearby, and Henry talked with him about the dance, and asked for a literal translation of the Palauan words. In John's simple explanation the group sang: You come to me, I come to you. We are good friends. Man and woman sleep together. I like to speak to you. I am not too big, not just medium, not too small (here the dancer demonstrates lowering himself over the other person.). Come sing with me. You are a friend (pointing the branch teasingly to some person in the crowd); but I love *you*! (For sleeping purposes, as he points to the final person of his choice).

"John," said Henry. "I think this is very fine dance. Can we get the best man dancer and best woman dancer to do this dance together?"

"I think so, Mr. Wahl. Goro is best man dancer, I think, and maybe Suzana. I speak to them, see if they will dance."

Goro agreed, and watched the dancing until the end of the one in progress. Then he sprang into the circle with a single bound like a great live cat. His black eyes glinted, and his mouth was pursed in a concentrated grin as he moved his head from side to side in the rhythm of the dance. He took the branch, and with lithe hip movements and bounding strides danced over to Suzana, proffering the branch in invitation. The whole crowd gathered in a tight circle around the two, singing the song and keeping time with clapping hands. They sent a number of furtive glances Henry's way to see how he was reacting; but when they were sure he was not laughing at them, or disapproving, they forgot him and were completely caught up in the excitement of the rhythm. Goro and Suzana faced each other and rocked almost to the floor. Up and down their hands moved, along their cheeks, down their torsos, now close to their hips, now extended, palms down as if to balance the rolling, rocking motion of their hips and knees and ankles. Never touching each other they circled and bounded and rocked around the enclosed circle. No one seemed to notice the close press of bodies around the dance floor, or the damp heat in the tight quarters.

When Goro and Suzana had danced for possibly five minutes they retired to the side, giving the floor over to other couples for the finale. Usually only two people danced at one time, changing partners as the dance progressed; but now everyone was excited and happy, and the *bai* was filled with the music and movement of "Ka day kee moh ny."

John came up to Henry during the noise and said, "Mr. Wahl. This the last Ka day kee moh ny tonight. You pick friend for this dance."

"Say again, John. I do not know what you mean."

"This time you dance this dance, Mr. Wahl. You pick friend for dance, and keep for your friend the rest of the night."

Suddenly Henry realized he was a little deeper in this thing than was comfortable, or compatible with his position. He glanced over his shoulder to where John kept pointing. Lined up at one end of the hall were about a dozen unmarried girls in the full bloom of maturity from whom he was expected to choose for the dance and his pleasure for the rest of the night. This called for some lightening fast thinking! His best bet, he figured rapidly, was to play dumb, not to understand the offer.

"Oh, I think I cannot dance so well, John. I like better to see you all dance. Anyway . . . " He glanced at his watch. "I think it is very late. I must go home now. This was Number One party, I think." He backed away as easily as possible, and beat a hasty retreat.

The next morning Tulop came in at the usual time. After passing the amenities of the morning he hesitated for a moment and looked quizzically at Henry.

"Hey, Meestahr Wahl, when your missus come?"

"Oh, I don't know yet, Tulop. Two months, maybe three months. Why?"

Tulop jumped up. "Hey, Meestahr Wahl, one month you be this place now. Two, three months before your wife come. Jeezchrise, Meestahr Wahl! Too long! Tonight I bring you woman!"

Henry broke into laughter and assured Tulop that he could wait, and though it was very kind of Tulop to think of him, Henry could not accept his offer.

The phrase "Jeezchrise, Meestahr Wahl! Too long!" became a classic which could be applied to the period between mail deliveries, or the time since we had had fresh strawberries or lettuce, or any other momentarily lamentable missed item.

CHAPTER THIRTEEN

Mariana

Lt. McDougall gave a long, low wolf whistle and stared over his shoulder as he walked. "Who is that purrity nut brown maiden, Wahl?"

"That," joked Henry, "is my mad money! Now come in the house and have a coke and keep your eyes off our house girl."

"Ye gods, she's one of the prettiest natives I've ever seen. You mean she works for you? I'll bet all the little boys go wild over her."

"I suppose so, but it's kind of hard to tell. She's one of the quietest, shyest girls we've seen around here. She's really a little queen. I've never seen an eighteen year old with such poise and assurance. She doesn't giggle or wriggle the way most of the girls do. And the man of the village seem to listen with respect when she has anything to say." Henry voiced our great enthusiasm and respect for Mariana, who had come to work for us when Cissie departed Angaur. She was all the visiting flight officer said, a lovely, soft brown girl, with wide eyes, a slow smile, and long, straight black hair. The daughter of a *rubak*, she had come home when Henry asked Uherbalau to find someone to do our housework and laundry.

Mariana was so shy that she seldom spoke more than three words at a time to us. She murmured polite good mornings and goodbyes when she came and went each day, and nodded her head and said "yess" with many "ses", as did all the natives, when she was asked to do something, whether she understood or not. But with the natives she was voluble and witty. During the hours when there was no work to do she sat under the banyan tree chattering like mad with some of the inevitable native group that would be there. When she came to us, Tulop explained that Antibus, her father, was pleased to have her work for Mr. Wahl, and that she should learn much English while she was with us.

Accordingly, we arranged a place at the lunch table for her and for several days she ate soup and sandwiches with us at noon while she pointed out various items, using the English words and asking her to give us the Palauan word so that we might learn the native language. She ate slowly and neatly, watched our use of silverware, and repeated the words carefully after us. But on the third day, as we were pumping up the camp stove and getting out the plates for lunch, Mariana stood by the back door for a long minute, screwed up her courage, and managed her first voluntary words to us.

"I go." she said breathlessly, and slipped out the back door and hurried toward her home nearby.

Mariana, our housegirl

"What's the matter, Henry? Do you suppose she doesn't like the work? We haven't done anything wrong, have we?"

"No, I think not, dear. More than likely she doesn't like American food, and is embarrassed to eat with us. I'll ask Tulop after lunch."

Henry was right; Mariana had gone home for taro and fish. She was back almost before we finished lunch, stacking the dishes in the kitchen, and putting a pan of water on the stove to heat. From then on she went home at noon every day.

We gave up the English lessons, too. Mariana was so quiet we could never tell if we were making progress or not. Every time we attempted to learn more Palauan from most of the villagers we ended up teaching them more English. Actually there was little need for speaking Palauan. The Angaur people had learned a great deal of English in the three years of American occupation. They were eager to speak English, and used it whenever possible. So the Palauan words and phrases we used were largely greetings, thankyous, and words applying to local items.

Mariana, as we could see, was a young woman of position in the village. Frequently, when she was in the house, anyone who came hunting Henry would call to her in Palauan, carry on a lengthy conversation, and leave, apparently having gotten the information he needed without seeing Henry.

It took a long time for the villagers to become informal and at ease in my presence. Even Mariana could tease and laugh with Henry, but when I was there they were most proper, polite, and deferential. Eventually we all grew better acquainted, and they took this strange white, light haired woman more for granted. Still Mariana never started a conversation. We learned by accident most of her various abilities.

She could do anything she set her mind to. Henry struggled every morning with the water heater outside the kitchen window. He knelt uncomfortably in the sand adjusting the valves, waited for the fuel to fill the cup, twisted papers and lighted them, and reached in gingerly to light the temperamental burner. Mariana usually stood by while he went through this muttering rite. One morning we had to leave in a hurry to catch the Peleliu tug. While we ate breakfast Henry asked Mariana if she could learn to light the heater.

"Yess," she murmured, and twisted a piece of wax paper into a torch as she went out. She squatted down comfortably in front of the heater, turned one valve, lit the torch and ignited the burner in a matter of seconds.

It was the same with the sewing machine. Tulop had brought his wife's Japanese treadle machine for me to use in making a dress. It took me some time to get used to the heavy needle and rusty works. Mariana watched intently while the pattern was being altered and the dress cut, and while the first seams were laboriously stitched. I carefully explained patterns and pattern cutting, and how I stitched. Mariana came nearer and nearer the machine while I gripped the material and forced it along slowly.

"Mariana, do you think you would like to try to sew this? You see how I do it?"

She looked quizzically at the machine and the material. "Yes, I can do." And she sat down and raced off one neat seam after another, an old hand at the job. It was my turn to be embarrassed.

Her own clothes were well fitted, and always immaculately clean. Like all the other Palauans she wore American style dresses and was most interested in pictures of style, and in pattern books. Whether the Angaur women had worked from paper patterns we did not know. But they made their own clothes with the several Japanese sewing machines in the village, or by hand using heavy thread and long running stitches. On Koror, Marian Christie taught classes in dressmaking and the use of patterns, and saw several of her pupils become excellent practical dressmakers. The women liked bright colors and prints, and used great quantities of the dyes they could buy from USCC. But Mariana, when faced with the choice of materials, always took white. Most of her small wardrobe was of white fabrics, her best clothes adorned with lovely Japanese embroidery or applique, which came from the pre-war days.

The Palauan female form is short and chunky. Few of the girls we saw were fat, but they had little shape at the waistline, and on the average, little bustline. They were strong girls, used to working in the garden and house. They loved fancy shoes, flaunting ornate straps or patent leather sandals whenever they could get them. But even Mariana's shoes were more austere than the other girl's. When she and Ballantina looked at the catalog, laughing and choosing the items they would like, Mariana chose the plain pumps, or the white oxfords. Skittery Ballantina, on the other hand, chose high heels, fancy bows, and bright leathers.

For the Palauan girls to learn to do housework the American way was a sudden changeover from their long established habits. Their own homes were neat and clean by any standard, but they went about their work in a different manner than we. At the same time it took the American women some little time to relax their customs to the easy-going life of the Palaus. Chief point of disagreement was in the use of hot water for dishes and laundry. The native girls ran cold water over dishes, and set them upside down to drain. The Navy wives, schooled in horror of germs of all kinds, and used to scalding water for dishwashing, resisted this as long as possible. Most of us finally gave in gracefully on the washing part, but tried to insist on scalding the dishes before wiping. Clothes were handled much the same way. It may have been a shortage of fresh water that made the girls wet the clothes thoroughly in cold water, rub with bar soap, and scrub as clean as possible; but the American method of plenty of hot, sudsy water was a better spot remover.

Any of us who had been persnickety housekeepers at home began to modify our ideas. The tropical relaxation and lassitude soon became a part of us. There was casual living in houses that were half screens; and other things assumed greater importance than sheets folded just so, or dustless corners, or spotless picture frames. Pictures, for that matter, were both unimportant and out of place on a curved quonset wall. The never to be forgotten sunsets, the drives through the jungle growth to watch the white herons and the monkeys, the headlong dash to the airstrip to meet surprise visitors: these were the important items on the day's program. Each of us learned when our girls were absent for a day or two that sweeping an eighty foot quonset, or washing yesterday's pile of soiled clothing was an enervating, perspiration-producing task that left us little pep for the rest of the day. And our respect for our housegirls grew by leaps and bounds.

According to Tulop, Mariana was going to be married soon. Never a word of this did we hear from her, nor did we ever see her alone with Matthias, the fine young chap to whom she was engaged. When they came to the Sunday evening parties they paid absolutely no attention to each other; and at village parties or gatherings Mariana was always with the girls and Matthias with the young men. We hunted out some lengths of material and some extra shoes to give Mariana for her trousseau, and received her usual pleased, quiet thanks. We envisioned a dress-up wedding as Fumiko and Johannes had, one at which we could more or less sponsor our favorite girl.

Fumiko was a gay, giggly girl of twenty, one of the happiest in the village. She and Johannes had dressed up within an inch of their lives for their wedding reception, which some of the Pomeroy men and we attended. In the Japanese style she wore a long white silk dress, and a veil with a headband of traditional pearlized orange blossoms. Little Fumiko, whose arms and legs seemed stunted, possibly from malnutrition during the war, wore a gold and lacquer necklace and earrings, a large costume jewelry ring, and a great deal of rouge and lipstick. And the fanciest Stateside patent leather shoes Angaur had ever seen, with high heels and straps around the ankles! These were borrowed from Kasau, whose prowess with the Henderson men was well known. Fumiko and Johannes each wore a large lavender silk artificial flower on their left shoulders. Johannes' suit was undoubtedly one of the few complete suits in the village, and obviously not his, for the sleeves stopped some six inches above his wrists. But he suffered in silence like any noble bridegroom.

None of us saw the actual wedding ceremony, if there was such. General custom was for the bride and groom and their families to hold a conference with the village chief, stating that they wished to be married. The chief would voice his approval, and discuss with the parents the proper bride price. This sum of money or valuables was paid by the groom to the bride's family, and was evaluated by the prestige of his family and of her family. If the marriage should fail, so said custom, by some fault of the bride, the groom's money was refunded. But if it should be his fault he forfeited the sum.

It seemed apparent that appearing before the village group as a couple was a part of the ceremony, for Johannes and Fumiko sat absolutely quiet for several hours at the head table in the village community house, their parents on either side of them, while the rest of the crowd laughed and ate and danced. Buck had insisted on furnishing an American supper for the villagers in honor of the occasion, and proceeded in his usual bull-like manner to run the affair, growing impatient when the easy going natives did not hurry fast enough to suit him. Strangest part of the feast was that the natives ate the American food, and the Americans sat down to a feast of native lobster and crab, far superior to the spaghetti on most of the plates.

After all this fanfare the marriage lasted only a month. We heard rumors among the young natives that fiery Fumiko had charmed Johannes into marriage just to prove she could get a man. Johannes was accepted by the USCC as a member of a group of native on-the-job trainees, and sailed off to Guam. And Fumiko was soon very ill and was sent up to the hospital at Koror on an emergency boat run. It was clear that she had produced an abortion by the native method, using an herb which Tulop described to us, but which we never saw. Fumiko was soon her gay, foolish self again, going to the gardens with the young girls, and laughing and singing "Little Mohee" at the Sunday evening parties.

This sort of behavior did not appeal to Mariana, it was easily seen, for she was seen less often with Fumiko nowadays. And we knew her marriage would be of a different sort, for she was carefully brought up and a devout Catholic. When Tulop first told us of Mariana's approaching marriage, it was to ask Henry for a pass for her to go to Koror to talk with the priest. We thought the marriage would take place as soon as Father John made his next visit to Angaur. But that visit came and went, and the next, and still there were no nuptials.

Then we learned that the villagers thought only single girls should work for the Americans, and that Mariana had decided she should not marry until we left Angaur. And though she was assured that it made no difference to us, and that we wanted her to go ahead with her plans, she only smiled and said to Henry, "No, Mr. Wahl. I stay here."

So she continued to run our house, to iron our clothes neatly, to clean the yard, hold the foolish dog so he wouldn't run after the jeep, and to play her part as a young woman of consequence in the village. At the village parties it was Mariana who stood in the middle of the line of dancing girls, called the name of the next dance, and counted cadence for the beginning. While the rest of the girls tugged at their skirts, and giggled nervously, Mariana looked them up and down calmly, smiling to herself, and waited till they were ready to begin. Tapping her right food, she counted, "One, two, three, four." Then Joe Mrar began the harmonica music. Her dancing was graceful but reserved; and though some of the other girls put more into their clog and shuffle steps to give a more rhythmic effect, none of them executed the steps and turns any better than Mariana.

Mariana rode to the post office at the Henderson camp the morning that fourteen boxes arrived from Uncle Bill and Aunt Pearl at home. She sat wedged in the back of the jeep with the packages and studied them curiously all the way back to the house. But she was too polite to ask questions.

Henry explained as we carted them in the house. "The packages come from my aunt and uncle, Mariana. Their church said to me, 'We want to do something for Angaur people. What would be best?' I said to them that Angaur people need many things hard to get . . . clothes, shoes, reading glasses.

"So my aunt and uncle have a big meeting at their church, and all the people bring something they think Angaur people will like. Now the packages are here, and we must find the best way for the men and women to get these things. I will go talk to Uherbalau. You and Mrs. Wahl unpack the boxes and put men's clothes in one pile, women's in one, children's...you know what I mean, Mariana?"

"Yess." She nodded, and began untying the cord on the first box. She squatted on the floor, going through the contents of each box carefully and with obvious enjoyment. Each dress was held up and appraised fore and aft, the material felt, and the size noted.

She lingered over the children's clothes, smiling at a tiny

A rare sight was the dance done by the older women.

beruffled pinafore, and carefully folding several new two-tone boy's cotton suits. Angaurese children wore few, if any, clothes in their early days, and graduated to trunks, tied with cord over match-thin hips, or short shifts hanging from the shoulders. Little effort seemed to be made by the mothers to keep the small fry dressed . . . for common sense reasons. Nevertheless the mothers loved to look at pictures of children's clothes. Whenever they came to the house they asked for the pattern book. Tarrying only briefly over their own size, they turned to the children's section. Mariana's pleasure over the contents of the packages would be shared by her friends.

The clothing lay stacked on the floor in the corner of the living room for several days while arrangements were being made for its disposition. Everyone who came into the room veered to that corner, where he looked through one or two stacks before he could keep his mind on the business of the moment.

It was decided that the garments should be given according to need, beginning with the oldest people in the village, who had no way of earning money or able relatives to provide such things, and working down through the families to the young people who had jobs either with Henderson or M.G. Accordingly Tulop and Joseph compiled the list to be used and passed the word around that everyone should gather at the Wahl's house at nine o'clock the next morning to choose the items they wanted.

By eight o'clock all the youngsters on Angaur were in the back yard, on the terrace playing ping pong, and cavorting on the sandy beach in front of the house. A half an hour later the adults had gathered, sitting in groups under the trees, holding the smallest babies, chewing betel nut, and visiting with their friends. By the appointed hour everyone in the village except the ones who worked for Henderson was waiting in our yard. There were older women we seldom, if ever, saw, for they stayed close by their homes. Even the middle aged women, who spent so much time in the gardens, were near strangers. We felt that we knew most of the villagers; but seeing them all together made us realize that our association was with only that minority which were leaders, and the men at that.

Under Mariana's direction the men laid papers on the sloping approach to the garage and carried out the piles of clothing and shoes, placing them carefully in order: women's, children's, men's items, shoes behind the stacks. Immediately the children surged in close, peering around the adults, between their legs, clambering up on the jeeps in the garage to get a clearer view from above. No manner of warnings from the adults could keep the curious kiddies away. They pointed out the gayest colored dresses, and the patent leather shoes, and laughed and called to each other about what they would choose if given a chance.

Uherbalau quieted the crowd to make his official speech of thanks for the gifts. "This day we are very happy," he began. "Mr. and Mrs. Wahl maybe two months ago write letter to their home that because of the war Angaur people do not have much clothes. When their relatives hear of this thing they say, 'We are Christians; Angaur people are Christians. Therefore the people of our village should gather clothing and send to Angaur Christians who have not yet much clothing.' These relatives of Mr. and Mrs. Wahl are Number One in their village and can do this thing. Uherbalau speaks for all the people of Angaur and thanks these relatives and their many friends who could make this thing be." He retired to a seat at one side where he remained during the rest of the proceedings with two grandchildren sitting on his knees, the perfect picture of a gentle patriarch.

Tulop and Joseph call the names.

Joseph put on his glasses and unfolded the sheet of paper holding the list of names while Tulop explained how the clothes would be distributed. Then Joseph began calling the names. One by one the women walked to the platform, bent over the piles of clothing, and looked through them until they selected a dress of pattern and size to suit themselves, or a piece of children's clothing. Each selection was accompanied by much chattered coaching from the sidelines. Several of the women passed their piece to a grandmother when they returned to the places, and it was pleasant to see some teenage girls pick a child's suit or dress and present it to a younger member of the family. It seemed a happy, sociable business, though serious, for each person wanted to make the best choice possible for this first new clothing in some time.

The crowd surged closer around the piles of clothing as each name was called, watching closely what each women chose, hoping that the pieces they were eyeing would still be there when their turn came. Except for the fact that only one at a time touched the items, the whole affair took on the look of a bustling bargain sale in the States.

NUMBER ONE PACIFIC ISLAND

When the turn came for the younger women and girls to make their choice they made straight for the dozen or so pairs of shoes. Regardless of size, they took the style they liked, for size trading could go on later. When the last pair was picked up a resigned murmur ran through the crowd.

The men came last. Most of them stood in the open four-jeep garage, back of Tulop and Joseph. Their choices were made in typical male fashion, without much shopping around. The pile of shirts dwindled quickly as each man stepped up, picked up an item, and returned to his place where he held it up for general approval. Beside the shirts there were a few pairs of wash trousers, some underwear, and some T shirts. When shy Santo bent over to make his selection he did it quickly, taking the first white piece of material his hand touched. He retired to his seat on the hood of one of the jeeps where he felt of the soft goods and then held it up to see what it looked like. His private pleasure changed suddenly to wide eyed embarrassment. He crumpled the cloth abruptly between his hands, and tucked it in his shirt as he took a furtive glance around to see if anyone had been watching him. His piece of clothing was an old fashioned, one piece B.V.D., and he had held the split rear right up in front for everyone to see!

"Oh, how dreadful, Henry. Let the poor man choose something else. Look how he's blushing, even under his dark skin."

Henry whispered that someone in the family would use the cloth to make a suit for the baby, or some other useful item, but that Santos wouldn't trade, once he had taken his choice.

We moved among the villagers, taking pictures of the occasion. There was wiry, ancient Takahashi, the Japanese woodcutter, strolling about the grounds carrying his granddaughter piggy-back. She wore her

Takahashi and his granddaughter

· 202 ·

best red velvet dress and carried a tiny Japanese doll. Dainty, two-year-old Tina sat shyly by her mother playing with a doll that was larger than she. The doll was of stuffed cotton, with a flat painted face whose features were worn dim with a good many years of use by other little girls.

Two small boys, the Pacific version of Penrod and Sam, lounged against the posts of the garage, slingshots dangling from their dirty paws. Their noses were runny, their bare feet sandy; and they hitched their loose trousers over nonexistent hips from time to time. They were curious about the events of the morning, but were keeping weather eyes out for fat green lizards. Tomas, the fisherman, knelt with his grandson to keep the boy from being frightened while their pictures were taken. The wide red mouth with its betel-nut blackened teeth, and the tiny trembling lips that finally parted for a brief toothless grin made an excellent contrast in the picture.

Finally the last name was called and the villagers rose to murmur thankyous and drift off to their own homes, and back to work in the gardens. The holiday spirit persisted even though it was only mid-morning of a week day.

Tulop and Mariana gathered up the few items that had not been chosen and took them back into the house. One or two worn and mended dresses remained, some hosiery and several brassieres which the native did not use. It must be added that the bras fit the wife of the M.G. representative, who was made happy by the package from Aunt Pearl and Uncle Bill.

"Well, they all had a fine time and chose very well," Henry commented after the crowd had gone. "You'll notice that with the exception of blushing Santos, the folks took only those items which they could use. I'm grateful there were so few things they didn't want. This is like any other kind of commodity the Palauans see. By golly, if they don't want it, you can't give it to them. And that's a good thing to remember in this kind of work."

CHAPTER FOURTEEN

Dog Days

Rosco was a problem child. A gangling, lovable rascal, but just a shade *non compos mentis*. His mother was a moron of the canine world, and half blind. Although she passed along to her first litter of eight the handsomeness of her pointer background, she also gave them more dominantly her vagueness and myopic vision. Rosco became ours through the process of elimination. Six of the family had been chosen by various natives and construction men for pets, leaving us brown and tan Heathcliff, who was an utter dumbbell, and bouncing black and white Rosco. We preferred handsome Heathcliff; but we gave up any hope of his even coming in out of the rain and passed him on to one of the men. Rosco we took into our family and affections, and though our peace was limited thereafter, we had days filled with laughter.

His chief accomplishments were sleeping on his back on the best davenport (feet straight up in the air) and his method of getting into a jeep. When he was six months old, and the size of a half grown horse, he still could not climb in the vehicle by himself. He had tried, it's true, but his one and only attempt to leap up on the seat had ended so ignominiously that never again did he make the effort. The puppy came bounding out of the house that morning in his best Disney form. Long floating leaps through the air, tongue lolling out, a happy smile stretching back to his flapping ears foretold the pleasure of a jeep ride.

"Hurry up Rosco. We can't wait. The plane will be down before we can get to the strip!" Heinie impatiently raced the motor.

Rosco made one long leap toward the front seat . . . and accordion-pleated himself into the side of the jeep. He bounced a full three feet onto his back, and skidded to a stop in the coral. It didn't seem to phase him, but from that moment on he had to be lifted into the jeep. That was all very well for him, but as he grew bigger and clumsier it was next to impossible for us. So we developed an ingenious method of leverage with which he cooperated to the full. He braced his forelegs against the side of the jeep and stiffened his neck and back. One of us then put a firm hand on the scruff of his neck and, using his paws for a fulcrum, teetered him into the jeep head first. There he sat proudly . . . tail wagging in our faces, until we banished him to the back seat.

Rosco was a one-man dog . . . -woman it would be better said. After Henry disciplined him once for making a puddle on the living room floor, the dog would have nothing to do with his so-called master. The fact that I gave him his food, a lot of sweet talk, and lifts into the jeep gave him a mother complex. Whenever Henry asked him to do something simple, like, "get out of here, you dull wad," Rosco would return the compliment with a disdainful toss of the head, and with tail wagging would come trotting to his mistress.

Rosco's existence centered around the jeep. It was at once his joy and his affliction. At an early age he suffered several falls from the moving jeep because he defied the laws of gravity to watch the wheels turning. He would be there in the back seat, leaning as far out as his short legs could push him, small puppy ears waving in the wind. And in another second the back seat would be empty. However many were his falls they never seemed to discourage him. He only developed, as he matured, an insatiable curiosity over passing trees and animals.

The day's greatest joy was to go riding through the jungle undergrowth at the north end of the island. Here the branches encroached on the road until they flipped into the passing jeep. Henry and I huddled toward the center of the front seat to avoid their wet, spider-webbed snap in our faces. But Rosco defied them ecstatically. He stood panting in the back seat, ready to leap from one side to the other, to snap at a passing branch. Keeping a weather eye ahead to see from which side the branches would attack him next, he growled and gruffed as he tried to bite off the menacing branch and pull it into the seat with him. Usually he caught only leaves, cobwebs, and spiders, but occasionally he got such a vice-like hold on a heavy branch that he nearly left the jeep with it. At the end of the ride he would be exhausted but happy, surrounded by a seat and floor full of leaves and twigs, and a few telltale leaf feathers sticking to his chops.

Along the abrupt ridge on the northwest corner of Angaur a band of goats lived, an old black, crusty Billy and his harem of some twenty women and kids. They belonged to the villagers, who left them to roam this uninhabited part of the island. The Angaurese milked the herd only when some woman of the village was unable to feed her infant. The goats saw few people and were so shy that the sound of an approaching jeep would sent them skittering across the road into the underbrush. Rosco had never seen the goats until one of our morning rides. As we topped a rise several of the herd trotted across in front of us, hurrying to hiding places. Rosco gave a delighted yip and took point, ears and tails at full attention. Suddenly he took off from the moving jeep in a long graceful arc, a hunter's bark forming as he flew. That bark was jerked from him in an agonized yelp, for Rosco suddenly "bit the dust." Head first he hit the rocks, tilted sharply up on his neck, and snapped over on his back.

Henry stopped the jeep so suddenly we nearly went through the windshield. "Migosh, he's killed!" he gasped. We started to back up to his aid. But before we got to him Rosco staggered to his feet. He stood unsteadily, spitting out bits of coral dust, working his tongue in and out to clean it of the dirt, and moving his head from side to side to see if it was still attached. He stood uncertainly a moment before he saw us. Without one look in the direction the goats had disappeared he limped slowly back to Henry's side of the jeep. He looked up at Henry, eyes wide and puzzled, and he half lifted one paw in a gesture of begging to be lifted in. A more nonplussed dog never lived. All the rest of the ride he ignored the flapping branches. He lay on the back cushions, shaking his head thoughtfully as if to say, "Whatever those animals were, they carried an awful wallop! I wonder what hit me?"

Someone in our family hadn't been able to say "fierce" when she was a child, and had transposed it to "fearus". That is the kind of watch dog Rosco was, fear-us! He could smell any crab at fifty paces, and growl, yip, and scratch at the offender till we came to see. Most of this business was carried on under the house, which rested on twelve inch coconut logs. And most of it came at odd hours of the night . . . muffled, frenzied barkings, followed by spurts of digging, which spattered sand against the underside of the floor, continuing until we stamped on the floor above Rosco's head or called him from the chase and shut him in the house. Not even a crab's claw clamped in his muzzle deterred him. But any person or animal could prowl around or into the house and Rosco was nowhere to be seen. Even his fellow dogs baffled him.

He approached any other dog with bouncing assurance, usually knocking the acquaintance over in his enthusiasm. But one wuff or growl from the other dog sent Rosco rolling on his back in abject terror, all four feet trembling and drooping over his prostrate form.

The greatest sport among the village youngsters was hunting wild cats or chickens with their bands of dogs. So popular did the sport become that Tulop came to Henry to say that many of the small boys were not attending school regularly. A checkup on the truants found them in the Henderson camp lassoing dogs cowboy style to take home for their hunts.

A cat game surged around our house one fine morning leaving us limp with laughter, and Rosco dizzy with confusion. We were suddenly assailed with a wild chorus or cries and barkings. Past the house ran fifteen or so small boys ranging in age from four to ten. Most of them were barefoot, garbed in loose hand-me-down shorts. Some of the smaller youngsters were in their birthday suits. The bigger boys were dragged along at the end of the rope leashes, their hounds straining after one small yellow and white bobtail cat that dashed under the garage.

All the dogs stuck their heads under the garage and barked wildly. The boys presented a row of brown bottoms to our view while they knelt and called excitedly, "Poos, poos, poos! Come poos!"

While they urged the dogs on, the cat escaped from the far side of the garage and, ears flattened against her head, raced past the house. Rosco finally discovered some excitement going on outside and trotted merrily out to join the fun. .Just as this point one of the youngsters saw the disappearing cat. He gave a cry, and the whole gang was up and after her. They surged over and around Rosco, leaving him flat on the ground. The big boys jumped over the gasoline drums which edge our terrace and were away. Smaller boys stepped up, aided by the pull of their dogs, and the smallest tots climbed up slowly on hands and knees to follow along. Before they were on their feet, and before Rosco had collected himself again, the tide came rolling back, led by the cat. Under the garage she went, and down went Rosco and the tiny brown boys. The puss finally escaped, and the small boys went off in search of fresher game. But poor, befuddled Rosco staggered back in the house for a long nap.

Napping was his long suit, and he made up for any lost action in his waking hours by the graphic dreams he had while asleep. In pantomime he ran, jumped, barked, and snorted. His tail thumped the davenport, and his tongue lolled out. He seemed to be enjoying himself thoroughly, and he hated to be wakened and ejected from the house, particularly at bedtime on rainy nights. On one of these nights he had lain cosily on the davenport all evening in his favorite pose, all four feet straight up. We had enjoyed him so hugely that we brought out the camera equipment noisily and took pictures of him, never waking him once. When bedtime came Henry called, "Hey, Rosco! Here boy, let's go outside." Rosco didn't stir.

I walked over to the davenport and leaned over him. "Come on, Stupid. It's time for you to go outside."

"Snort!" he answered disdainfully, not moving a foot.

"Listen silly, wake up and get going!"

Rosco rolled over on his side and put one paw over his eyes . . . sound asleep, can't you see . . . no comprende . . . can't hear you!

At that we rolled him bodily off the davenport. He assumed the air of an injured householder being evicted, and slumped out onto the protected terrace, leaving us to enjoy a hearty laugh at his expense.

While Rosco was having his dog days, his owners were struggling over their housekeeping problems, which were many. We frequently muttered about roughing it on a faraway island, because the rusting quonset hut took a great deal of attention to keep it water and mosquito proof, and we had had to scrounge most of our furniture and equipment. Actually we wanted for nothing essential, and were comfortable in the finest sense of the word. There were just the constant annoying little things like the refrigerator's temperament and the trouble with the stoves.

When we first setup housekeeping in February the kitchen was filled by that monstrous field range which leaked gasoline copiously over the floor, and accommodated only five to ten gallon pans. It was obvious we could not cook for two people on that treacherous number.

We began, therefore, to fry our bacon and warm our soups in a large ladle placed precariously over a Number 10 peanut butter tin out in the yard. The tin was filled with sand, which was saturated with gasoline, and fired. A piece of screen was placed over the top and the cooking utensil set thereon. This worked admirably for a few items; but we ate lots of sandwiches in those days, and were grateful that we could fall back on already cooked items we could get from the Henderson mess hall.

After three weeks of that, Henry discovered a Coleman camp stove on Peleliu and arranged a trading deal with its owner. At last we could cook inside, on two burners, too. The fallacy of this method was soon apparent. The stove needed constant pumping to retain enough pressure to make a cooking flame. Accordingly Henry manned the pump, raising heavy callouses on his hands, and I fried or boiled whatever food we were having. Naturally we didn't go into any involved or slow-cooking items, for we would be too weary to eat by the time they were done.

But we ate a larger variety of food now than in the first days. When the LSM came in with Richards we had several people at a time for dinner. They had to wait till the very social hour of eight to eat, because it took us so long to struggle through the meal preparation. The last day Richards was in the house, before he left for Koror, he showed a great deal of interest in our little stove and wanted to know how it worked. So he turned all the valves and screws; and, being a hefty man, he accidentally stripped the threads on the gasoline pressure pump. That was the end of that stove. And though we didn't care much because it was such a tiring nuisance to operate, we were faced again with the problem of cooking.

The Henderson mechanics came to the rescue, as usual. Red Mills dismantled the old field range, finally taking the hulking steel frame out of the kitchen. He worked over the firing unit till it operated quite well, set it up on the kitchen counter, and placed a heavy iron plate over the top as a cooking surface.

This was luxury! We could put on two large pans, and the smaller, flat-bottomed ladle pan at once. Dinner could be served at a more reasonable hour, and the pumping was no longer necessary. But since the stove was fired by gasoline under pressure, and was such a complicated problem to start, we decided it would be wise to start it only when both of us were there, in case it should explode.

When Henry's group of officers came to the Palaus, the first thing they did was order stoves for all the dependent houses yet to be built. The months crept on with no sign of the stoves from Guam. Word seeped down that they had been ordered, that they had been diverted elsewhere, that they were sitting on the dock at Guam rusting out because no shipping orders had been issued, that they were on the way, that they were not on the way . . . all the forms of scuttlebutt possible. Every time an inspection party came down from Guam its members kindly asked what we in the provinces needed, and what they could do for us on Guam. The first cry was, "Stoves! Get us the stoves!" But still they didn't come.

In June when the Henderson company was getting ready to leave Angaur, they hooked up an extra jeep generator in the garage at our house so that we might have lights any time we wished. Along with this loan came a large size two-burner hot plate. With the village lights on only from seven to eleven in the evening, and low powered lights at that, we had never been able to have a hot plate before. This was speedy cooking, and highly efficient. Now that we could run out to the garage, push the button to start the generator motor, and switch the house wiring system over the small generator, we could use the toaster, and make coffee quickly. We took to having coffee and toast in mid morning after the radio check.

This little method of cooking had its trials too. The wiring was cock-eyed, and both burners of the stove plus the toaster in use usually blew a fuse. And with the fuses out and the box turned off we would still get a dim candle glow from every light bulb in the house. About this time Joe Mrar came in from his house at the far end of the village with a problem. "Mr. Wahl! This is very funny thing. Sometimes morning, sometimes noon, light in my house go on. Village dinky is not on, no light in any house. But in my house . . . lights!"

We went over the wiring a dozen times and could find nothing visibly wrong. The only answer seemed to be a ground somewhere in the line that connected up with the village power line.

Through June and July, and part of August we used the hot plate. We could get bread from the construction company bakery until they left, and then from the major's kitchen. We tired a little of fried and pan-broiled meats, but the local fresh fish was delectable. There was always a stalk of small, sweet bananas hanging in the kitchen, and by daily searching we found enough papayas to keep us in fresh fruit. Using all the contents of a Number 10 tin of food was always difficult, but since that was the way in which most canned foods are packed for mess hall use, we had no choice of smaller cans. Consequently we spent a great deal of time shuffling the cans around in the refrigerator, putting the contents in several smaller coffee tins or jars, and finally throwing out a third of a can of, say, beets, or dried out cheese because we couldn't face another meal with the same menu.

Supplemented by the fresh fruits we found on the island, and occasional limes and oranges from Kayangel and Babelthaup, we fared well. But, like all the other Americans in the islands, we sighed now and then over the fresh things we were missing. "Have you heard," someone would say when we spent an evening with friends at Koror, "the next reefer ship is going to bring FRESH tomatoes! And frozen strawberries. And maybe lettuce!" Those items never materialized, but we kept on dreaming. Perhaps the conversation would turn longingly to favorite foods. "What is the first thing you're going to eat when you get home, Heinie?"

"Eat? I'm going to drink! Milk, fresh milk, gallons of it!"

Evelyn would chime in, "I am going to have a cool, crisp lettuce and tomato sandwich. Doesn't that sound heavenly? Cec, what about you?"

"A jumbo-sized fresh strawberry sundae! Henry's folks wrote all during the spring that they were having so many strawberries that they didn't know what to do with them. Breakfast, dinner, and supper . . . strawberries, strawberries. They were so bored with it all. And we drooled over every letter until we could hardly stand it."

And so we went back to our canned vegetables and fruit, with an occasional fresh head of cabbage or a case of old, moldy carrots. We discovered that shredded green papaya was the finest crisp fresh salad imaginable. And we reveled over the few green onions and leaves of lettuce that were coaxed out of the USCC garden at Koror. We supplemented our diet with vitamins every day and added extra amounts of salt to our food. And we all thrived. The American children at Koror were healthy and brown. They drank canned milk or Toddy, ran in the sun, and suffered only from occasional infected mosquito bites or worms, in rare cases. Henry had an occasional fierce headache brought on by too much sun on a boat trip, and I suffered only from sunburn.

In mid August the kerosene stoves came from Guam. There was great rejoicing at Koror, and much ceremony over the first use of the stoves in each house. The news trickled down to us on Angaur, and we hastened to Koror to get our stove.

"Good lord, no," said the supply officer, "there aren't any more stoves. Was your name on the list?"

"No stoves!" I croaked. "That did it! I've burned my fingers and the soup, raised callouses pumping, substituted and done without because there were no stoves. I've waited for the mail, and I've gotten used to cold showers, all without too much complaining. But now I'm mad. There's got to be a stove!"

So we checked through all the warehouses ourselves. The stoves were there, of course. They'd just been moved from the first warehouse to an unused one after the issue to the Koror families.

After that, we concentrated on roasts, biscuits, and baked desserts. One good way to help use a half-gallon can of apricots was to make an upside down cake. We tried jelly rolls, and cakes, which were often quite flat because the baking powder was not much good. But they were tasty treats after the long dry spell. So for the last two months of our stay on Angaur we had a real stove. Without making dinner a collaborative affair, or letting one course cool while the other one cooked, we could have a real meal. And best of all, I think, we could cook in the daytime while Henry was busy without having the noise of the generator drown out all attempts at conversation.

Our electric light business was most involved. Angaur was the only Palau village blessed, if such may be the correct term, with electricity. The generators used by the Army for their hospital area were still in operation when the people moved back into the area. So with their natural mechanical skill and their leaning toward things American, they tried to keep the machines in running order. There were no spare parts, and the machines were gradually wearing out. The running hours had to be decreased, and the machines tinkered with more and more. By the time we got to the island the lights were on only from seven to eleven in the evening. From seven to eleven every bulb in every house burned; the people never switched their lights off. If they wanted to sleep during this time they did so with the lights shining in their faces. A full load was thus carried on the generators, and the use of any additional equipment, say an iron, dimmed all the lights appreciably. Often the phonograph would not play at full speed, but would whine and groan through a piece of music until it was turned off. Reading was an eye-straining affair when the lights were dim. But for a few days after the dinky had been overhauled the lights would be bright and the power strong.

Knowing that once the lights went out at eleven there would be no light the rest of the night built a psychological fear in my mind during the early days when Angaur was still a little strange to me. Mine was strictly a daytime-electric light bravado. We could sit all evening reading or playing cards, only slightly aware of the surf, the construction camp noises, and the voices of the natives along the beach. But when we got to bed, right by the screen, I suddenly would awaken and hear all manner of strange sounds. The surf would roll in an ever-increasing crescendo, a canvas screen cover would flap raggedly somewhere along the house, and a rat would begin crunching on one of the beams in the bathroom. They conspired against me, timing their noises to catch me just as I let my reserve down and reached that stage of half wakefulness. It wasn't the fear of being attacked in the dark; there were no belligerent Japs on Angaur, and the Angaurese were only curious, never forward. My worst pictures were of the furry spiders falling down on the bed, or the surf rolling into the room, or a rat climbing up to nibble on a toe. I never forgave the construction man who told about waking to find a rat chewing on his thumb nail.

Of course none of these things happened. I was only afraid of being afraid. But the flashlight was always within reach, and some nights was a cramping but comforting bump under the pillow. I was always certain that if anyone appeared at the screen and called to Henry I would jump so high they'd have to pull me down from the overhead. But the few times when Tulop did appear during the night in need of Henry he spoke softly and I was immediately awake and quite calm, trying to waken Henry, the heavy sleeper of the family.

One night, after we had been asleep a short while, there was a stealthy tiptoeing through the house. I wakened in panic and held my breath a moment to find exactly where the tic-tac noise was. My heart gave a tremendous thump when I realized it was right in the bedroom with us. The natives would never think of entering the house. It couldn't be sissy Rosco. I fumbled for the flashlight and threw a beam of light around the room at bed level. No one in sight. I flashed it on the floor and found, frozen in the beam of light, in the dead center of the room, a young land crab, one claw raised in the air ready to tic down for the next step. Where he had come from I never knew . . . nor where he went!

I sat in bed giggling with relief until Henry sleepily demanded to know what in the world possessed me. He roused enough then to see the gray crab standing dead still in the rays of light. We pondered half heartedly how to get rid of the rascal, but we could find no logical means. I wouldn't have picked him up in my hands and risked a cutting clamp from his claws for love or money. There were no shoes near the bed to slip on in order to kick the pest out of the house. So we simplified the solution by lying down, turning off the flashlight, and promptly falling off to sleep again, leaving the lost crab to find his way off the hard plywood floor and back to familiar sand. There was no sign of him in the morning.

Henry sprayed the bedroom with the freon bomb copiously each night just before we went to bed. Thus the mosquitos which pestered him were discouraged, and so were the fuzzy spiders between the plasterboard walls. The "bomb" was part of the regular going-to-bed equipment, along with the flashlight, for Henry often used it three or four times during the night to ward off the mosquitos that ate him alive. They seldom touched me, which made the annoyance even more maddening to him.

"Why those things will fly right over your nice white skin and chew on my tough hide is more than I'll ever know," he'd mutter as he boxed his ears and face against their nocturnal attack. Fortunately the Palau mosquitos were not malarial, so we had only the bites and the scratching to annoy us.

One night just after the lights went out we were puzzled by a steady tap or drip somewhere in the room. As usual we began the process of elimination to determine the cause. It wasn't raining, so there could be no water dripping on the floor. The noise was too regular to be a rat. Finally Henry swung the flashlight beam around the floor till he found a hard shelled brown bug "hopped on" on the freon we had just sprayed in all the corners of the room. He was hopped up in more ways than one, for he was jumping nearly a foot in the air and landing, plog! back on the plywood again.

The rats were always a problem. I had always prided myself that bugs and worms didn't bother me in the true female sense. Even the big spiders soon became only items of interesting speculation. But the rats I never got used to. At the sight of one I would involuntarily emit a cross between a gasp and a gurgle; and Henry claims that I have bested the world's record for the standing backward broad jump on more than one occasion when we were trying to corner one of the beasts. I did manage to overcome my fear enough to bait traps and to chase rats with a broom when the case demanded; but they still sent a chill up my arms and back.

The rats were kept at a minimum on Angaur because the village was very clean and the construction men kept their traps set. We seemed to have epidemics of them, catching half a dozen in two or three days, and then having no trouble for some weeks until a new litter came along. At our house they lived between the flat roofing and the ceiling of the bathroom, a spot from which we could never clean them out. They ran along the inside of the quonset roof to the kitchen where they skittered down the beams to find any open food. We had to keep all our boxes and dishes of food closed tightly. Even then the nuisances managed to gnaw through cardboard boxes on the open shelves. We'd set the traps up high on the beams after boiling them and tying the bait on very securely. Only by keeping human smell off the traps could we be sure the rats would approach the bait. We'd no sooner be in bed then a trap would explode with a loud BLAM! And fall ten feet to the floor. Henry would sigh, put on his slippers, grab the flashlight and go to the kitchen to be sure the rat was dead.

Crrunch . . . scrr-r-ape . . . they'd start gnawing on the overhead beams in the bathroom. A pillow over the ears couldn't drown out the noise. I would grab Henry and beg hysterically that he do something about it. He would bang on the floor a couple times with his shoe, bringing momentary silence. I would try to settle down to recapture sleep. After several months of this behavior I became a hardened character. I could listen to the rasping sound, and then mutter, "Okay for you, buddy. As long as I hear you I know where you are. You'll be in the trap before morning, I'll bet. Now 'sheddup,' so I can go to sleep." Then, paradoxically, I'd carefully tuck my toes under the cover, make sure my hand wasn't hanging over the edge of the bed, and drift off to sleep.

It was amazing what a big, brave girl I could be when someone else was a little more frightened or uncertain than I! Some people who came to Angaur for a few days were terrified by the rats. They stated that if they were living in that house they'd move all the equipment warehouses nearby to get those terrible rats away, never realizing that it was the food in the kitchen the rodents were after. I pooh-poohed all their fears, refraining from telling the story about the fingernails being chewed; and I set and emptied traps blithely as if I were throwing out the garbage. It was something you had to get used to, I reasoned, and there was no sense being hysterical about it.

Unfortunately when the guests went to Koror they spread the story that when they had walked into our house for the first time there was a rat on the table. When the gang found out how worried they had been, loud and luscious conversations were carried on about the horrors of rats. The climax came when Ted, the group's greatest punster, greeted Marian Christie.

"Hi, Marian. Had any trouble with mice in your ice box lately?"

"Mice in the ice box? Good heaven, no!" she said, biting hard. "Have you?"

"Yep. I opened the refrigerator this morning and found a little mouse inside. So I said to him. 'What'n'ell are you doing here?'

'Well, isn't this a Westinghouse?' he asked.

'Yes,' I said.

'Well, then,' he answered, 'I'm just westing!'"

Ordinarily our visitors took a different view of Angaur. For those who came down occasionally from Koror, it was a change of scenery and routine from the headquarter island, and the horrible roads. Angaur was their rest spa of the Palaus, where they could swim from the front terrace, sleep, or read to their heart's content without interruption.

For the three small blonde McCarthy girls, aged four, three, and two, who came with their mother from Koror, it was a strange, happy place where the schoolyard right across the drive was full of swings and teeter totters, and the sandy beach had more shells than they could carry. Dozens of native children hung by the door all day, fascinated with these dainty white children with the fair hair. Kathryn, Carolyn, and Marilyn were carried any place they wanted to go, usually by Palauan youngsters tinier than there were, it seemed. It was a glorious holiday for all.

For us, the visitors who came to Angaur were one of the most memorable parts of our stay. There was someone new almost every week, a fascinating stream of ship captains, army and navy personnel, construction officials, "-ologists" of all kinds. These were the world travelers, a hybrid genus of people who had always wanted to see "the other side of the mountain" and who had stories and philosophies worth listening to. And people asked us how we could stand the lonesomeness of Angaur!

There was the lieutenant colonel who came with an inspection party from Tokyo to look over the phosphate mining. When he walked into our living room, the first thing he spotted was a large calendar with a view of the heart of the campus at Indiana University.

Before we could even be introduced he pointed to the picture.

The crowd that appeared every time the three blonde
little Murphys stepped out of the house.

"My god! This is the last place I ever expected to see that picture! Where did you get it?"

We explained, and said we'd gone to school there, and did he know the place?"

"Know the place! It's my home town!"

"Ours too," we yelled. And we promptly ignored the senior officers of the party to go off into a happy exchange of familiar places and names.

There were Miss Esther and Miss Julia, the two lady geologists who came down from Tokyo too. They studied the formations of the islands, and searched the reef for marine life during the several happy days of their stay. In the evenings Henry took enough practical lessons in geology from Miss Esther to start him off on a new reading hobby.

NUMBER ONE PACIFIC ISLAND

Julia Gardner, a tiny, vital woman, at the age when most women, and men too, retire to a rocking chair by the fire, had found a paradise in the Pacific and was spending happy, exciting days on the reefs, water up to her knees, a tropical helmet on her gray head, adding to her collection of shells and corals. When she had returned to her job at the National Museum, she said, she could dream of the typical tropical island she had found in the Palaus.

Miss Esther Aberdeen more than completed the pair of most interesting conversationalists we had on Angaur. A vigorous, handsome career woman, she worked in khaki trousers, shirt, and heavy boots, right alongside the men of the survey party.

We gave all our guests what we called "the two-dollar tour" of the island: the mining areas, the airstrip, the crumbled Jap lighthouse on the ridge, the village, and the camp, boasting all the while about our fine roads and lack of mud. They saw how difficult the gardening was, and how the area had to be grubbed out of the rocky, tangled sections of undergrowth. They relaxed when they knew there were no malarial mosquitos, no scorpions or centipedes, and no poisonous snakes. We saw only two snakes while we were on Angaur, both medium sized, grayish-brown land snakes. And one of those was in the mouth of a four foot long monitor lizard, its natural enemy. We watched the raucous, blue kingfishers, and the flashy redheaded and breasted honeyeater birds that flashed in and out of the shrubs. When it was a rainy week, with rough waters that precluded any beach activity, we drowsed, and talked, and played double and triple solitaire until we saw the cards in our sleep.

Ned Elliott came down when the house was full of other company. We had looked forward to his visit for months, and had planned every time we went to Koror, all the things we'd do when he came home with us. It was being a hectic, involved week, and we had little time to ourselves. We were at the tag end of the beer supply, too. But we did play the records he'd been waiting to hear, gave him a chance to swim, and waited until late evening to do our visiting. After the lights were out, and everyone else in bed, we'd slip into the living room where Ned was bunking on the davenport, light a candle, divide two beers three ways, and talk in whispers for an hour or so. It gave us such a gay, clandestine feeling that we enjoyed his visit even more.

Scarcely one of our guests failed to react violently to the sound effects which came with our house. We had been scared out of our boots at first, too, when the objects bounced off the tin roof; eventually we paid little attention to them. But just as we were going to sleep one night, there was a rustle-rustle-rustle in the trees above the house. Then suddenly a loud report, as a hard, apparently heavy object crashed against the roof and bounced in flattening arcs to the ground, where it landed with a sandy thud. Henry was up in an instant.

"Good night, somebody's throwing rocks again!" he whispered frenziedly, as he hunted for his shoes and trousers in the dark. "You stay here, and I'll scout around to see if I can find what the trouble is now."

I lay trembling in bed, ears alerted for any sound around the house, certain that the first noise would frighten me out of my skin. I hoped the rustling I heard out in the dark was Henry, but I couldn't see a thing. Then the noise came again . . . rustle-ss-ss-ssss-cr-rash! Bang-bang-bang . . . thud. Even the birds in the tree above the house seemed startled now, for there was a rustling of wings.

Just then Henry whistled at the back door and came into the house chuckling.

"There was another one!" I informed him breathlessly. "What's so funny about it? I was scared silly, and you had the flashlight."

"No rocks, joe," he said. "It's the fruit bats in the big tree above us. They knock loose the seed pods that are ripening and are about the size and hardness of a golf ball. I picked up that last one when it hit the ground. So we don't need to worry, just get used to it."

The visitors reacted just as violently as we had, jumping a foot, and yipping, "What's that!"

"Oh, nothing," we'd assure them blithely, "just the bats in the trees above the house. You'll get used to it too!"

CHAPTER FIFTEEN

Angaur, Here's to You.

Every morning while we were having our fruit juice we could watch the flag raising ceremony in the schoolyard across the drive. Two small boys with the flag and a whistle tramped out to the flag pole, carefully snapped the ensign on the hooks, blew the whistle for attention, and slowly raised the American flag to the top of the pole. The flag detail changed from week to week, all the boys taking turns at raising it in the morning, and lowering it at sundown, long after all the school children had gone home. When the tiniest boys who were assigned the duty came to take down the flag they approached the folding business in a slightly unorthodox, but highly practical manner. The flag was an unusually large one which billowed over the boys' head and arms when they tried to catch it. So each took an end, and they carefully laid it out on the ground. Then they folded it exactly in the proper prescribed fashion.

The flag raising in the morning was the beginning of the day at school. This was followed by a period of ground cleaning, during which all the children manned long, handleless brooms made of the stripped stalks of coconut fronds bundled together. The yard was swept clean, and all new weeds pulled, until the place looked immaculate.

This was the daily program in all the Palau schools. Whether the buildings were quonset huts erected since the war, the bombed out concrete block house buildings of Babelthaup, now patched with tin, or the big school building at Koror which had once been a Japanese hospital, the children were responsible for keeping the grounds and the building clean.

Most of the schools had five grades where the children were taught English, arithmetic, elementary science, a little geography, music, and handicraft. These subjects were taught by natives who had had little training except in the pre-war Japanese schools. But in fourteen schools where the pupils numbered from thirteen to one hundred eight-nine students these teachers did a very creditable job. As the teacher training programs at Koror and at Guam got under way a definite improvement in the teacher caliber became evident. However, in the meantime, there was no lack of zeal among the young men and women who were teaching the children of the various villages. The people who were in charge of the schools had a surprisingly good knowledge of educational procedures; the discipline was superior. They had the mechanics and the goal; we gave them the wherewithal and encouragement needed.

While Gullivert was headmaster at Angaur, he came daily for an English lesson. We were always surprised at the advanced words he was learning so he could teach them to the students. He wrote out ten rather involved sentences such as, "Are you departing the train at the next station?" Or, "I intend to visit my parents in the near future." There was always the Japanese bookish sound to the sentences, showing that they had been taken from some Japanese text. With both Gullivert and his successor, John, the change of pronunciation from the time they learned a word till the time it came out of the mouths of the students was both amazing and delightful. In the National Anthem, they sang of "the twee-light's last gleaming;: and in "America" of "sweet land of lie-bur-tee," or "rocks and riles, pinted hiles, and rapture thriles."

There was much of the Japanese in the schools, and it was slow to leave. There was extreme deference for the teacher, rising and bowing when he came into the room or called on a pupil, the excited cries of "yess, yess" instead of mere hand raising when the teacher wanted an answer to a problem. There was always a lineup outside the school in the morning, with inspection for dirty hands or ears, and for general neatness. Then there were calisthenics, which reminded us of all the newsreels of Japanese schools we had seen in the peaceful years between the wars.

A field day at the Koror school featured many of these calisthenic exercises, plus all the races and competitions we might have seen at a stateside graduation day. There were sprint races by the various age groups, a three-legged race, an exciting race by ten-year-old girls who balanced on their heads tall saki bottles half filled with sand, and then ran around the track. There was a relay in which the youngsters held tall paper dunce caps on their heads, ran the appointed distance, knelt down and crawled between the rungs of a ladder lying on its side, and then raced back. In the funniest relay of all, the youngsters held the open end of a three-foot long dunce cap over their faces, looked through the small hole at the end of the cone to find a volley ball, and then kicked the ball to the end of the course and back. It was side-splitting to watch the youngsters squatting down, peering through a long cone trying to find a volleyball, which was more than likely between the end of the paper and their bodies. They peered all around themselves in circles, bumped into each other, and quite accidentally found the ball now and then.

The last number on the program was executed by a group of older children who sang "Old Folks at Home" in harmony, while a double circle of teen-age girls, all dressed in white, held large white paper rosettes for effect, posed, and danced. It was most effective and graceful.

The Palauans have few natural art forms as we know them. Such artifacts as wooden utensils, combs, implements with shell edges which had been known in the older days had now disappeared, because manufactured items were now obtainable from western economies. The sad thing, we felt, was that the younger people no longer remembered what these old items were like.

One of the two most indigenous art forms of the Palaus is its monkey men. Little statues carved of wood, the grotesque men and women with receding foreheads, strong arms and haunches, and unmistakable sex, were very popular among the souvenir-hunting Americans. Even these were not strictly Palauan, but were made by some of the people of Sonsorol, an island one hundred eighty miles to the south, who were now living in the Palaus.

The other art form is the drawing on the walls of the *bais*, the men's houses of older days, where lusty tales of love, conquest, and history were shown in primitive pictures. A *bais* were passing customs too, so there were few of the pictographs left. And only the older *rubak* could relate the stories . . . if they wanted to. The children copied the same kind of art in simpler story form on packing box boards. Sometimes the story would be very clear: two groups of people, two villages, facing each other across an open stretch of water. Much shaking of spears, and many zig-zags for harsh words told of a very strong fight. Or one small man in an outrigger, wrestling a tremendous fish would tell the story of the biggest fish anyone in the village ever caught. The figures were cut in the board with knives, and the whole picture colored with lime and other naturally made paints.

The people were wonderfully generous with the handicraft items they made. Hardly a week went by that some student or adult did not stop at the house with a purse or a cigarette case as a "presento." Usually they were the pandanus items, but occasionally there would be one woven of extra-quality, fine white strips of the coconut fronds. Gus, the son of Erademel, the Chief of Peleliu, came with an exquisitely done bust of coconut wood, a female with an intricate hairdo, and a necklace of inlaid trocus shell. Another fine item was a large ornamental comb made of tortoise shell, with a catseye set in between my cutout initials, C.W. Whenever there was a special occasion or holiday, or if the chief felt we had done some special thing for Angaur, he would come limping in with many smiles and thanks, and would proffer a newspaper-wrapped salad set, several purses, or an especially large, colorful suitcase type pandanus bag.

The handicraft work which the children did at school was along the line of saleable articles through USCC to the Americans. They stripped the pandanus trees, rolled the fronds, and boiled them.

Then they laid the strips out flat in the school yard to dry. After this, the strips were dyed, usually with American dyes purchased at the village store. Then they were fashioned into table mats, cigarette cases, purses, beach bags, and now and then floor mats. Sometimes a youngster made a belt and cigarette case set with the same pattern woven in. The younger group very seldom did the carving work which the elders sold. The salad sets and model canoes of ironwood needed rather intricate work.

The Japanese had forbidden the teaching of Palauan history and language when they had been in charge of the schools. Consequently many of the old customs and stories had disappeared. Now a Palau background for Palauans was being encouraged again, and the little first, second, and third graders were learning some things about the islands, the vegetables, and their own language.

One note of interest is that there are no Palauan books as such, so far as we know. They apparently had no written language until the colonizing nations came in. The only Palauan booklet of any age was a collection of religious rituals and prayers, which was made during the Spanish time. Because of this lack of written language, or encouragement for it, all their folklore and history was passed on by word of mouth. We were pleased to see several of the folklore tales being put down in English by Rudim, the headmaster at the Koror school. He went to a great deal of effort to get some of the old *rubak* to tell him the stories. This could be the opening step in getting others of the Palau legends and eventually, we hoped, the oral stories to accompany the picture stories from the *bais*. We even offered prizes to the students who could bring in some of the stories; but none came. It was not so much that they were reluctant to tell the stories, we felt, but that there was such an effort involved to write them in Palauan, then Japanese, and then to translate them to English.

Here are the three stories we got from Rudim and the Military Government Unit at Koror.

* * *

ANGAUR, HERE'S TO YOU.

THE MAN AND THE BIRD

A long time ago there was an old hunter named Ngeramerang. One day the old man went hunting birds far away with his blowgun. As he walked along he found a snake holding a bird tight with its body. The poor bird was in misery; and when he saw the old man approach, it was an answer to his prayer.

The brave old man killed the snake and set the bird free. The bird was very happy then and flew to a tree, far away. Ngeramerang caught many birds and returned home. But he soon became very sick because the snake had bitten him when he had saved the bird.

While the old man was sick, the same bird flew down to a small tree near the house and said to him, "The other day you saved my life, so now I will help you. Take one leaf of this tree and eat it."

The old hunter ate one leaf of the tree and soon recovered. He was very happy and sang this song, "The bird helped me because the other day I helped him when I went hunting birds."

A LITTLE BOY

Once there was a little boy who lived with his old parents in a very little house. When the boy was sixteen years old he did a bad thing. He ran away from his father and mother. His parents waited and waited for him, but he did not come back. They were the poorest people in the hamlet. The roof of their house had many leaks, and the walls and the floors became bad. But nobody could help them. When the rains came, the poor people had to move from place to place. The people of the hamlet looked for the boy but they could not find him. They said that the son was ungrateful because he left his parents.

All this time the boy was living with a man in another hamlet. After a time he married; and one day while he was fishing his wife bore a child. When the boy returned he saw his wife holding the baby, and her mother was sitting nearby. His wife gave the baby to him, and he held the child and looked at him a long time. Suddenly he cried and cried and gave the baby back to his wife. Then he said, "Oh, I remember my mother, who bore me. She looked as you do with our baby. Where are they now? I will have to find them."

So he took some fish and went to find his old father and mother. He asked the people in the hamlet where they were and at last found them in a small house. He told his father and mother that he was sorry he had left them, and he built a better house for them.

THE MOTHER AND HER BOYS

A long time ago there were many people living on Bliliou. They were in great fear of a terrible old woman named Mluadelchur, who lived in a hole on a mountain and who ate men. Because the people did not know how they could kill the terrible old woman, they thought it would be better to flee. So they prepared to leave Bliliou by canoes and go to another island.

One mother and her two boys did not have a canoe and could not leave because nobody would help them. After all the other people left, these three lived in a hole under a big tree.

When the boys were grown the mother said to them, "My boys, I would like to tell you the history of Bliliou. When you were little boys there were many people here. But there was a big old woman here named Mluadelchur, who ate men. Therefore, the people fled. But we were left behind because we did not have a canoe. We had a house, but we could not live there. So we came to live in this hole for safety. You cannot go away from our hiding place because if the big woman finds you she will eat you.

But one day while their mother was sleeping, the boys went fishing. Mluadelchur found them there and said in a big voice, "Now I will catch you! For a long time I could not find any food; but now I am very happy." She came toward them, and when she was near one of the boys jumped into her stomach and made it swell and swell. It was so hard for her to walk then that she fell on the rocks. The other boy cut the old woman's stomach open and his brother came out. They put the stomach on a plate and said to it, "We will let you go. If somebody finds you, he will ask, 'Who are you?' If he asks, 'Are you a snake's stomach?' you will not swell. But if he asks, 'Are you Mluadelchur's stomach?' then you will swell."

The stomach ran to Ngerkebesang, where the people of Bliliou were now living. They found the stomach and asked it many questions. When they asked, "Are you Mluadelchur's stomach?" the stomach swelled. Then they knew Mluadelchur was dead.

So the people went from Ngerkebesang to Bliliou; but the mother and her boys would not let them come on the island. Then the people made an application and they were allowed to return. So the boys who had been left behind on Bliliou and had killed the terrible old Mluadelchur became the head men of the island.

* * *

Tulop and Henry were in the midst of a serious discussion when I walked into the office one morning in May.

"But why do they do this, Meestahr Wahl?" Tulop was saying. "Do the Angaur people not take good care of the American cemetery? My people try very hard."

Tulop is asking about the removal of the American military cemetery," Henry explained. "I had been telling him about the graves registration group that was here yesterday, and explaining that they would come soon with a group of Philippine Scouts to dig up the graves and take the bodies to the Philippines for ultimate shipment to the States."

"Yes," I said, joining the conversation, "this is too bad, Tulop. You know, and we know, that these Navy and Army and Marine boys have a beautiful place to sleep here, and that it makes everybody very sad to have them taken away. But, you see, in the States many of the people whose sons died in the war say, 'I want my boy to come back home even if he no longer lives. Then I can take care of his grave.'"

Henry added to this. "You see, Tulop, some of these people whose sons are here on Angaur do not know what a fine island it is, or that the Angaur people take such good care of the graves. They see their sons far away, maybe in a big jungle, with nobody thinking about them.

"You tell the Chief that the Angaur people take very good care of this cemetery, and that we are very happy about what they do. When the cemetery is gone the land will belong to the Angaur people again."

"That is okay, Meestahr Wahl. But after people go die this place we cannot use the land again. I think we will keep the flag pole and the small church at this place. Maybe the women will use this small church to stay out of the rain when they go work at gardens near this place. When you think they will take the bodies away?"

"I think maybe three weeks, Tulop. The Army man says they will begin to work next week."

Tulop pondered the strange situation for a moment. Then he said, "When they take all these men away, Meestahr Wahl, I think my people want to make a ceremony to say they are sorry to see them go. I think school children will make many flowers to go with the men."

And so it was. The last few days the graves registration men were on Angaur, the children worked in our garage long after school hours fashioning four huge wreaths of dried grass and coconut fronds. The night before the ceremony was spent in gathering large bunches of every kind of flower on the island and fastening them on the wreath bases. The finished products were exquisite red and pink and white floral pieces that would have done credit to any fine florist.

The sad little canvas packets of bones that were the American soldiers and sailors were placed in the small open boat to be taken to a larger ship waiting at Peleliu. The workers and their gear were all gathered dockside, and the two Army officers joined the large crowd of construction men and natives by the boat.

Then a long column of children came marching down the road, two abreast, tallest first, tapering down to the tiniest first graders. They were all dressed in their best clothes and shoes, and were

81st Division Cemetery, Angaur

church-solemn. The first four pairs of girls carried high above their heads the floral tributes which they had all made.

The crowd on the dock formed an open square, the Chief and the Army captain on one side, the Philippine soldiers on the left, and the crowd on the right. Silence fell on the group as the children marched into the open space and placed the wreaths between Uherbalau and Captain Rogers.

Uherbalau made his speech saying that these men had done much to liberate the people of Angaur, more than could be repaid. All we could do was take care of their cemetery after they had died, being thankful for their coming. The Angaur people had not and would not forget these Americans, even when they were gone. The school had made these wreaths as a token of remembrance for the Americans, and the flowers were to be tossed to the sea when the bodies finally left the island.

The captain then stepped forward to make a reply. He added the one light note to the morning's ceremonies, for he said, "I am unaccustomed to making speeches, and I am not prepared for this." Whereupon he pulled a two-page written speech from his breast pocket, and proceeded to give the Armed Forces' very kind thanks to the people of the Palaus for taking care of the Americans during the war, and of these soldiers after they had died.

Several pictures were taken of the ceremony, and then the captain and his men boarded the boat, and the four wreaths were placed on top of the boat load of bodies. The children then lined the dock in single file, drew out their white handkerchiefs and began waving them and singing as the boat pulled away,

> Should old akeensance be forgot,
> And nevair brought to mind . . .

We had been strongly against the removal of the bodies, Henry and I, for we felt that it would start the whole train of grief over again for the folks at home. We had known what a peaceful resting place the men had, and we believed that they would feel, having paid such a high price for twelve square feet of sandy soil on Angaur, that they would prefer to stay there. But when we stood in the sun with the little group of quiet people watching the touching ceremony it didn't matter so much anymore. It was all right now because with the singing of "Auld Lang Syne" the Angaur people made an outward expression of an inarticulate understanding that freedom is a vital right and that it applies to everyone in the world. What better appreciation and remembrance could be given the American solders who were leaving this morning than the understanding and appreciation of the island people whose lives they had touched so briefly. With their innate kindness and ability to do the right thing at the right time the school children of Angaur had made an indelible impression in the minds of all of us present that morning.

Graduation was due very shortly after this ceremony, and we were drawn into the excitement of preparing awards for the best scholars, and inviting people from the headquarter island for the exercises.

ANGAUR, HERE'S TO YOU.

John Telei, the headmaster, came in one morning to show us the prizes and to talk over plans. There were lengths of dress goods for the girls, new shorts for the boys, flashlights, hair ribbons, and some books. We added several prizes from our stock of odds and ends . . . pocket knives, rubber balls for the first graders, sets of zippers, buttons and thread, and some costume jewelry.

"Mr. Wahl, Chief say next week Number One M.G. man come to graduation at Angaur school. Also Chief Aibeduul, Number One Chief of all Palaus. This is so?" John was laying careful plans.

"Yes, John Telei. I think one, maybe two big officers come from Koror for your school graduation."

"Mr. Wahl, Angaur has very fine school, best all Palaus Islands. But we must make show this to Number One. My students make very good graduation. We make prizes for best pupils in every class, for girl and boy who do best work for their father and mother. But, Mr. Wahl, we would like to have song for Angaur school, song we can sing at graduation when these people come from Koror, song we can sing every year. Can you teach us this song?"

Henry turned this problem over to me, and together we leafed through the one small songbook we had with us. The natives already knew several Stephen Foster songs, and we felt they weren't just right for a school song. There were no marching songs in the book, and we drew blanks when we tried to recall any. I favored my favorite hymn, "Oh beautiful for spacious skies," but Henry pointed out that the Angaurese would scarcely understand all the words since they had no "amber waves of grain." He went to the other extreme by bursting into parody of the Illini Fight Song, which every other high school in the States uses . . . "We're loyull to you, Angaur High . . . " and we gave up for the moment in laughing despair.

Well, if they can do it at home, why not here, I found myself thinking. Why not a new version of our own alma mater song at Indiana, via Cornell. We could say, "our beloved Island Mother," instead of Alma Mater." And so it emerged.

· 233 ·

> Come and join in song together,
> Should with might and main.
> Our beloved Island Mother
> Sound her praise again.
>
> Gloriana! Frangipana!
> Here's to her, be true.
> She's the pride of all the islands,
> Angaur, here's to you.

Henry approved heartily and went off to find John Telei to arrange for the youngsters to come for practice that evening.

We were considerably surprised during the afternoon to find a half dozen of the young men of the village at our back door with the battered piano which had been at the community house.

Takime spoke. "Mr. Wahl, we bring this piano so Angaur children can learn new song much better. You think Meesus can play for us?"

"Meesus" was so rusty it was embarrassing. Outside the familiar songs in the "Everybody Sing" book she could play only three selections from memory. And the tinniness of the upright piano, acquired after many months without tuning, and the dampness of the tropics did not enhance the renditions.

The children trooped into our living room after supper, almost the whole school population, until there was scarcely room to move. We helped them relax by playing the songs we had heard them sing at school the past mornings, and asking them to join in. Their repertoire had come from the G.I.s, for they sang "You Are My Sunshine," "God Bless America," "Somebody Loves Me," and their old favorite, "Auld Lang Syne."

They learned the new song quickly, a phrase at a time, following the copies we had made for them, with stiff fingers on each word. We worked on shouting "Angaur, here's to you!" with much might and main till the plywood floor shook, and foolish Rosco beat a wild retreat under the garage.

Every morning for a week we heard them rehearse their new

song for almost an hour. John was nothing if not an exacting teacher. But he was puzzled about one phrase after they had worked on it for several days.

"Mr. Wahl, this 'gloriana frangipana.' What this mean?"

"Gloriana means everything very fine, I think, John. And frangipana is a good word for here. You know beautiful white flower that grows over by village cemetery. It has four petals, is yellow down inside flower, and smells, oh, very good? That is frangipana. But maybe you would like to make some Angaur words for that line. Something that says how happy you are that this is graduation, and that everyone loves Angaur school."

"Ah! I think so. I think that very good. We will see."

As commencement approached the school and the grounds took on a new gleam. The children cleaned every inch of the yard, removing weeds, and brushing it clean with their short whisk brooms.

When the great morning arrived we found every child dressed in his cleanest outfit, hair slicked back, face gleaming. John was sweating it out in a full suit, but too proud to let his discomfort bother him. The dignitaries were there in force, chiefs from several other islands, and Aibeduul, the high chief of the Palaus. M.G. had a representative from headquarters, though the commanding officer was unable to be there.

The prizes were received with wide eyes and solemn smiles. The littlest boys trying ever so hard to stand, step forward, receive their present, and turn, tripped over their own feet and were stricken with terror. But the program moved as smoothly as John had planned it. His own two sons received the prizes that were their due; and his proud, whispered "Well done, my son" was the most beautiful part of the program.

Then came the speeches. Each dignitary in his turn added his congratulations of the day to the Angaur students. They were all made in Palauan, but we could understand from the gestures and inflection what was being said. The Peleliu headmaster was the most articulate of the group. He stepped up to the desk where a large bouquet of flowers was placed. Pointing to the buds and flowers, he said that the school takes

Left, Chief Aibeduul, number one chief of the Palaus, and the Airii chief.

the bud of the flower, the small child, and trains him through the years. Now the finished product graduates as the full blooming blossom to take his place in his community and to be an honor and credit to his people and the Palau Islands.

At last came the singing of the new song. The children rose as one, and almost as one gave us a sidelong glance before they began. Being a sentimentalist, I thought I would surely weep a bit when they began to sing. But the subtle pronunciation changes which had crept into the song as the children learned it in their newly acquired English were so delightful that we could only smile as we listened.

>   Kahm and jhoin in song togather,
>   Shot wiss might and mine.
>   Ar belahved ilahnd mahzzer
>   Sond her prize agine.

Kay-doot-kayoo. Ritial sils.
(We are very happy today).
Hairs to her be troo.
Shays the pride off all de ilahnds.
ANGAHR! HAIRS TO YOU!

We had scarcely arrived home from the ceremony, and the picture taking afterwards, when John Telei came running to the back door in much consternation.

"Oh, Mr. Wahl, much trouble about this graduation!"

"Why, John, what is wrong? Everything was Number One, I thought."

"Oh, Mr. Wahl. I have many things to do to make this graduation good, and I forget to make my speech for you!" He pulled the handwritten paper from his coat pocket in much embarrassment and handed it to Henry.

"This is the speech I want to make for you; but I forget, so I give it to you now."

Henry read it, face reddening as his eyes went down the page, for he was pleased, but overwhelmed, with the rhetorical praise.

"Ah, John, *mal ungil*! This is too good. You say too many things about me. I think it is better that you do not say them out loud. Thank you many times for bringing this to me. I will keep it always."

"Let me see," I clamored, as soon as John had gone. "What on earth has he said! I never saw a man so embarrassed at a slip as he was."

The speech was a beauty, which we have read many times, and prize highly.

"Ladies and gentlemen. I have the honor to express our heartful feeling of gratitude to gentlemen of U.S.N. Military Government especially our kind leader Mr. Wahl of U.S. Civil Administration. Angaur taking the opportunity of the good remarkable day.

"We, the residents of this Island, were used have very poor knowledges about other side of the world so that we did not know how to live our lives usefully to become the member of peaceful world.

"We were so miserable as the crew of the ship, sailing in the raging waves of great ocean in a cloudy stormy night neither one compass nor a piece of chart. But, very fortunately after long dangerous voyage we could get the merciful salvation of our Lord. Our Lord gave us a skilled captain. He give us a kind Mr. Wahl as the Military Governor of our Island.

"It was Mr. Wahl who taught us very very kindly about every question we had met to deal with. He gave us nice clean dwellings in our village. He gave us splendid school like this. He also gave us many nice prizes congratulating this good day.

"I'm very glad to say that we are enjoying our lives in these days under the protection of his powerful arms.

"Mr. Wahl I express here agin our feeling of gratitude, representing all students assembled here today. Thank you, thousand and million thanks to you."

CHAPTER SIXTEEN

Going to Town

A visit to Koror was like going to town on Saturday . . . walking up one side of the street and down the other until you had seen everyone, and they you. Like looking in all the store windows to see what was new since you had been in from the country the last time . . . did USCC have any new material or dyes or wooden monkey men or flash-light batteries. Like having a frosted malt at the drug store, surrounded by all the crowd . . . the Sanders had open house at all hours. And like eating out in a swank restaurant after enduring your own home cooking for weeks . . . the Christies concocted the most luscious epicurean meals imaginable: India curries, or Steaks Stanley, accompanied by shredded green papaya salad with bits of bacon and french dressing *au fines herbes*, steaming coffee, no dessert. These were not only delicious and imaginative meals but amazing in a world of monotonous fare.

That was what Koror was in retrospect. It was also many other things less reminiscent and romantic. Koror was, for one thing, the department of utter confusion. In the first place the roads were unspeakable. The Japanese must have put down a good road bed, for the topping was completely worn off, and the bed itself was standing up remarkably under the wear and tear of jeeps and rain-washing. It was full of large chunks of rock, and of chuck holes. A ride from one end of the island to the other, perhaps three miles, was enough to leave tempers ragged the rest of the day. Some of the men had developed backside jeep sores and kidney ailments that lasted months.

Nothing ever seemed to get done. Used to a small island where the people worked well together, we found the larger island seemingly confused. The Navy headquarters were jammed together in a dark, small quonset with the screechings and rattling of the communications department overpowering any attempt at conversation. When it rained there was a great deal more mud than we had on Angaur, and everyone sloshed around in ponchos and dirty shoes.

But Koror was beautiful, too. The dark green hills rose abruptly from the water to points and bumps like icing on an ornate cake. Even now, when it was a shambles from the bombings of the war, the island showed evidence of having been a beautiful city. There were remains of formal gardens and terracing, which told of a tropical capital of the Nippon empire that could easily have been, as they said, the place many Japs came for their vacations. From the hills of Koror, where the Navy dependent housing now was going up, the view of the bay was a symphony of changing colors, as the tides moved in and out . . . emerald green, intense blue, lavender, chartreuse, gray; and the hills of Babelthaup rolled hazily away to the north. The island was a lush spot with bougainvillea in flaming spears, gardenias, poinciana, torch ginger, and many red hibiscus.

On our first trip to Koror we had the enthusiasm to go bouncing around the island sightseeing. After that we sat in the homes of our friends and took things easily. We inched our way along the road to the Babelthaup dock past overhanging cliffs which had bristled with Japanese gun emplacements. We prowled around the old "M" dock where there were derelict tuna fishing boats and pearl divers masks, marks of the Japanese pre-war industry in the Palaus.

South of Koror, and running across the string of islands, is Malakal Harbor. Protected on both east and west by reefs and narrow channels, the harbor held a concentration of the Japanese fleet during the war. There is vast anchorage space to the west between the islands and the barrier reef; and in the caves in the cliffs at the entrance to the inner harbor are mounted large caliber Jap guns which sighted directly down the mouth of the entering channels. It was a perfect natural defense. But the Japanese hadn't counted on the swift appearance of the American air power one morning in March of 1944. Now the harbor was full of rusty hulks rising from the water or visible below. One repair ship lies on the bottom, her top decks and masts accessible above the water line. All around the shallower parts of the harbor are the curves of capsized ship hulls, everything from war ships to sampans, which had sunk quickly. The abrupt hills all around the bay now had a young, lighter green foliage rising like flames toward the hill tops. Flames had been the cause of this color variant. When the many ships had been sunk, oil burned so furiously on the surface, and licked up the face of the hills so that most of the trees from the water line up to the ridges were destroyed. What a conflagration the Palauans and Japanese must have seen when the fighting was beginning to work its way up to the Palaus.

Ngerkebesang and Malakal, two small islands adjoining Koror on the harbor side, had held most of the area's military installations. On Ngerkebesang there was the twisted steel wreckage of two seaplane bases, the hangars a swept-up pile of serpentine steel, looking like the morning after New Year's Eve; the cave offices dank and deserted. The wide cement ramps where the seaplanes had come lumbering up from the water were good places for swimming and sunning. We discovered on one trip that there were numerous good-sized fluted Tridacna sea shells attached to the straight edge of the concrete on either side of the ramp. They would be just the thing, we though, to place decoratively along the edge of the terrace at our Angaur house. We lay flat on the cement and tried to reach down over the edge to get the shells. We didn't come near them. So I held Henry's feet and levered him over. He could reach the shells but couldn't pry them loose.

"Well, the most sensible thing to do is get in the water and get them," I said.

"Yes, I know, dear; but this is my only set of clean khakis. I don't want to get wet."

We though a minute about all the angles. "The tide's not very deep. Why don't I just take off my slacks and shorts and have you lower me down. I wouldn't have to take off my blouse."

That was a good idea, except for the fact that when he tried to swing me over the corner of concrete my legs got badly scratched. "Ouch! Darn it! I can't do that. Let me just wade down the angle of the ramp and then around here to the edge."

I pattered down the slope. Just as I reached the water's edge, Heinie called, "Say, better watch that cement, it may be slick under water . . ."

The last words were too late, and were lost to me as I hit slimy underwater growth on the ramp. My feet slid out from under me and I sat down with a thud, softened only slightly by the splash of water. I slid all the way down the ramp, wet to the neck! What difference did it make then about getting wet. I waded to the spot where Henry stood above me, howling at my plight, and struggled to loosen the shells, which I handed up to him.

A postscript to the incident must be added. When we went home to Angaur we forgot the shells and never saw them again. Heinie had taken a color picture of his soaking wife proudly displaying the booty of the day. And when the roll came back from processing there was a brief note enclosed. "One of the pictures in this roll is not of suitable matter to mail to you. If you will send us your permission we will destroy the transparency." No Esquire girl, I!

Along the eastern curve of Koror is a lagoon dotted with the tiny mushroom islets so typical of the Palaus. From a distance they appear to be fingers of hill reaching out into the water; but when we floated among them in a small boat we found a maze of hillocks that rose fifty or sixty feet above the water. At low tide the rocky under-curve and the "stem" of the mushroom were visible. There was a stern reminder of how deeply the Japanese were entrenched in the area. As we passed the many little islands, the native boatmen pointed out rope ladders disappearing up into the trees, or the remnants of a machine shop, or a fuel storage dump visible in the crags. Several of the formations had water-worn caves where two or three small boats could seek refuge. There were machine gun emplacements and anti-aircraft platforms. We shuddered to think how nearly impossible it would have been to wrench the enemy from their position. Taking Peleliu and Angaur had been expensive enough.

The present stillness and beauty of the lagoon was breathtaking. Leaning over the edge of the boat we could look down to a sandy bottom filled with corals, sea slugs, and star fish, and shot through with many interesting fish. Suddenly the bottom would drop off to great, dark depths, and as dizzily rise up again till it seemed it would strike the boat bottom.

The Navy houses were on a high ridge which overlooked both the bay and the lagoon. Overlooked Drive, Ted McCarthy had dubbed it, for reasons other than the beauty of the area. The houses had gone up slowly while the men waited impatiently for their wives to come out from the States. It was hard to think of some of them as quonsets, for they had been very well constructed and arranged. But they leaked as only quonsets can through the many nail holes in the tin roof. And the rain misted in the screens, sending everyone dashing to lower the canvas covers. From the outside the houses looked awkward, set up on concrete posts, with off-pieces of canvas and flaps of tin protruding here and there.

Inside, the women had attained various degrees of house decorating. Joe and Marie Havenner held to the sound theory that since they would be in the Navy for a good many years to come, moving from place to place, they were going to make each house they lived in a real home, having with them the accouterments of pleasant living. Their records and books were well used, and they managed to keep a steady stream of interesting food tidbits coming from the States for the enjoyment of their friends and themselves. Others felt that their Koror house was only a temporary place for them, so why fix it up. We'll live out of the boxes and barrels, they said, and use our worn out things here.

Henry and I weren't exactly as one on the problem. He felt, and reasonably I knew, that we should bring nothing to the area we did not count expendable, because of the rough handling the household effects would get en route, the possibility of storms drenching and ruining everything, and the certainty that the heat and moisture of the tropics would mildew things of quality. I subscribed to this part way; but mine was the female dependency upon some familiar things. And in eight years of marriage we had still to use a great many of our wedding gifts. So I had come to the stage where I felt that if they wore out or were lost, all right, I would still like to have a few of our nice things with us. Navy wives never gather without bewailing the horrible condition of their crockery and furniture after shipment; but we were lucky. We lost not a single record from our collection, and had only the minor breakage of dishes that is bound to happen.

It was fun to see the houses take shape at Koror. When the women brought out the sewing machines and fashioned slip covers from the materials they could buy at USCC or had sent from home, each house took on its own personality. There was dyeing in wholesale lots. The best way, Jo Sanders maintained, was to heat water in a wash tub over an outside fire, dump it into the wash machine with the dye, and slosh the fabric around till the desired color was reached. The color ran like mad; but then it was easy to dye it again, possibly another color, whenever the spirit moved her. Consequently her muslin slipcovers moved through a wondrous range of color from yellow, to rose, to raspberry, to brown.

To most of the people who passed through this part of the world the Sanders' and the Christies' homes were synonymous with the words Koror and hospitality. The doors were always open to callers, and another bed could be found somewhere. A newcomer felt within minutes that he had known them forever. They had been on the island longer than any of the rest of us, and their houses were most comfortable, even though they were constantly undergoing remodeling processes. But they suffered from the shortages as did everyone else. The Sanders, for instance, never had a refrigerator that could be counted on twenty-four hours at a time. And they rather gloried in the fact that they could keep a bulging household going with much recalcitrant fixtures. They felt about it the way we did about our lack of decent stoves on Angaur.

GOING TO TOWN

John and Jo Sanders were outstanding characters in a world of interesting people. There was scarcely a place in the world where Sandy had not been at some time, and he had a natural knowledge of boats and native peoples that was unsurpassable. He had a wealth of fabulous travel stories which we always clamored to hear. But Sandy was such a quiet soul in a noisy crowd that he seldom could be urged to talk. Once in awhile when the group was small, or it was a cozy, stay-at-home night, or some bit of conversation reminded him of a choice tidbit, he would launch into a story . . . boats and pearl diving in Tahiti, mining in Alaska, shore leave in Australia, shipping and ships the world over. It might be any of these, for he knew them first hand. All these experiences gave him an understanding of the Palauans and an ability to deal with them which furthered the natives' cause tremendously.

Jo, his wife, was an active, militant woman, an extrovert who loved to gather people and causes about her and whip them all together in the excitement of living. There were never too many people for a meal or a drink, and she could entertain people as they dropped in all day, and then spend the night typing reports, and letters for her husband. She could talk like a literateur, or fling out the words of a dock walloper in equally effective fashion. Their household was a delightfully informal jumble of people, pets, and work. There was Janie, their nine-year old daughter, the picture of both of them . . . long, stringy, and precocious, a child who understood and spoke Palauan better than any American adult in the islands, who went off on three- or four-day trips with the natives, and who read books far beyond her years. There were three Palauan house girls to do different jobs, a yard man, and a couple extra workers always on hand. Add Princess, the dog, Victoria and Pierre, two perverted cats, and don't forget Yakojon, the sulphur-crested cockatoo who ruled the whole roost. Mix well with coffee, liquor, and many guests, and you have the Sanders menage.

That Yakojon was a real character, too. A raucous white bird with a yellow crest and underwing markings, he lived in the wreckage of a Japanese house adjoining the Sanders' quonset. There he "owned" a pile of glass window panes, and beware the man or animal who trespassed. Yako had been known to attack the intruder, and bite a hole through the toe of a heavy work shoe, or to rip the seat out of the pants of the unsuspecting scrounger. He had chewed a hole through a plywood wall at one end of the house, and he made his entrance there, swinging all the way around as he climbed through, jumping down to the floor and waddling across toward the family room. On a desk in this extra bedroom was an unused telephone. It was a ritual with Yako, who had been trained by the Japanese, to climb, beak over claw, up the leg of the desk, step to the telephone, stick his beak in the mouthpiece and scream, "Mushi, mushi!" Then he carried on a long business conversation in Japanese, after which he said goodbye, hopped off the desk and proceeded on his way to find Sandy. Yako could wake the whole island and the dead, we swore, with his early morning screams of joyous living. He made every one of us long for a bird just like him.

The Sanders and the Christies seemed permanent fixtures on Koror, for they had been there when all of our group came, and they were to stay through many changes of Naval personnel. They were civilians (to differentiate from the Navy people, though in the islands people were people, with no rank or stigma attached) who were managing the business of the United States Commercial Company. Their concern was building a trade store for the Palauans where they could sell copra, trepang, trochus shell, and handicraft, and be able to buy items which they needed.

Max and Marian Christie had the most fabulous house in the Western Pacific, and they matched their surroundings. Handsome, ultra-smart sophisticates, they made their Hawaiian-type home a blend of unusual color combinations and tropical comfort. Marian had an eye for clothes design and interior decorating that made every woman on the island want to copy her. But she also was so far ahead of the rest of us that by the time we had copied a dress, or a hairdo, or a kind of drapery, she had adopted a far more advanced design. Their meals have already been mentioned; but not the details of dining, Oriental fashion, on cushions before a low chow table, with candlelight, music, and flowers, and relaxed conversation. The Christies both possessed a keen, sharp sense of humor and a conversational ability that flattered their guests' intelligence and kept them on their toes.

These were not all the families we knew or enjoyed, but they were the ones of whom all the visitors, as well as the people who lived there, thought of when Koror was mentioned. Everyone on the island had traits which were enjoyed and appreciated by the rest of us; and if relations were ever strained it was because we were living in a strange, hybrid society, completely isolated, and too small for the normal American outlets. The largest trouble was that everyone knew everyone else too well because we were so interdependent for our recreation and social life. At home a man sees even his best friends only when he wants to, sharing the pleasures of friendship and not necessarily the drab details of everyday life . . . of washing clothes, and hair . . . of having stomach aches or a tendency to over-drinking . . . of seeing the same drooping petticoat day in and day out . . . of annoying mannerisms. These small things are the pitfalls of a small social group.

All the component parts of any group were present: the super housekeepers, the ones who hated housework, the ones who liked serious literature and philosophical discussions, and the ones who read *True Confessions* and discussed movie stars; the women who liked children, and the women who liked M-E-N. It was a normal cross section of America. But, pointed up by its close confines, each personality became a topic of conversation and discussion, and . . . gossip.

No one missed out on the gossip; even the children remembered all they heard. It was after a handsome lad from one of the ships had been known to be spending his time on shore at the house of one of the more willing Palauan girls, that we were gathered at the McCarthy's one evening. Harrison, the man, dropped in for a cup of after-dinner coffee. And while we chatted amiably, Kathy, the four-year-old daughter of the house, climbed over our laps and played with anyone who would join her. She had skipped Lt. Harrison, though, and her father thought to make her mind her manners.

"Kathy, you remember Lt. Harrison, don't you? You haven't spoken to him yet," Ted said sternly.

"Oh, yes, Daddy, I know him," she answered confidently. "He's the man who lives down by Augusta's."

Six adults bit their lips in a wild attempt to keep straight-faced, and the subject was quickly changed!

The women at Koror entertained themselves, outside of the usual routine of home and family, which took a bit of doing because of shortages, by chitchat more than by any other recreation. It was natural, and fun too, to join someone for a coffee in the morning, and to talk over the affairs of the previous evening. This was essentially female, whether it was constructive or not! There was a good deal of bridge played, by family couples and by the bachelors, seldom by the women alone. For awhile we were all in the grip of Liverpool Rum, playing it at every gathering. But again, the smallness of the group came into the picture, and someone would be saying, "I'll be damned if I'll play with Ethel again; she hasn't got the sense God gave green apples, and besides, all she cares about is the M-O-N-E-Y!" Or, "Honestly, he takes every card in the deck, won't let you have a one, and then he fusses when he loses." So the popularity of Liverpool waned, and something else was taken up.

Possibly the most consistently popular avocation was scrounging Japanese dishes. This means going to the ruins of the many pre-war houses on the island, and digging among the rubble to find saki cups, flower vases, small bowls that could be used for salt dishes or ash trays, and decorative tiles. It became an obsession with some of the crowd, who spent many hot hours digging, lugging home, cleaning, and admiring or trading off with their neighbors.

The business reached rather embarrassing proportions at times. At the native feasts, or at the meals fed us on field trips there might be one lovely Japanese-made vase or ash tray decorating the center of the table. Or on each tray a covered compote would be given the place of honor. The rest of the dishes would be very plain, even cracked and chipped. It was obvious that the people had brought out their limited "best" for us. Unfortunately there were women who did not seem to understand the losses which the natives had had during the war, or their difficulty in housekeeping now. They would exclaim over the beauty of the dish, wish loudly they might have it to add to their collection, and even send the interpreter to see if they could buy the dish. From these shuddering *faux pas* the rest of us evolved a typical conversation which we carried on whenever we visited friends. "Oh, dahling," one of us would say, "look at that lovely silver tea set the Christies have on their table. Wherever do you suppose they got it?"

"Oh, scrounged it, I suppose. Where else could they get anything so nice. I'd just love to have it. How much do you think it's worth?"

"Oh, surely not more than a quarter, do you think? Let's ask George to see if they'll sell it. It'd just match a salt shaker I have at home." This was dreadful humor, but to the point.

It must be said proudly for the Koror group that they kept any differences of ill feelings under cover. There were the natural personal and family feuds that might be expected to arise, but they never broke into the open. This helped the group tremendously toward keeping on an even keel. Unlike another one of the islands where a real knock-down, hair-pulling contest developed among the women, leaving the last three on the island not on speaking terms. Koror groups always met genially and properly.

The women were bound together by their mutual problems of housekeeping and lack of supplies. Preparing for the sojourn in the Palaus had been a real problem because we had no precedent on which to set up our inventories. When the men had been in training at Stanford a lecture had been prepared for the wives by a Navy nurse who had spent several pre-war years on Guam. It was a helpful hour, albeit filled with information about a social Navy life. She spoke of wearing only washable clothes, preferably cotton, that sanitary napkins might be hard to procure, and that tampons might mildew, that all electrical equipment and leather goods should be kept in hot lockers to avoid rust and mildew. The mothers with small children were the most concerned group, for they feared a lack of milk and baby food, and they had heard frightening stories about barefooted children getting hookworm and some of the more scrofulous diseases. The nurse's words to them were encouraging; and they were borne out by the fact that the children who came to the Palaus thrived beautifully. But the statement that stuck with us the longest, for some foolish reason, and the one at which we laughed ironically many times while we were splashing around Koror in muddy shoes, clad in shorts and shirt under a form-enveloping poncho, hair dripping in our faces, was this: "You will find that you'll want two or three formals, and that a broad-brimmed garden hat will be needed for late afternoon lawn or cocktail parties."

"Yes," we'd snort in our discomfort, "a leghorn hat, a long dress, and boondocker shoes underneath the whole charming ensemble!"

The real answer was that each woman had to figure her own needs for the particular island to which she went. Every one of us made miscalculations. We threw away our rayon lingerie, buying a whole new set of cotton shorts and slips. The knit rayon things would have been fine. The main trouble was that elastic wore out faster than any other part of the clothing. Someone could always be found clutching frantically at her waistline to catch a slipping item of apparel.

On some islands formal attire was never worn, and the crisp cotton formals wilted in the closet. Most of us misjudged the amount of pedal pushers or shorts and cool blouses that we would need. And we found that once we were settled, the things we sent for oftenest were food specialties: jars of cheese, mushroom soup, tuna, spices, nuts, good crackers. No one ever had enough scarves, for we used them either in turban or peasant fashion every time we rode in the open jeeps. We all dressed most informally, chuckling among ourselves at the women who arrived from the States dressed in elaborate silk dresses, wearing high heels and hose, and a hat. Yes, even remembering how we ourselves had dressed up for the moment of arrival, we smiled. The first time was the only time we wore anything but slacks and sensible shoes for boat or plane travel.

When evening came everyone showered and dressed up a little. Not in the classic British form of "dressing for dinner," but in clean clothes, dresses not shorts, and for the men fresh khakis. It was surprising what a lift to the morale it was to be clean, combed, and crisp.

The Koror parties were memorable affairs, for each hostess who gathered the crowd together for a long dress evening made special efforts toward having some refreshment or bit of unusual entertainment. The pattern of the parties varied little however, for we usually gathered to talk in small groups, while we "bent elbows" at the host's bar, wandered around the room joining each conversation for awhile, and then congregated with the singing crowd in the corner. The singers were an ever-changing group of harmony devotees, some who could sing beautifully, the rest who would add tone-deaf voices for a few bars until everyone was out of key, and then wander off to talk to someone else. The groups at the parties always varied because there would be either a visiting fireman from Guam or the officers of the ship in the harbor to add to the Koror family.

One of the visiting ship's officers afforded us the best laugh of the year at a Saturday night party. The occasion was the birthday of one of the Koror crowd, and Joe and Marie Havenner had built an impromptu party. Everyone was gathered, dressed in his best, and the cocktail hour, for which we had been invited, had long since passed. In the mellow mid evening the singers gathered in a circle on the floor and began running through their repertoire of old-time and slightly shady songs. We were joined by a very young ensign from an LST which had come in that morning. He was a quiet lad, for whom most of the women immediately felt a protective urge, for he was constantly bedeviled by the also young, but domineering, captain of his ship. This night he was out to assert his own personality, and he was helping the cause along with a long, tall glass of some volatile liquid. He wandered over to join the group, sat down tailor fashion, and used his glass as a baton to direct us all. We ran through "You Tell Me Your Dream," "Someone's In the Kitchen With Dinah," "Goodbye to Homosexuality," and a loud chorus of Casey Jones; we were all naming our next favorites. A sudden hush fell over the room just as the visiting ensign raised his glass and began to sing loudly to the tune of the last song:

> Ooh, she was goin' down the hill
> Doing ninety miles an hour,
> When the wheel on her bicycle broke.
> She was found in the grass
> With the sprocket in her pocket
> And was tickled to death by the spoke.
> Woo-woo!

The whole room broke into wild laughter, and the singing circle grew immediately, much enlarged by people clamoring to learn the words of the new song.

There were very few women who came to the Palaus who did not enjoy their stay fully. It was a stimulating experience in a beautiful, different world. Our health was excellent. There were a few people who had little resistance to mosquito bites or cuts, and they had infections from time to time. But there were certainly no dread diseases which originated in the area and struck hard at the Americans.

We felt that it did take a certain kind of temperament to be happy and interested in a stay in the tropics. To the people who were desperately homesick or who could see no place to live but "the old home town," the two years' tour of duty could be a miserable, frustrated experience. The islands are no place for a neurotic or a hypochondriac; for the informal living conditions, the rather monotonous diet, the narrow choice of recreation could start that man or woman complaining, and then brooding, and then being actually ill. A neurotic woman will worry if her husband is away from her for some time, but she will be better off in the familiar routine of home and the States; her husband will do a better job for not having been whipped up emotionally by her worries.

The prime requisites, we believe, for anyone coming to work with the peoples of the Trust Territory, are a consuming interest in seeing other parts of the world than the United Sates, a real liking for the people, and adjustability to any circumstance.

Our visits to Koror were undoubtedly more fun for us than for our hosts. There was no guest house on the island, so every week when we went up we had to foist ourselves off on some kind family who could give us bed and board. This was a real treat for us, for we could enjoy the company and the food. We tried to move up and down the road, staying at all the places we had been invited; but I am sure that the Koror families grew to dread the sight of the picket boat coming in from Angaur. We could always look forward to a day or two of good visiting, a hot shower after our sticky trip, and, when we were ready to start home, one of Marie Havenner's very special picnic lunches.

But as much fun as Koror was, we found it good to get home again after the trips. Often we were detained at the headquarters island on business, when there were urgent things to be done on Angaur at the same time. We never could judge the amount or kind of clothing we would need at Koror. If we took a formal outfit, the party would be informal; if we took one change of clothes we stayed two weeks. It never seemed to fail. We went home always a little tired of the hustle and bustle at Koror . . . and of the bad roads. So the sight of Angaur lying secure across the Peleliu channel was always a welcome view, as we made the glad trip southward. It was fun to go to town on Saturday night. But after its pleasures, we greeted the quiet first days of the new week gratefully.

CHAPTER SEVENTEEN

Safari!

Shortly before the end of Henry's tour of duty in the Palaus we used the picket boat for a four-day field trip around the biggest island of the group, Babelthaup. The commanding officer at Koror wanted to make a trip to the native village on the north island; and since our boat was the only one in the islands in good running order, Henry was called upon to bring it up to Koror to prepare for the trip. Being coxswain did not bother him a bit, for it meant we could both make the trip. We were delighted with the chance to get up north, for Henry had been field officer when he first came to the Palaus and had seen and loved the small, remote villages along the coast of Babelthaup. I had seen all the other islands with this exception.

The natives chose their best crew to handle the boat: Singinari for the wheel, Tomas as navigator, Charlie Eduardo as chief engineer, plus old Suus and young Antonio to spell Singi at the wheel, and to handle the lines. Tomas and Suus were *rubak*, so they would attend the official meetings in each village as we went along. Antonio was chosen because he was from Kayangel, a small island north of Babelthaup, and knew the reefs along the way, and also because he could combine his work with a visit to his mother whom, he had not seen for many months. To Singinari and Charlie Eduardo fell most of the watches on the boat; Charlie never left her the four days we were out. Neither he nor Singi had ever been to Kayangel, or to the village of Ngerelong, but despite their obvious eagerness to see these new places they never faltered in their allegiance to the boat.

The preparations were wondrous and without end. When the white man goes on safari, he must have all the fittings of his daily life from ice water to an arm chair for the small native boats we would use for ferry trips across shallow water to the shore. There were six officers in all, plus the wives of three, and the young daugh-

SAFARI!

ter of one. Two native housegirls went along to take care of the women and Mary Jane, and ostensibly to prepare our food.

An open LCM followed our boat, carrying a full-size kerosene stove and all the food, carefully thought out ahead of time, to feed us all for four days. That supply was scarcely touched, for at every village we were served a fabulous native meal of lobster, crab, chicken, taro, tapioca, bananas, oranges, and coconut milk. To take our own food among the most naturally polite, charming people in the world was a waste of time and material. But we might have been courteous enough to leave some of our supply behind to replenish the natives' stock instead of carrying it all home again.

We set off along the west side of Babelthaup and began our calls at the small villages of the strange names: Ngeremlengui, Ngerelong, Ngertmau, Aimeliik. The skipper changed to his white uniform as we reached each stop, and all the officers trooped off with the delegates from the village for a meeting. The doctor and his native aides inspected any patients and gave the villagers a pep talk about sanitation in their homes, and keeping their *benjoes* well screened so flies could not carry the germs away into the village. The native affairs officer usually handled the meetings, introducing the various other officers, each of whom made short speeches of welcome and praise.

The ice water ran out the first afternoon, and there was much fussing by our passengers over roughing it in a rocky boat. Some of the women felt we must make a good impression on the villagers as we went along, appearing always as the *grande dame*, and dressing the part in high-heeled shoes and sun-back dresses. This was all very well, but the long walk up to the first village from the pier resulted in several feet full of blisters. And the sun got in its licks on the bare shoulders. Tempers flared frequently, and *mal de mer* made its appearance. The Wahls stayed in the front cabin with the native pilots and enjoyed themselves thoroughly. I'd learned early that I had to stay away from the sun or its reflection on the water; I knew what kind of clothing I had to wear for hiking. So I'm afraid I made a rather unladylike appearance among the nicely

NUMBER ONE PACIFIC ISLAND

garbed party in my khaki riding pants, flat hiking shoes, long sleeved shirt, scarf tied over my hair, dark glasses, and extra portions of sun burn cream applied frequently. But I was completely comfortable, and loved every minute of the trip.

The rusty, raw hills of Babelthaup rose from the water and, fringed with towering coconut palms, climbed as high as six hundred fifty feet above the sea. How different we had found the various islands of the Palaus: Angaur and Peleliu flat coral and limestone; the central uninhabited islands rising abruptly from the water, green mushrooms with their stems submerged; Koror a volcanic island, lush green with reddish soil; and the large mass of Babelthaup far enough from the water that its hills were rolling brown pasture land.

Then there was Kayangel, a perfect jewel of a tiny island, some fifteen miles removed to the north from the rest of the group. A circular reef a couple miles in diameter stands alone in the open sea. Poles mark the channel through the reef at one side and steer us straight across the lagoon to a string of four small islands, graduated in size like a necklace of green pearls. Towering palms arched over rolling white, sandy beaches, and great banyan trees cast their shade along the sand and shallow aqua water. The village lies along the inside waterfront from which springs a long, gray pier of heavy rocks. The center of the village, just behind the pier, is an ancient, giant tree of the fig family. The limbs spread out forty or fifty feet on each side, and around the gnarled old trunk a platform has been built of stones, and benches backed all around the trunk. A completely remote village, it was spotlessly clean, and it boasted a spacious, grassy avenue through the length of the village lined with perfect specimen coconut and betelnut palms under which bloomed a fragrant lower fringe of plumeria.

We walked leisurely along the heavenly avenue to see one of the few remaining *a bais* in the Palaus. A relic of earlier times, *a bais* are men's houses of a primitive society. Hewn from heavy beams with shell instruments, and perched on huge stone some three feet above the ground, these long, thatched roof structures provided a meeting place and club house for the men. The roof points sharply upward, and at each end under its point are crude drawings carved in the wood. Of phallic or historical significance, the figures tinted with clays or plant dyes still dance dimly across the rough-hewn beams. Inside were the pictographs of which we spoke earlier. There were only a few of these structures left in the islands, and the men were now gathering in unromantic quonset structures.

It was a rude shock to step back from this fragrant, faraway world to the schedule of the field trip and the crowded boat. We admitted to ourselves that we'd been alone on Angaur long enough that we enjoyed our own company and that of the natives best. When we traveled with the big entourage, we didn't have enough time to explore the beauties of the small villages, to watch the birds, and to note the flowers.

But we came home from the field trip with a separate package of delightful mental pictures for our album of the Palaus. We met the little girl at Ngeremlengui who was my namesake. When Henry had traveled that way some months before, he was asked politely by a native to suggest a name for his newborn daughter. Henry came up with two choices: Anne, his sister-in-law's name, and Cecilia, his wife's. We found a Palauan adaptation, Sisiniya.

At Ngertmau, we found a remarkable old character of a native of unknown age, who had worked as a hand on the old English

Little Sisiniya, who was named for Cecilia

sailing vessels that touched the islands many decades ago. Now gnarled and humped, he must have been almost a hundred. He still spoke a chipper brand of pidgin English, and when someone asked him if he'd like to go to sea again, he came forth spiritedly with, "Hell, NO!"

We women spent the first night of the trip on the boat. Exhausted from the first day at sea, we were ready for bed by nightfall. The men had all departed for the village on the hill above us, where they were to sleep in the school house. But it was deemed wise not to carry all our gear the long mile up the hill. We boiled hot dogs and had poor excuses for sandwiches along with cups of scalding coffee, and then literally fell into our bunks.

Singinari was elected to stand by the boat that night, and it was he who helped me make up the four bunks in the after cabin for the two women, the young girl, and one native girl. The other housegirl slept on a pallet on the deck of the front cabin where I spread my sheets on the bunk. Singi flipped out my sheet, tucked it in at the end, and handed me my pillow. The beds made, he helped straighten up the mess of dirty cups and plates. When we had everything ship-shape, and the ladies were settled in the back cabin, he stood at the hatchway of the front cabin, viewed the candlelit scene and giggled, "Ah, Meesus Wahl . . . this Stateside! This boat of ours!"

I had barely fallen off to heavy sleep, when a voice roused me. "Cec! Cec, are you awake?" A stage whisper came in through the window above me, and I struggled up to find Henry leaning in the window. He had walked the mile down the hill after all the men were asleep to see that we were all right and that his crew of boys had places to sleep. The boys had not found the camp cots which were boxed on the deck of the picket boat for them. And they had politely said nothing to me, but had settled down on the rocky beach. Henry hacked open the crate and set up the cots on the beach for all the boys. Then he came back on deck, and we watched for a time the full moon send its path along the water to the boat, talked over the new things we'd seen that day, and snickered over the discomforts of the Americans roughing it in the wilds of the Pacific. When his cigarette was finished he leaned through the window, kissed me a nice moonlit goodnight, and left to hike back up the hill to his bunk. Next morning the women moaned about uncomfortable bunks and not being able to sleep a wink all night. But they had to admit they'd not heard Henry cracking open the box of cots.

The second night we stayed at the schoolhouse in the village of Ulimong, on the east side of Babelthaup. Here everyone in the settlement had donated his only sheet or pillow or mattress till there were enough to make mosquito-netted beds for us in two rooms of the concrete block building. We left our boat out at the reef and were poled in small boats through the dark to the village. It was a pleasant, quiet ride, and we could see the reflection of stars in the water as we drifted along.

After dinner we were led to the main school room where all the village children sat ready to entertain us. It was an airy, open room lit with candles and lanterns at the front, and reaching back to shadowy darkness at the rear. Fifty children watched us curiously with wide open eyes. Fifty children who looked like any other group of school children in the world, until they stood as one at the command of their teacher and burst forth with the "Star Spangled Banner" in the most spine-tingling four-part harmony ever invented. We were all so completely thrilled by this astounding performance that we stood dumb for a few minutes before we could lift our hands to applaud. In a tiny Palau village where there were no musical instruments whatsoever, a gifted young native had trained his students to sing American anthems and folk songs familiar to their audience, and strange to themselves. They had even composed an original song in Palauan praising the American flag.

This program was the high spot of the trip. But at each village we found the same eager, polite, brown people bustling about to make us comfortable. Much less sophisticated than the people of the southern Palau islands, these natives still clung to many of their old customs, and lived with fewer of the accouterments of civilization. The southern Palauans had had contact with the Americans for three or four years now and had become skilled mechanically, fond of cokes and movies, and much less formal in their treatment of their village chiefs and *rubak*. Here on Babelthaup in the villages of the strange names were more houses with thatched roofs, direct living from the land and the sea, obeisance before the chief. The youngsters were more shy, but more curious of the white man than the Angaur kiddies we saw around our door. But the trim villages, the slower way of life, the few houses and flowers untouched by the wounds of war made us believe that this was the way mankind was meant to live.

At Melekeok we sat on freshly made bamboo benches under the palms along the beach and were served fresh picked oranges with the peel slit and turned back to make it look like flower petals. As we sat cooling off, the natives passed trays of the oranges and topped green coconuts so we might have refreshing drinks of the coconut milk from individual containers.

In every village we found the grassy trail, overhung with palms and hibiscus or plumeria, winding up the hill to the old *a bai* or a view of the ocean. We slipped away from the crowd whenever we could during those four busy days to walk along these trails. At Melekeok we sat, the two of us, watching the sunset on the final day of the trip, and Henry voiced his theory about the native people of the Pacific, gathered from his few short years of war and peace in the area.

These are smart, happy people, he said. Give them medical aid and education to a certain point and we'll have fulfilled our assignment here. Why should we force them to an American, hustling way of life when it is alien to all they know? It's uneconomical to make them earn money to buy American goods, when the cost of bringing it seven thousand miles from the States is prohibitive. Since the Palauans stem from the Malayan States originally, and have been under Japanese influence so long, theirs is an Oriental culture.

In the Solomons, for instance, native peoples were forced by

SAFARI!

missionaries to wear clothes on islands hotter and more humid than these. Nature decreed that they were more healthy without. But they began to wear clothes. The clothes got dirty, and the natives washed them on the rocks, the only way they knew how. The clothing fell apart. So to preserve them, they wore them without washing; and they got sores, they got wet from the rains and contracted colds and T.B., which decimated their ranks. They'd have been better off in their original state.

Nature has been the basis of most of the social and economic laws of these peoples. All laws must have some reason for being other than the mere fact that they are law. So I can't see why we should force a whole code of our laws on the natives, which they'll never understand, or, more important, have reason to use.

If we could give them enough education to increase their skills in fishing, gardening, carpentering, and mechanics, a general knowledge of the world and its people, and concentration on their own background and arts, we'd be doing them a service. There is a point past which we'd be making them dissatisfied. Say we imbue Tulop, our right hand man, with a desire to move to the States, and we teach him all manner of skills to use there. He'd move to America and probably be killed immediately by some virus to which we've all built up immunity, but to which he has none. Here he is upper class, living in his own country; in our land he'd be a displaced person, and because of his color placed in a lower social group. This is tragic; but it's true. Wouldn't it be vastly better to give him the medical aid and the skills to make his life easier and more pleasant here?

When I see these wonderful people living in this natural, beautiful way, I can't bear the thought of going home and settling down to some mundane job, down to the rut of catching the 8:05 bus every morning, of hanging my hat up and sitting down at a desk at exactly the same time every day, of having my whole life run by the clock. There's so much to be done here, and in all the overcrowded, underprivileged countries of the world. And we've barely begun. Since we've been given the responsibility of taking care of these islands, we must do the job well. We've been here a year, and we just now are beginning to understand the people and their needs . . . we think! We Americans have barged ahead in our own brash way. I hope we're not moving too rapidly. In many cases we have been too eager and generous; and if we're not careful we may end up drowning the people with kindness instead of setting them on their own feet again. It's like knowing how much water a certain plant in your garden needs. Unlimited amounts may kill it instead of making it grow. We must make it right with these Palauans.

You know, if I had to go home with the knowledge that I'd never see another strange country, Henry mused, never find another spot so lush and fragrant and untouched as these islands, never meet more of the people like the natives here and some of the world travelers we've met while we've been here . . . if we could never travel again I'd feel caged, as if I were beating my head against a blank wall. We've got to find a way to do it somehow.

But we were far away from the realities of the moment. It was time to get back and check on the boat and join the crowd for the evening.

The Melekeok meeting was the last, and we hated to move away from the palm studded beach because we knew we'd not be back. Most of the group was excited at seeing the hills of Koror rise up ahead of us, for they longed for their own beds again, and were sending radio messages ahead to have transportation waiting at the dock and steak dinners at home. The mail plane passed over us as we neared Koror, making our return more promising. But it also returned us to the modern, American world and tore us protestingly from the fairy tale world we had seen for the past four days. We had had a fleeting glimpse into an isolated society, just enough to catch the atmosphere; and then we were gone. We were left with a certain sadness because we would never see the spot again.

The mail plane also brought Henry's replacement officer and his wife, so we knew that our days in the Palaus were short. Henry was detained at Koror on official business. So when we started home for Angaur the next morning with the high tide, I felt it my duty to acclimate the new couple to their home and job, and to begin to tell them the things we knew about the islands. I was most eager that the trip be perfect and that our boatmen show their greatest skill and happiest mood, for I wanted the Stocktons to see what a wonderful world they had come to.

The lieutenant was pleased with the general appearance of the islands, but was definitely not impressed by the boat. Nervously and disapprovingly, he watched Singinari wheel out of the Koror harbor and turn homeward toward Angaur. Although he said nothing, it was apparent that he thought the boat unseaworthy for the open channel. But he had many enthusiastic ideas about the things he wanted to do, and we talked of these as we moved along.

We were scarcely under way when I noticed something was wrong with Singinari. Singinari was crying. There was no doubt about it. That was why he faced stiffly forward brushing at his eyes with the back of his hand. Presently he opened the window in front of the wheel and called to old Tomas. "Tomas, come take the boat." He slipped out of the cabin as quickly as possible, turning carefully away so that we could not see his face.

During the rest of the trip he did not return to the cabin, but sat disconsolately on the prow playing mournfully on his harmonica the tunes that were usually happy . . . "I am just a little ba-a-arfly, with a beer bottle for a home." And "Smile the while you kiss me sad adieu . . ."

As soon as I could, I moved up on deck and sat down by him. "Singinari, you do not feel so good. You sick today?"

"Oh, no, Meesus." He fiddled with the harmonica, and experimentally blew a couple minor notes.

"You maybe have trouble with your Koror girl, Singi?"

He giggled briefly. "Oh, no! Koror girls okay."

His face clouded again, and he spit into the water. Then he blurted out, "Meesus, what happen now to our boat? Mr. Wahl say it is okay with the boat as long as he is here; but after that he not know.

Now you go away. This new man come. Maybe now they take our boat away." He ran his hand along the brass rail. "Our Number One Boat, all Palau Islands!"

I was near tears, too. The boat was a symbol. It exemplified all the efforts we had made toward rehabilitation for the natives, all the gains we had hoped could be made. Now it was out of our hands. We had every reason to believe things would be increasingly better for the Palauans, but we could not be sure that the constant changes of American personnel would always bring understanding men who were truly interested in the welfare of the natives. All I could think to say to Singinari was that maybe Mr. Wahl could fix it somehow, and that I was sure everything would be all right.

I sat with Singinari for awhile, forgetting the blistering sun, and letting the salt spray stiffen my face while my mind slipped back over our days in the Palaus. . . .

CHAPTER EIGHTEEN

"Back Home Again"

We floated away from Angaur on my tears. Sentimentalist that I am, I had known all during the preparation for our return to the States that when the time came to leave our island, I would weep profusely, for the Angaur people and the boat had become so dear to us that the thought of not keeping contact with them, and possibly of not seeing these islands again, was very sad.

Tulop went around with a long face too. He had said that he would leave Angaur when we did, but we noticed no signs of moving day at his house. So we accepted his compliment to Henry at its face value and talked much with him about the future of the island people as he saw it, and how we hoped we had helped the people along a little bit while we had been there.

The night before we left, the villagers brought a sumptuous feast to our terrace. Just before dinnertime many people came walking across the road from their houses carrying packages. One by one they came into the room where we were packing, said a few words, and placed their paper-wrapped packages on a cot. Pandanus purses, larger suitcases, salad sets, shell necklaces and bracelets, grass skirts . . . each man brought the best his family had to offer in the way of a farewell gift for us. We were overcome. The whole cot was covered with presents, and the pile grew higher. Gullivert came last with a king-size salad set, beautifully fashioned and polished of dark wood. The tips of the handles were elongated Navy eagles, a scroll held in their teeth and the legend inscribed thereon: "Recallect of Angaur Island." These were too big to use for salads, but were the kind to cross above the mantel with the rest of the trophies.

Uherbalau and the village *rubak* joined us for dinner, a quiet, candlelit affair with the usual verbose speeches of thanks from all sides. Later the young people came and danced their dances for us.

NUMBER ONE PACIFIC ISLAND

We sat talking with our many friends until very late. Everyone stayed, and the village lights were left on till midnight by order of the Chief.

When we got to the dock the next morning with the last of our luggage, nearly everyone in the village was there. Major Bruce had brought down his record player, hooked it up with a public address system, and had "Anchors Aweigh" booming out over the harbor areas. But it was not until the older men, and the women whom we seldom saw, lined up to shake our hands firmly and to say goodbye that the cascade of tears came. Henry was admittedly a little dewy-eyed, too, though he was able to contain himself far better than I.

We stepped aboard the picket boat for the last trip. Singinari saluted sharply and said, "All ready, sir?"

"All ready, captain; give her the gun," Henry smiled back in an attempt at their usual buffoonery; but it fell a little short on both ends. We moved away from the dock while everyone waved handkerchiefs and the music roared a farewell. It was a good thing the major had brought the records. Without them the young folks would probably have sung "Should old akeensance be forgot . . ." That would really have done us in!

As we moved along the northwest point of the island we could see two truckloads of wildly waving youngsters moving along the road. And when we rounded the point into the open channel the children had jumped out of the vehicles and ranged themselves along the sharp rocks. From this vantage point they waved until the boat was half way to Peleliu. The last we could see of the children was their fluttering white handkerchiefs.

Through the winter months it was good to be home among our families, reveling in the fresh foods we had missed, visiting our friends, and enjoying stores, theaters, and the farm. But when the warm weather returned, the feel of the tropics was on us again. Then the hills of Indiana began to be the verdant island hills rising from the water, and fields of ripening winter wheat became the undulating Pacific. We could see and feel our island every place we turned, and the nostalgia was so great we were restless to be returning.

Then, we went to our class reunion at the university, where much jollity and good fellowship reigned. When the banquet was over and the round of hearty speeches, the master of ceremonies announced the program would be closed by the group singing the Alma Mater song. And when we rose to sing, "Come and join in song together," my throat tightened, the familiar stinging came behind the eyelids, and I could only listen. We looked at each other and far away, for we were back, Henry and I, at the quonset school house on Angaur; and the children were shouting at the tops of their voices,

"ANGAUR! HERE'S TO YOU!"

Epilogue

Henry and I visited Palau again a few years later, and this time stayed at Koror. Henry went on a tour of Koror to see how much had changed. The first thing was a small boat basin and salvage yard. There he found to his consternation our beloved Mail-boat 5. She looked a forlorn figure, and the bow and deck area were damaged beyond repair. So when Tulop came for a visit, our first question was, "What happened to Mail-boat 5?"

Tulop was expressionless. Very quietly he told us, "Meester Wahl, you know Angaur people no good on ocean, not good boat people, not good mechanics. The day after you leave Palau, radio message came, 'Bring mail-boat to Koror.'"

"People not good with boat."

"Come very very fast to dock, hit big stone, break off bow, and boat sink."

Henry replied, deadpan, "Too bad boat crew no good."